GLOBAL MARX

Studies in Critical Social Sciences Book Series

Haymarket Books is proud to be working with Brill Academic Publishers (www.brill.nl) to republish the *Studies in Critical Social Sciences* book series in paperback editions. This peer-reviewed book series offers insights into our current reality by exploring the content and consequences of power relationships under capitalism, and by considering the spaces of opposition and resistance to these changes that have been defining our new age. Our full catalog of *SCSS* volumes can be viewed at https://www.haymarketbooks .org/series_collections/4-studies-in-critical-social-sciences.

GLOBAL MARX

History and Critique of the Social Movement in the World Market

EDITED BY

MATTEO BATTISTINI
ELEONORA CAPPUCCILLI
MAURIZIO RICCIARDI

Haymarket Books
Chicago, IL

First published in 2022 by Brill Academic Publishers, The Netherlands
© 2022 Koninklijke Brill NV, Leiden, The Netherlands

Published in paperback in 2023 by
Haymarket Books
P.O. Box 180165
Chicago, IL 60618
773-583-7884
www.haymarketbooks.org

ISBN: 979-8-88890-016-1

Distributed to the trade in the US through Consortium Book Sales and
Distribution (www.cbsd.com) and internationally through Ingram Publisher
Services International (www.ingramcontent.com).

This book was published with the generous support of Lannan Foundation,
Wallace Action Fund, and the Marguerite Casey Foundation.

Special discounts are available for bulk purchases by organizations and
institutions. Please call 773-583-7884 or email info@haymarketbooks.org for more
information.

Cover design by Jamie Kerry and Ragina Johnson.

Printed in the United States.

Library of Congress Cataloging-in-Publication data is available.

This volume is collectively dedicated to the memory of Benedetto Vecchi

∵

Contents

PART 2
Spaces and World: States, Revolutions, Social Movement

Preface

This book is not a collection of scattered essays, but the outcome of a lengthy collective research project aimed at investigating the way Marx reconstructed the spatial and temporal coordinates of capital's world domination. Although the terms *global* and *worldwide* are now often taken as synonyms, we do not intend to establish the possibilities and limits of Marxian discourse under the conditions of present-day globalization; researching the possible ways of making Marx and Marxism global today (Spivak 2018; Hoff 2017) falls outside the scope of this volume. Our aim is rather to identify the factors that make Marxian discourse global in its very formulation. The underlying hypothesis is that, in spite of its many limitations and antinomies, Marx's political epistemology allows us to go beyond specific spaces and the hegemonic subjects within them, and thus is itself global.

The different chapters are arranged along a double axis. The first axis explores some of the disciplinary languages that Marx encounters, uses and criticizes in more or less explicit ways in order to produce his own political epistemology. The second interrogates the political spaces on which he focuses, in different ways and with different levels of intensity. In an apparently intermediate position, and with a connecting function with respect to these two axes, is the investigation of political processes and structures such as the city, patriarchy, colonization, and technology, which, although widely present in Marxian texts, have until now attracted little interest.

We are aware that a lot is missing, but the book does not claim to be encyclopaedic in nature. To give just a couple of examples of what is lacking, there is no adequate analysis of the importance of the hard sciences in the building of the Marxian discourse, just as there is no analysis of the political relevance that Poland had for Marx and Engels. However, our global Marx is not limited to his analyses of geographical spaces but focuses on how his global approach affects his conceptual framework and his critique of the scholarly disciplines that were establishing themselves as the scientific knowledge of capitalist society. From our point of view, Marx's epistemology is a political epistemology of antithesis that aims to define the cleavages that characterize capitalist society in all its spaces. Precisely for this reason, it is crucially determined by his critical confrontation with those disciplines that were preparing the forms of the governance of capitalist society through the scientific description of the *social*.

This seemed even more relevant to us in light of the centrality of the concept of the world market in Marx's discourse, understood not simply as the extension of trade to ever larger parts of the planet, but as the structure of a communicative, economic and institutional power that repeatedly redefines the geography of capital, setting the changing coordinates of the forms and figures of the exploitation of wage labour through the subordination of ever larger masses of individuals.

The exploitation of wage labour is obviously a function of the valorization of capital, which cannot exist without continuously reproducing its conditions of possibility, which are not always strictly economic and are neither delimited to the areas where exploitation is most evident or intense. It is precisely for this reason that Marx argues the world market is not simply the progressive outcome of so-called capitalist development, but the political presupposition of its very existence. On the other hand, in 1858 Marx stated that the process of the globalization of capital was complete. There were no lands that could still be considered outside of its range of action. The geography of bourgeois society seemed to have fulfilled its historical task, which, however, opened up a political problem that did not concern the spaces of capital, but the time of revolution.

> The proper task of bourgeois society is the creation of the world market, at least in outline, and of the production based on that market. Since the world is round, the colonization of California and Australia and the opening up of China and Japan would seem to have completed this process. For us, the difficult QUESTION is this: on the Continent revolution is imminent and will, moreover, instantly assume a socialist character. Will it not necessarily be CRUSHED in this little corner of the earth, since the MOVEMENT of bourgeois society is still in the ASCENDANT over a far greater area?.
>
> MARX to ENGELS 10/8/1858 in MECW 40: 347

In the years that followed, Marx attempted to solve this small geometric paradox, this corner in a round body, through investigating the social movement that traversed the world market and tormented the structures guaranteeing its continuity. In this regard, it has been rightly observed that 'the most fragile part of Marx [is] the predictive Eurocentric scenario' (Spivak 1993: 142). At the same time, however, a growing literature has shown that this scenario is not given once and for all (Shanin 1983; Nimtz 2004; Anderson 2010; Basso 2015; Pradella 2015; Musto 2020). It changes over time and is affected by events that, although not happening in Europe, are not recorded by Marx as secondary facts or expressions of a still 'immature' history, but as symptoms of the structural instability of the world market. To fully assume the political dominance of the latter means recognizing that the presence of the social movement is not determined in a binding way by the national form of the market and that its dynamics turn against the historical, geographical, gender and racial hierarchies that capital constantly recuperates.

The Marxian perspective clearly hints at the possibility that the fate of Europe could be decided outside of Europe due to capital's ability to continuously impose its own specific temporality. For Marx, the government of time is the most important vector of the spatialization of capital. This emerges clearly in his dialogue with the French historians, thanks to which the very possibility of class struggle – the true Marxian criterion of the political – is freed from any universal historical meaning, as well as from any functionalist interpretation. The class struggle is not, nor can it be reduced to, an element of the infinite progression of bourgeois civil society.

The structural connection established by the world market is the very form of the global domination of capital, which produces and confirms power relations that, although they may have older histories, are politically re-signified by the logic of capital. This process of re-signification primarily occurs through distributing the time of subordination within different hierarchical spaces. Scientific disciplines play a central role within this process, establishing the canon of development and 'modernity' that presides over the specific dynamics not only of different political spaces, but also of power structures such as land and movable property, law and patriarchy, slavery and race, nation and city, technology and, last but not least, the state. Despite some infrequent optimistic assertions, and despite arguing for the radical novelty of the capitalist mode of production over previous modes, Marx soon sees that those structures are constantly being reused because of their proven ability to produce discipline and power.

As much in his works on history and the critique of political economy as in his vast activity as a *political* publicist, Marx's intention is never simply analytical and descriptive, but is always directed towards finding possibilities for *reading* the movements capable of overturning the legitimacy of the structures that continuously defer or suspend the possibility of crisis. Both in the 1840s, when his journalism had an immediately political character, and in the two following decades, when he struggled with the rules dictated by his employer, *The New York Daily Tribune*, Marx ended up investigating the varied geography of the times of capital, a 'temporal geography' that showed the inexorable expansion of capitalist society, with the opening of new markets and financial crises, diplomatic traffic and wars, and, most importantly, its fractures: for Marx the world market went hand in hand with its always possible crises. And this connection continuously opened up new scenarios. Marx argued that the globalization of capital was not the form of its stabilization, but that of its

constant transformation and of the political possibilities that this transformation opened up. Thus, the history of the capitalist mode of production prevents
the geography of capitalism from becoming a mere topography. Cartography
must also include an aerial perspective that allows for the different sites of
exploitation and class struggle to be captured in all their dimensions, so that
each has its part to play in the narrative of global capitalist society.

Connecting time and space, history and geography is thus the political task
that Marx sets himself in his global research, as is already clear in his 1858 letter
to Engels cited above. The potentially chaotic difference of historical experiences is unified by capital with the violence of its development, and the revolutionary process must necessarily deal with that. On the other hand, as Latin
America demonstrates, even parts of the earth that may now seem marginal
have not only played a fundamental role in the genetic history of capital, but
their political forms and modes of exploitation are perfectly consistent with
contemporary capitalism. The concern that Europe may end up paying the
price of the revolution stands alongside the reminder that, from the perspective of class struggle, the most relevant social movements do not necessarily arise in Europe. The chapter on Marx and the colonies must therefore be
placed next to that on Marx and colonization, because only in this way can the
relevance of the former be grasped. Precisely because he is not interested in
assigning a role in the world theatre to each part of the globe, Marx identifies
in colonization one of the constituent processes that allows the global establishment of the world market. This is because it consolidates a difference that
is a historically integral part of the condition that combines dispossession and
exploitation.

Dispossession, after having involved many European populations, was the
destiny of non-European populations from Asia to Latin America, becoming
the foundation of the capitalist mode of production. The direct act of rob-
bery was in fact functional to the formation of fully capitalist land ownership.
Colonization also reinforced the conditions of the constant separation of
workers from the means of production. Finally, it represented a fundamental
process for the capitalist appropriation of the state, which for Marx is far more
relevant than the history built around the democratic and liberal evolution of
forms of government.

Thus, only two years later, Marx wrote: 'the most momentous thing happening in the world today is the slave movement – on the one hand, in America,
started by the death of Brown, and in Russia, on the other' (Marx to Engels
1/11/1860 in MECW 41: 4). Russia was indeed a place where the *temporal geography* of capital could show its limits, just as it was asserting its most classical forms in an apparently decentralized global space. Marx argued that the

processes of insubordination that did not take place at the highest point of capitalist development, but outside Europe, or in the colonial space that connected and divided Britain and Ireland, had decisive importance for 'the whole social movement'. The latter was the practical answer to the bourgeoisie's claims, that historical progress had established its course, showing its indisputable universal character, and achieving the ultimate goal of freedom through the representative form assumed by the state (Marx 1852b: 330). Within and against the global movement of society, therefore, another movement arose, the political character of which could not be denied, as soon as it affected the constituent foundations of society itself, such as that of slavery, servitude and the length of the working day. In the Napoleon III's France, the interest of the bourgeoisie was to use the state machine to 'mistrustfully mutilate, cripple, the independent organs of the social movement' (Marx 1852a: 139). At first, Marx considered the demand for the abolition of the Anglo-Irish Union as a purely political movement. Indeed, he contrasted that demand with the agitation of the land tenants, which would instead be a 'deep-rooted social movement' (Marx 1853a: 505). In later years, however, he argued that the political priority of the social movement of the British working class was the Repeal of the Act of Union. And again: recognizing their fundamental importance as 'centres of organization of the working class', Marx criticized the trade unions for having 'kept too much aloof from general social and political movements' (Marx 1867d: 191), stubbornly dealing only with local struggles. The social movement is political when it directly challenges the forms of command that characterize capitalist society. Marx claimed that the knowledge of this movement was not the product of a specific science, arguing against Bakunin that he used 'scientific socialism' 'only in contrast to utopian socialism which wishes to foist new illusions onto the people instead of confining its scientific investigations to the social movement created by the people itself' (Marx 1875b: 520). The 'relationship between political action and the social movement of the working class' prevents the latter from being understood as a form of identity; it establishes the coordinates of what should be the political reverse of the world market, revealing the existence of global connections that go beyond the single claim and the single territory. For Marx, the social movement is political when it starts to deploy a 'socially binding force'.

This movement must not only confront the 'automatic' movements of capital in the world market, but also the hierarchy of individual states that guarantee its concrete articulation. For Marx there is no possibility of relying on any autonomy of the political. The State as an institution cannot free itself from the constitutive bureaucratic and authoritarian content that allowed its affirmation in the ancient society of estates. It is one of those anachronisms that capital manages to constantly use. This does not mean that, in certain circumstances, the state cannot become a significant area of struggle, but, as the class struggles in France demonstrated, the state soon becomes a tool to block them rather than allowing them to be amplified. It is precisely when it is faced with the most intense conflict that the state intensifies its bureaucratization and relies on the solitary power of the executive.

If the state cannot establish global limits on the action of the world market, the latter does not, however, represent the model for the automatic regulation of the social relation of capital. Under no circumstances can it be reduced to a series of peaceful mercantile relations, designed according to the ostensible symmetries of the contract, because it is precisely economic relations that ultimately require recourse to political regulation. Much more than political representation, presented as an indisputable mechanism of political unification, it is money's domination that constantly reproduces the conditions for the extension of individual and collective relations of subordination. While polemically establishing the radical historicity of the capital relation, the Marxian confrontation with economists thus affirms the political character of exploitation, that is, its being the effect of a power that is based neither on economic technique nor on societal competence.

Patriarchy and law are historical structures of power that establish and preserve the normative forms of what is presented as a specific societal competence, i.e. as the indisputable prerogative of occupying a certain position in that society. Both are now inseparable from private appropriation and create constant hierarchization, continuously reproducing the fundamental anthropology of capitalist society. While precisely defining the characteristics of the private form of appropriation, the law also consistently violates the link between the individual worker and their activity and especially between individuals working collectively and the fruit of their cooperation. Marx thus has a historical critique of both law and patriarchy. He is not concerned with establishing the possibility of a 'more just' law or showing the way to more equitable future relations between the sexes. Rather, his problem is how they have historically formed a type of subordination that is perfectly functional to the domination of capital and in what way they act hierarchically.

The nation is also a historical structure that operates by establishing internal and external hierarchies. This emerges not only explicitly in the Manifesto, but also in the critique of claims to national independence that Marx continues to make after 1848. As the cases of Ireland, a colony in the very heart of Europe, Italy and Latin America show in different ways, these claims are linked to the intensification of class struggle within the world market, so that a single national struggle becomes more relevant on the global level than on the level of the affirmation of the nation. Despite the obvious differences in context, Marx also reads Indian and Chinese history from this perspective, in which British colonial rule, while showing its ferocity and the intensification of the world market, incubates the germs of its crisis. For Marx, even the transformations of the city and in technology are political processes that can change the history that produced them, presenting the possibility of relationships that go beyond the capital relation. If the Commune appears to him as the truth of city politics, the critical history of technology aims to deny the dominance of the machine and the neutrality that technique claims. The problem that Marx always poses is how to go beyond the social relation of capital, which, even in the structural connection established by the world market, cannot disregard the state, as the latter is ultimately an important structure of power that ensures the market's concrete articulation.

The history of the state as traced by Marx is devoid of the glory it is usually assigned. However, by denying the state as the representation of the universal, he recognizes it as the place of executive power and of a struggle for democracy, possible only by exercising pressure from without, given the impossibility – in Germany as well as in France and Britain – of changing the material conditions of exploitation and subjugation only on a national level. For Marx, however, it is the International that constitutes the organized response to the world market, the attempt to act against it on its own scale. The International is the political opposite of the world market, designed to counter its systemic order. Global Marx cannot be understood without an effort to constantly connect the struggles against capital in Europe and in other areas of the world. There is in Marx no sense of a hypothetical division of revolutionary labour between the British working class and the French proletariat. Global Marx shows that figures of subordination and insubordination cannot be classified geographically, economically, or sociologically.

Only within this organizational and political perspective can we understand why Marx interprets the American Civil War as a global historical fact. It does not establish a tendency to be later shared by others, but the possibility of a connection between slave and free labour, black and white skin, at the moment when slavery becomes a problem for wage labourers in Europe and vice versa. That same political connection that he had tried to produce between Irish and British workers, is for Marx what makes the Civil War in the United States an empirically universal fact. It produces lines of connection between conditions that would otherwise necessarily remain distant and separate, making emancipation a materially global concept and removing it at least in part from its original legal definition. The social movement requalifies emancipation on a level that completely escapes its state and legal definition and national destiny.

Global Marx does not identify any *global* working class, nor a *centre* of power to be conquered. Instead, he recognizes that, within and against the global movement that the world market imposes on capitalist society, there is a social movement that is irreducible to any form of identity or to a single area from whose perspective one can write a universal history of class struggle. The global gaze of political Marx is thus always aimed at finding the possibility of undoing the legitimacy of the power structures that defer the crisis of the world domination of capital. It is 'neither a local nor a national, but a social problem' (Marx 1864a: 14).

Abbreviations

MECW   *Marx Engels Collected Works*. London: Lawrence and Wishart; New York: International Publishers, 1975–2004.

Notes on Contributors

Luca Basso

Ph.D (2004), studied in Padua and in Berlin. He is Professor of Political Philosophy and Coordinator of the Doctorate in Philosophy at the Universiy of Padua. His research interests are early modern philosophy, Marx, Marxism, contemporary French philosophy. His monographs include Individuo e comunità nella filosofia politica di G. W. Leibniz (Rubbettino, 2005), Marx and Singularity; From the Early Writings to the Grundrisse (Brill, 2012), Marx and the Common: From Capital to the Late Writings (Brill, 2015), Inventare il nuovo. Storia e politica in Jean-Paul Sartre (ombre corte, 2016).

Michele Basso

is researcher at the Department of Political Sciences, Law and International Studies, University of Padua. Ph. D. in Political Philosophy and History of Political Thought, he studied at the University of Padua, at the Max-Planck-Institute for Legal History and Legal Theory and at the Ludwig-Maximilian University of Munich. His research interests range from political philosophy, history of political thought, legal history and classical sociology. He has written two books on Max Weber and essays on Marx and Troeltsch. He translated and edited the Italian version of Tönnies' On Custom (2019) and Lederer's On the Sociology of World War (2022).

Matteo Battistini

Ph.D. (2008), University of Bologna, Department of Political and Social Sciences, is Associate Professor of U.S. History at that university. He has been visiting scholar at the Department of History of Columbia University and at the Tamiment Cold War Center of the New York University. His research interests are mainly directed to the history of U.S. political thought and social sciences. He has published monographs and articles on political and intellectual history of the United States, including Middle Class: An Intellectual History through Social Sciences. An American Fetish from its Origins to Globalization (Brill 2022).

Eleonora Cappuccilli

Ph.D (2016), University of Bologna, is core research fellow at Villa I Tatti, The Harvard University Center for Italian Renaissance Studies and has previously been postdoctoral fellow in History of Ideas at the University of Oslo. Her research interests are women's political and religious thought in Renaissance and early modern Europe, feminist political theory and the history and critique of patriarchy. She published two monographs: La critica imprevista. Politica, teologia e patriarcato in Mary Astell and La strega di Dio. Profezia politica, storia e riforma in Caterina da Racconigi (2020).

Michele Cento

Ph.D (2013), University of Bologna, is research fellow at the University of Bergamo, after having hold the same position at the University of Bologna. He has previously been postdoctoral fellow at the Istituto Italiano di Studi Storici "Benedetto Croce". His research interests are modern Italian history in a transnational/transatlantic perspective and the political, economic, and intellectual history of the 1960s/1970s. Among his publications: (with Roberta Ferrari) Il socialismo ai margini: classe e nazione in Sud Italia e in Irlanda (Soveria Mannelli 2018), and Tra capitalismo e amministrazione: il liberalismo atlantico di Nitti (il Mulino 2017).

Luca Cobbe

Ph.D (2008), University of Macerata, is research fellow in History of Political Thought at the University of Rome 'Sapienza'. His interests focus on the political thought of the Scottish Enlightenment with reference to David Hume; on the genesis and evolution of social sciences in nineteenth and twentieth century France and Great Britain and their effects on political theory. He published two monographs: Il governo dell'opinione. Politica e costituzione in David Hume (EUM 2014), and L'arcano della società. L'opinione e il segreto della politica moderna (Mimesis 2020).

Isabella Consolati

Ph.D. (2015), University of Pavia and University of Innsbruck, is Senior Assistant Professor at the Interuniversity Department of Regional and Urban Studies and Planning of the Polytechnic of Turin. Her research interests are the history of spatial representations, German history of concepts and constitutional history, Marxian theory of history, and the politics of digital technology. Among her publications: Dominare tempi inquieti. Storia costituzionale, politica e tradizione europea in Otto Brunner (il Mulino 2020) and La prospettiva geografica. Spazio e politica in Germania tra il 1815 e il 1871 (Edizioni di Storia e Letteratura 2016).

Niccolò Cuppini

Ph.D. (2016), University of Bologna, is lecturer at the University of Applied Sciences and Arts of Southern Switzerland (SUPSI). His research is oriented towards a trans-disciplinary approach within the urban studies and the history of political doctrines fields. Moreover, he researches on logistics and digital platforms. Niccolò is part of the research group 'Into the Black Box' (www.into theblackbox.com) and he is a member of the editorial board of the journal Scienza & Politica (https://scienzaepolitica.unibo.it). His latest book is Nel vortice del presente: Voci, scorrimenti e sorvoli tra movimenti, logistica, urban-izzazione (Ledizioni 2020).

Roberta Ferrari

is researcher in History of Political Thought. Her research focuses on socialist thought in England and Ireland and on the concept of planning in Europe, the USSR and the United States in the 1920s and 1930s. She also works on fem-inist theory and Karl Marx's theory. Her current research is exploring the con-nections between the concept of planning and the transformation imposed by algorithmic programmability. Among her publications: Beatrice Potter e il capitalismo senza civiltà (Viella 2017) and Plan-based Thought. From the New Civilization to the Global System of Power in Scienza & Politica 2019.

Michele Filippini

is Associate Professor at the University of Bologna. His research activity covers mainly the history of political thought and political philosophy. His main line of research involves the history of Marxism and the forms of political legiti-mation and political power. He has been PI of gramsciproject.org. He wrote several books and articles on Antonio Gramsci, the Italian autonomist tradi-tion and the political theory of Ernesto Laclau. Among his recent books: Using Gramsci: A New Approach (Pluto Press 2017); Una politica di massa (Carocci 2015); and co-edited Mario Tronti, Il demone della politica (il Mulino 2017).

Giorgio Grappi

Ph.D (2007). His recent research interests focus on migration and the role of logistics in reshaping politics and political spaces. Previously he has worked also on United States' constitutionalism and the development of postcolonial state in India. He has been involved in several international research proj-ects, including the EU funded Horizon 2020 project GLOBUS (Reconsidering European Contribution to Global Justice) and the tricontinental project Logistical Worlds: Infrastructure, Software, Labour. His publications include the books Logistica (Ediesse 2016) and Migration and the Contested Politics of Justice (Routledge 2021).

Maurizio Merlo

is Associate Professor in Political Philosophy at the University of Padua. He has studied the relationship between the historiography of political discourse and the conceptual History (Begriffsgeschichte). He has been member of Centro Interuniversitario di Ricerca sul Lessico Politico e Giuridico Europeo (CIRLPGE) and collaborates with journals such as Filosofia politica and Scienza & Politica. His research interests are the threshold between medieval political philosophy and modern political thought, from Nicolaus of Cues to Marsilius of Padua and John Locke. His last monograph is dedicated to the problem of obligation in Francisco Suarez's thought.

Mario Piccinini

PhD (1992), University of Pisa, teaches Legal History and Political and Legal Concepts at the University of Padua. His main research interests are the relations between social and legal normativities and their connections with political concepts. He is the author of a monograph on Henry Sumner Maine and of many contributions on the history of the English idea of political body, on Thomas Hobbes, F.W. Maitland, Harold Laski, Leo Strauss and Ernst Troeltsch. He is currently working on a book on panic and politics.

Fabio Raimondi

teaches 'Forms of Political and Institutional Innovation' at the Department of Law of the University of Udine. He is member of the editorial board of the journal Storia del pensiero politico (il Mulino edition). His main fields of research are the political thought of the Renaissance (Machiavelli and Bruno in particular), Marx, Engels and Marxism. He is the author of numerous essays in journals and collective volumes. Among his latest books: Constituting Freedom. Machiavelli and Florence (Oxford University Press 2018).

Maurizio Ricciardi

Ph.D. (1996), is Associate professor of History of Political Thought at the University of Bologna. He has been visiting scholar at the Leibniz-Institut für Europäische Geschichte in Mainz, at the Max-Planck-Institut für europäische Rechtsgeschichte in Frankfurt am Main and Berlin. He is chief editor of the journal Scienza & Politica (https://scienzaepolitica.unibo.it). He has published articles and monographs on the history of political and social concepts and modern political thought. His latest book is Il potere temporaneo. Karl Marx e la politica come critica della società (Meltemi editore 2019).

Paola Rudan

is Associate professor in History of Political Thought at the Department of History and Culture, University of Bologna. She is the author of monographs on Simón Bolívar's (2007) and Jeremy Bentham's (2013) social and political thought, and on the history and critique of the concept of woman (2020). Her research activity also addresses contemporary political theory, the history of women's political thought, and the problem of power in gender and feminist studies. Currently, her research focuses on the relationship between women and new technologies and the feminist critique of techno-societal relations.

Federico Tomasello

is Senior Research Fellow at Ca' Foscari University of Venice. He is also post-doctoral researcher at the Université de Neuchatel, visiting fellow at the European University Institute, and guest researcher at the WZB-Berlin Social Science Centre. He edited the volume Violenza e Politica. Dopo il Novecento (il Mulino 2020) and published the monograph L'ordine della città. Violenza e Spazio Urbano (Manifestolibri 2020). He is the author of the forthcoming monograph for Routledge, Labour and Citizenship in Post-Revolutionary France: The Beginning of Work.

PART 1

Disciplines and Structures: Time, History, Mutations

∴

CHAPTER 1

On Possession and Property

Marx, Gans and the Law

Michele Basso

Possession *per se*, in its origin, is a mere fact:
   but it is equally certain that through the effect of laws, there are
legal consequences connected with it.

   VON SAVIGNY 1803

• • •

The true basis of private property, possession, is a *fact*, an inexplicable fact, *not a right.*

   MARX 1843

• • •

The populace is a fact, not a right.

   GANS 1832–1833

• •
•

Marx began as a scholar of law. Whilst, in the overall scheme of his output, legal questions have a role that is undoubtedly important, albeit collateral in relation to others, it is nonetheless in legal disciplines that one must look for certain patterns and primary motives of his thinking. This chapter will seek to highlight the importance of his studies in the legal sphere: more exactly, it will look at a crucial question of law, namely the relationship between property and possession. In this subject, comparison with the jurist Eduard Gans will be given close attention, as it is of primary importance in understanding certain points of Marxian reasoning. In particular, it was on certain promptings in the words of Gans that Marx felt the need to advance from a primarily legal and in part journalistic approach, to his first analytical explorations into the area of political economy, and then his wildly ambitious attempt to find ways of thinking about that 'world market' which constitutes the horizon of expansion from which the capitalist system can be understood.

Marx enrols to study jurisprudence in Bonn, 1835, then moves to Berlin the following year. In a letter of 1837 to his father (Marx to his Father 11/10–11/1837 in MECW 1: 10–21), he says that he is having to 'wrestle with philosophy' in order to study jurisprudence. This conflict is not surprising; indeed, it is typical of the close links that existed at the time between law and philosophy studies (Fioravanti 1979; Kelley 1976; Xifaras 2002), which Marx simply accepted, and into which he channelled his first efforts in terms of thought and output. It is also of interest, however, to mention the first failure endured by the youthful Marx. Likewise in the letter to his father, Marx says that he is trying to elaborate 'a philosophy of law covering the whole field of law'. He decides to abandon his first attempt (Marx to his Father 11/10–11/1837 in MECW 1: 17) having reached the end of a section on 'material private law', stating that he was no longer able to force the concepts of Roman law into the 'Kantian' system he had sought to construct. At this point he sees 'the falsity of the whole thing' and abandons the project (Breckman 1999; Cornu 1971: 104–106; Kelley 1978: 354–356). The 'where' of this abandonment is not insignificant. Marx decides to interrupt his quest at the end of the section dedicated to the 'laws of persons, of things, and of persons in relation to property'. What disillusions him, convincing him as to the pointlessness of his work, is a certain conception of the relationship between person and property, and the mediation of the state in guaranteeing it and making it possible, which in his eyes hides a basic falsehood. This view of the relationship in question is that embodied in the Civil Code of 1804, which would spread inexorably beyond French territory and, albeit with greater difficulty, even into the state of Prussia (Koselleck 1988; Bertani 2004; Canale 2000). It is that specifically bourgeois, but also peculiarly modern conception of the relationship between thing and person, and the resulting personal and real rights. As Marx would explicitly acknowledge later on, it is the conception of relationship in question that would do most to foster and favour the emergence of a capitalist mode of production. A couple of remarks, before moving on: in the letter, Marx cites Savigny, whose 'learned work on possession' he claims to have read, and from whom he admits that he inherited certain errors in his approach, when drafting the *philosophy of law*, that forced him ultimately, as intimated, to discontinue the project. The style of discussion is not that of Savigny, however, as indeed neither are the repeated references to 'conceptual development', to 'purely finite provisions' and to the 'formation of the concept of law'. It is not difficult to detect certain implied accents of Hegel here, which Marx in all probability would have taken on board thanks to his 'exceptionally assiduous attendance', during the year the letter was written, of the course in civil law given by Eduard Gans (Breckman 1999: 261; Kelley 1978: 351–352; Cornu 1971).

1   Possession

During the years of the young Marx's education, these two masters of his first law studies, Gans and Savigny, were engaged in a fierce, at times almost litigious debate. The dispute became official in 1839 but had been brewing for some years (Kelley 1978: 352; Braun 1980; Rückert 2002); it hinged in particular on the notion of possession, and the connection between possession and property. The reflection on the notion of possession has something to do with the chagrin related by Marx in the letter to his father, and the significant clue in this regard is the point at which Marx decides to stop and abandon his project. To reiterate, Marx interrupts his research on broaching the legal question of the relationship between things and persons, and the notion of possession is definable legally as the first form of relationship between person and property. Moreover, it is when reading Savigny's treatise on possession that Marx realizes he has inherited certain errors from it along the way and must abandon the three hundred pages he has written. Perhaps there is something in his head that tells him to move way from Savigny and nearer to Gans, and, by way of Gans, to Hegel. In general terms, Marx embarks on a journey here that will lead him to rethink the entire structure of the law, and, to this end, reflecting on possession affords an opportunity to dwell on the very foundations of legal thought. Notions of possession and property relate to the legal thinking of Marx in the same way that commodities and labour force relate to his economic thinking.

In the self-critical content of Marx's draft for the 'metaphysics of law', which a-critically separates 'basic principles, reflections, definition of concepts … from all actual law and from every actual form of law' (Marx to his Father 11/10–11/1837 in MECW 1: 10), Kelley presumes to discern a prefiguration of Marx's historical materialism (Kelley 1978: 355). Conceptually, one can also see a division in the understanding of *Recht* (a term which in German covers the meaning both of 'right' and of 'just, correct, proper'), that is to say a *recht* (*just*, in the adjectival sense) of law as distinct from, or not necessarily coinciding with, a *recht* which for the moment we might define as *social*. It is worthwhile exploring this separation, starting from the foundations, or indeed from the actual notion of possession.

In his *Besitzrecht* (Savigny 1865), Savigny defends the theory whereby possession, in its primary form, that is to say mere retention, should be considered as a mere fact, and placed outside the sphere of the law. As Savigny sees it, mere retention is not an *'objet juridique' [juristischer Gegenstand]*. The passage from fact to law, hence the passage from possession to property, would come about by way of two different legal institutions: positive prescription and interdictions. In the first instance, the passage would be determined mainly by time, or rather, by uninterrupted possession of the property for a period of at least two years (Savigny 1865: 29ff). In the second, one has the situation of possession claimed by another party. Since possession is a fact existing outside the sphere of law, it would not be possible for the claimant to undertake any kind of legal action. However, if someone uses violence against another party, the act of violence becomes unlawful and can be punished. According to Gans, it is precisely in considering possession as a mere fact that Savigny commits a basic error. Nothing, in the sphere of the law, can be seen as merely 'factual'. And if one does take this view, like Savigny, one finds oneself necessarily hampered by the impossibility of connecting the fact to the law. If we accept that possession is purely factual in nature, says Gans, the very definition of an act of violence against a possession considered to be wrong is logically inconceivable. In effect, if an act is definable as outside the sphere of the law, any associated violence cannot be seen as wrong. It is interesting – not least in the light of Marx's subsequent thinking – to observe the biting tone with which Savigny's reasoning is dismissed by Gans:

> The entire reasoning leads to this chain of logic: only the owner has the right of possession; another party, who is not the owner, has no such right; he is protected, however, since he who assaults, by using violence, commits an unjust act.
>
> GANS 2005: 82

That which is factual is devoid of any form of subjectivity, hence also of any link with volition (Gans 1839: 349). Possession, however, originates from an act of volition, and as such, it cannot in any sense be excluded from the sphere of law. The point at issue, rather, is to understand what the legal nature of possession might be. It is, in effect, 'the first of the relationships of the person with the thing' (Gans 1827: § 104). In a course of natural law, Gans also defines possession as the 'first realization of the person in a thing', the first 'contact between person and thing'. The first contact between 'my volition' and a thing defines the 'right of possession' [*Besitzrecht*] (Gans 2005: 81; Reissner 1965: 125ff). Possession is therefore a right, but only on the strength of individual, and therefore abstract volition. To be fully recognized as possession, it must be established within its particular context, its determined universality, and thus become *property* [*Eigentum*]. On this basis, Gans defines possession as 'the beginning of property', or as 'property from the standpoint of particular volition' (Gans 2005: 83). An example, taken from Gans himself, can help advantageously to unravel his self-evidently Hegelian language. If we were to think of a man – a completely solitary man – who possesses something, we might say that his possession is the same as property. In effect, as there is but one volition involved, particular volition and universal volition would here be one and the same. Clearly, the example in question is a logically absurd abstraction, serving purely for the purposes of clarification. Considering the relational situation in which the man necessarily finds himself, one of *mere possession*, the standpoints of particular volition and universal volition are in reality divided. And it is only when this possession is recognized that the particular volition will also be recognized in its universality, and the possession can become property (Gans' notes on Hegel's *Elements of the Philosophy of Right*, from this moment on: Gans on Hegel 1991, § 51, 81–82). Simplifying further: I can *want* to possess a thing, have *animus res sibi habendi*, but this is not enough for me to be the owner of that thing. I become the owner only when my possession is recognized within the scope of a (legally) determinate universality. This once again highlights the decisive importance of volition in determining what constitutes law. Again, arguing against Savigny, Gans shows how mere retention does not equate to possession. Should a thing that belongs to someone else fall into my hands, this does not mean that I am a thief. Only when I express the intention to keep it for myself do I become a thief. So, the doctrine of possession, Gans reminds us, 'is not positive, but is a doctrine that rests on the nature of the Spirit or the Will' (Gans 2005: 81).

It makes sense to imagine that Marx will have pondered this theoretical question. It is something rather more than an erudite declamation on a legal nicety. The point at issue is, in fact, the starting point of the law. From the legacy of Marx's writings, we can put forward the case that, in the wake of Gans, Marx distanced himself early from Savigny and other exponents of the historical school in their approach to the law. Marx agrees with Gans on the point that the risk in the approach of the historical school is one of 'remaining steeped in the accidental' [*beim blossen Sein*] and reducing history to a sort of 'knowledge of detail', consisting in the 'mere enumeration of facts' (Ballarin 1985–1986: 17). This 'micrological' approach brings with it a notable risk: that of 'celebrating the positive' (Ballarin 1985–1986: 17, 19), that is to say recognizing as law – ultimately in acritical mode – that which in the sources appears to be defined as such. What is missing, and what Marx on the other hand feels is needed, is a reflection on the very nature of law, such as will be fully able to embrace, historically and logically, the sources to which the history of the law gives us access. This is one of the main reasons for the attention given by Marx the student of law to Gans and to Hegel.

Care must be taken, however, not to dismiss the influence of Savigny too lightly (Levine 1987; Raggi 1980). As intimated, the study of possession brings with it the question of where the law begins, and of what might be the element, the fact or whatever else that allows something to be considered 'legally relevant'. Taking the approach of Savigny, the logical impossibility of going from possession (fact) to lawful ownership brings the risk that the law will be imposed by an external agent as something from outside, something given. In other words, since there is no *nature propre* of right or law, one has the risk that it could become whatever anyone, generally someone powerful, decides that it should be. On the subject of possession, the question is peculiarly apparent: it is surely conceivable that those who have succeeded in taking what they want for themselves by force, will also have thought about transforming their possession of what they have acquired into lawful ownership. In the case of possession, a possible original connection between law and violence appears more noticeably, as also does the division, mentioned previously, between *recht* in the sense of 'just' and a *Recht* in the sense of 'law' (the law of someone, one might say, or simply the law of the strongest).

The move by Marx toward the Hegelian approach is concerned not least with the attempt to avoid this potential drift of a law founded ultimately on mere *Gewalt*. However, the possibility that not even Hegel could fully resolve the basic question as to the origin of the law remains entrenched – at least as a possibility – in Marx's own head, and it would emerge later on, as history shows, in a conception of the nature of the law arrived at by way of Hegel, beyond Hegel (Clochec 2019). As Marx continued to shape this conception of the law, a decisive part in its development would still be played, as we shall see, by the contributions of the young Gans, and indeed of Savigny too, to an extent.

2 Thefts of Wood

The question of possession and property is also central to articles published by Marx in the *Rheinische Zeitung* and concerned with the debate on the law against the theft of wood. The approach is journalistic, with parts of the discourse descending into a rhetoric that spills over at times into eristic sarcasm. Nonetheless, Marx would remember these pieces as marking the moment when he began to look on legal studies as a 'subject subordinated to philosophy and history', with a shift in focus toward economic matters, so much so that he would define them as the first occasion when his attention was turned to 'material interests' and, in effect, to 'economy' (Marx 1859a: 261–262). Reading the articles, it is clear how Marx still has a much greater mastery of legal language than of economic language (Guastini 1974). Even so, one can discern a shift in approach to the questions of possession and property which, as we will see, becomes interlaced with questions of an anthropological nature, and in particular, a deeper reflection on the theme of action.

Marx is scathing in his attacks on the deputies of the Rhenish *Landtag*, busily utilizing the modern notion of exclusive land ownership to defend the feudal tenures which they themselves held. In this sense, the articles represent an interesting historical documentation of the conflict in progress between the manner of conceiving relationships between persons and things in modern codifications, and previously existing methods of viewing these relationships, with particular reference to customary forms established in common law (Xifaras 2002; Mascat 2019).

From time immemorial, it had become common practice in the Rhineland, among the poorer strata of the population, to gather dead woodshed naturally by trees, in the same way as berries and forest fruits would be gathered. An act of taking possession which, by dint of usage, resulted in the wood becoming the property of the gatherers. The permissibility of such an appropriation was assured by the consuetudinary nature of part of the law, and at the same time – as Marx did not fail to point out – by the equivocal nature of how property was conceived in common law (Marx 1842a: 232). The aim of the deputies of the Rhenish Diet was to enforce the right of exclusive land ownership so as to eliminate this customary practice which, under the new economic conditions of land management, had become an annoying hindrance. The means by which the provincial assembly sought to achieve this aim was quite clear: the gathering of wood, or whatever else, would be defined as trespassing, hence tantamount to theft. It is clear enough from several standpoints that the reasons for the Diet taking such a drastic decision were to a large extent economic in character, albeit the most prominent of these was concerned not with wood, but with myrtle berries and other forest fruits: the custom of gathering these items, carried on '*since time immemorial*' by the 'children of the poor', now had to be prevented, because 'the berries in this region have already been commercialized and are shipped by the barrel to Holland' (Marx 1842a: 234–235).

During this period, Marx finds a firm answer in the writings of Hegel to the question of the nature of the law, and many passages in the newspaper articles clearly show this faith in the strength of the law as a means of bringing out 'the general obligation to tell the truth', and determining the 'legal nature of things'

(Marx 1842a: 227). This brings a correlated confidence in the role of the state, an ethical whole in which confrontation between parties must find a necessary and higher reconciliation, made possible precisely by the universal instruments of codified law. And yet, at the same time, Marx appears unsettled. It seems at times that, through codification, the 'legal nature of things' could be violated further, rather than finally protected. Above all, it is clear that the deputies of the Rhenish Diet are utilizing instruments of the law, in particular the right of exclusive land ownership, to defend their interests against those of the impoverished classes. From the debates of the Diet, it appears that the right to the exclusive ownership of land is nothing other than a legal recognition of an act of violence on the part of the landowners. And if this same violence were really to be the origin and foundation of the law?

The need to clear up this doubt convinces Marx to study the question in greater depth and to search for conceptual tools that will enable him to overcome the *impasse*. It could be that the concepts of jurisprudence may not be sufficient for the purpose, as likewise Hegel's philosophy of right may not suffice, at least in part. Indeed, it was his researches in the field of economics, combined with a reflection on the anthropological significance of human action, that would enable Marx to resolve at least some of his doubts. And the decisive mediation in this process would come through the writings of Eduard Gans.

It is significant that Gans himself had felt the need, in his review of Hegel's *Lineaments*, to insist in particular on a reappraisal of the doctrine of possession. It is even more significant if one considers that one of the criticisms levelled by Gans against Hegel is that of not having given sufficient thought to an 'extreme case' of possession: theft (Bertani 2004: 286ff). The theme of possession is one of the levers on which Marx leans hard in his attempt to give deeper thought to the question of the sense of the law, and consequently, that which makes the law what it is, namely human volition and action.

Looking at Marx's construction of the questions of action and labour, which would find its purest expression in the writing of *Das Kapital*, one of the essential catalysts is discernible in comparison with the review by Gans of Hegel's doctrine on possession. Reading the thoughts of Gans on possession in conjunction with certain pieces by Marx from the period in question would appear to confirm this theory.

One of the fundamental questions that Gans takes up attentively is that of *Ergreifung*, i.e., 'taking possession' in its most literal sense, that is to say the physical, bodily sense: the movement of the body which, in carrying through an intention, an act of volition, takes possession of a thing. The part of the body used to take possession is predominantly the hand. Volition is thus manifested primarily through the movement of the hand, which is the body part that most readily distinguishes human from animal. However, this 'taking of possession' is in effect something 'quite singular': if on the one hand, 'I take possession of no more than I can touch with my body', it is self-evident on the other that 'external objects [*Dinge*] extend further than I can grasp' (Gans on Hegel 1991, § 55, 85). If I grasp the handle of a door, what can I claim to possess? The handle, the door, or the entire dwelling? In this regard, says Gans, nothing further can be deduced from the concept pure and simple, and positive law must make its own provisions.

From these few passages alone, it is clear that the meditation of Gans does not begin directly with the person, as in the case of Hegel, but dwells longer on the question of the body, leaving the focus on the person – associated inevitably with property – to emerge only at a later stage. This greater insistence on the question of the body would be important for Marx as well.

Before considering the thoughts of Marx, it is worthwhile drawing attention to a further passage of the Gans doctrine on possession. If one asks, what is it that makes a thing the possession of someone, it is probable that the most classic of references on the question will spring to mind, one that finds its canonical formulation in the *Second Treatise on Civil Government* by John Locke: what comes into my possession, becomes *mine*, is what I manage to make with my own hands. This poses the familiar and immediately consequential problem that possession should extend only as far as the limit of my capacity for labour, and no further. There is no reference of this type in the comments by Gans. The word 'labour' does not appear, and is replaced by 'giving form' [*Formierung*] to something. For Gans, the true vehicle for taking possession is not labour, but the ability to 'make a *sign*' on something. 'Giving form' is inevitably an act of *changing* the form that existed previously, hence sending a signal that the thing belongs to whoever has *fashioned* it differently to how it was before. Associating possession with the ability to 'make a sign', it is clear that any limit determined by labour is to a large extent avoided. To possess a field, one need not necessarily work the land; it can be enough to redraw the boundaries. The example given by Gans, in effect, is not Locke's ideal of working the land, but that of a simple sign, like the 'cockade', which indicates citizenship of a given state. It is not by virtue of labour, but by dint of the ability to 'make a sign' that 'human beings display their mastery over things' (Gans on Hegel 1991, § 58, 88). Thus, while referencing the theme of the body, the question of possession is resolved ultimately by Gans in terms of representation. From this perspective, Gans proceeds entirely in keeping with the Hegelian dialectic of persons and things: the former cannot exist without the possibility of manifesting themselves in the latter, thereby possessing them, and having this possession recognized. It follows therefore, of necessity, that 'everyone should have property' (Gans on Hegel 1991, § 49, 81).

It is to this point that Marx directs his attention, and while not denying the legal necessity for the representation of possession and property, he reveals its alienating dynamic, within the process of bourgeois appropriation and codification. To this end, Marx moves away from legal construction, returning to it only later, and dwells more on the question of the body and of *Ergreifung*. Already, in the area of the debates on wood theft, there is manifestly a clash between those who hold *possession* because they have done the *labour* of gathering (protected legally by long-standing custom) and those who, on the basis of codified law, claim possession of land by reason of having placed a sign on it. Taking this conflict as the starting point, Marx asks the question, what behaviour might correspond truly to the legal nature of things, and, consequently, what should be the approach taken by the lawmaker in this regard? It is significant, in this regard, to emphasize how certain fundamental notions of the subsequent economic discussion, like the distinction between possessors only of their own body and possessors of capital, and the fundamental concept of *value,* are already formulated to a degree in the articles published in the *Rhenish Gazette* (Marx 1842a: 229, 233ff). These early formulations are not yet exact, but – perhaps more interestingly – they are still connoted legally, and they show how that which would become the economic thinking of Marx finds a matrix within certain legal notions, at least in part.

3   Possession, Property, Labour and the Powerlessness of the State

The question of possession is thus reappraised by Marx beginning with the body and its activity. This is a period during which his thinking can be described broadly as anthropological in character, interwoven thereafter with ultimately thorough explorations of the economic sphere. The person-and-thing relationship is still discussed but expressed differently: it is no longer the legal relation that occupies the forefront; a new line of thought now comes in, which could be defined as primarily economic-social in character. In this dimension, Marx also reconsiders the question of the body and its activity, a significant part of which is qualified as *labour*, conceived here as a bodily activity channelled into productive ends.

It is with this approach that Marx once again, in his *Economic and Philosophic Manuscripts of 1844,* addresses the questions of possession, property, and the relationship between people and things. People *act*, using their mental and physical faculties to pursue productive ends. However, they do not have possession of their activity, as it has been sold beforehand to someone else, who does not claim to be the owner of this or that object that has been produced, but of the actual source of the activity that produced it, namely the labour. This creates the possibility for a peculiar kind of appropriation: the owner does not simply take possession of a given thing or object but establishes control – if only for a finite period (the working day) – of the *actual movement* that goes from externalization of one's activity, through possession, to property. And yet, in the light of Hegel's thinking, this movement was precisely the factor that made it possible for man to think of himself as a *person* (Sereni 2007). If a working man cannot become a *person*, he remains a mere body, and, as long as he is at work, his very life is incorporated into the activity of production. What is more, he cannot escape from this gradual process of alienation from himself; indeed, he has become a part of the process precisely because he found himself in the position of being *freely* in possession only of his own body and of his activity. Here, the taking of possession founded on *Gewalt* is replaced by the taking of possession founded on *need*, which in this case however is not the need for this or that commodity, but the very need to ensure survival (Marx 1844d: 220). And so, the placement of a mark or sign, guaranteed by the instrument of the contract and establishing legal recognition of property, appears necessarily, from the standpoint of the worker, as the application of an external sign, or, in the words of Marx, 'a mere *condition* external to man' (Marx 1844a: 290). It certainly comes within the dialectic between possessor of one's own body and possessor of the means of production, but, as it renders mutual recognition between person and thing impossible, it cannot come within the *Recht* of the state, in the sense that Hegel saw it. Things themselves, by reason of an *Ergreifung* that is never for oneself, but for others, now become enemies: unknown and dehumanized if not altogether rivalrous. Marx begins here to discern that the state is not or cannot any longer be that ethical whole which is able to guarantee the creation of political and legal rationality (Ballarin 1985–1986: 263). If anything, the state represents the 'present structure [*Einrichtung*] of society', a society founded on certain models of property and on a certain method of production, one that causes the civil life of at least a part of the population to be rendered 'unsocial', and in respect of which the state administration cannot be anything other than absolutely powerless (Marx 1844e: 198–199).

The strong change of perspective in the way that Marx comes to regard the state is identifiable in the separation, which underpins the capitalist system, between that peculiar activity of the mind and body known as 'labour' and the resulting 'possession' of the actual fruit of labour, which is now legitimately appropriated by the owner through a contract. On this point, the mediation of the state runs into difficulty. In effect, the state is no longer able to guarantee that singularity which made it possible to embrace the concept – essential to the logic of the Hegelian state – of 'person'. The identity of the person is shaped through the movement of constant appropriation, which goes from exteriority to interiority and vice-versa and is thus manifested in the legal concepts of possession and property, without which it would not even be imaginable. Now, this movement is blocked at source by appropriation – immediate and guaranteed through the instrument of the contract – of the activity of the body of the worker by the possessor of the labour produced, who is legitimated in law by the state, no less. As part of Marx's complex and frenetic research during the early 1840s, he would progress from a reading of Hegel mediated by the writings of Gans, to a direct reading of the selfsame Hegel, combined with initial attempts to address economic questions. At the same time, he makes a defence of the liberal state (seen inevitably more from the perspective of Gans than of Hegel) against the corporate state and the idea of a theologically founded state, which goes on to critique the foundations of the selfsame liberal state and, inevitably, the law on which it is founded. It is on this latter passage, in particular, that the questioning of possession and property seems especially important. On this point, having agreed formerly with Gans, in part against Savigny and above all as concerning the interpretation of Hegel's writings, Marx now takes a stand against his teacher; and he does so precisely by renewing that attack on the theme of body *and Ergreifung* that Gans himself had made in comments on the *Lineaments* of Hegel, mediated and in the end completely reinterpreted in the light of his incipient economic considerations. If the notion of possession is not reflected uniquely in the relationship between volition and (first) appropriation, but rather, defined constitutively also by a movement of the body, then the 'cockade', the placement of a sign as a distinguishing mark of appropriation – here, the labour contract – at the same time inevitably becomes an act of expropriation against whoever materially accomplished the movement: the worker. It follows that the institution of property, which underpins the notion of the person, and indeed of the bourgeois state (Basso 2008: 52ff), is an original act of usurpation. The act of *Gewalt* is thus the true origin of the law, or at any rate of that *Recht* on which the state is founded. Just as the corporate state could guarantee neither the universality of the law nor the ethical whole of the state, being reduced to an unmediated conflict between particular interests, the same is true for a state founded along bourgeois lines, which reintroduces a rift in the very foundation of its institution. Here too, one sees the conflict between general interests and particular interests that had already characterized the corporate state (Marx 1844e: 198). Naturally, this is a conflict founded on completely different standpoints, having significant consequences in the areas of the economy and politics, and above all, that of the political struggle.

First of all, the origin of the state is now identifiable with a separation between proprietor and proletarian, that is, between those able to generate the movement that goes from possession to property (and ultimately, to capital) and those who inevitably possess nothing more than labour force. According to the logic of Hegel's ethical state, if the possessor of mere labour force is excluded from property, he is also inevitably excluded from the political community. In one part of the *Kritische Randglossen* Marx would be very clear on this point: the exclusion of the worker from his own labour places him in a state of isolation from the political community and that of the state. This very isolation from the community is at the heart of every rebellion: just as the French Revolution had its origins in the isolation of French citizens from the political community, so in these times the 'rebellion' begins with the isolation of the workers (Marx 1844e: 204). Consistently with his reappraisal of the role of the state, Marx makes the point that the goal of the rebellion – which, significantly, he also refers to as 'industrial revolt' – can no longer be the political community, the state, or at least not this alone. A political revolt would retain a 'parochial spirit', whereas only an industrial revolt, partial though it may appear, in reality has a *'universal* soul' (Marx 1844e: 205). In the passage mentioned here, this universality is still defined in terms of a 'human essence', which Marx refers to as the true 'communal essence' [*Gemeinwesen*]. Marx is still expressing his thoughts using a broadly anthropological language, typical of this first period of his research. The reduction of the political role attributed to the state, given its inability to mediate the relationship between persons and things in the emerging system of social relations shaped by the new industrial milieu, is plain to see. The division between the two meanings of the adjective *recht* in the sense of legal [*rechtlich*] and of right [*recht*] is inevitable. The breach created by this division, discussed here still in generally anthropological terms, would soon prompt the consideration of a broader horizon for social relations, with the state representing only one component, albeit a hugely important one: the horizon would quickly become that of the world market.

CHAPTER 2

Breaking the Chain of Time

Marx and the French Historians

Isabella Consolati

Marx was, throughout his life, a voracious reader of history books, on any period, on disparate topics and on almost every point on the globe (Mosolov 1973; Rubel 1957; Krätke 2018). The tension to appropriate historical material is unrelenting, even if this knowledge only partly emerges in his published works. Eric Hobsbawm is right when he states that Marx uses history, but not as a historian (Hobsbawm 1984: 107). Marx not only rejects the philosophy of history, but also the boundaries by virtue of which history became a discipline in the 19th century: the distinction between history and 'this nonsensical pre-history' (Marx and Engels 1845–1846: 42), between history and nature, between political history and special histories. This is also why the Marxian conception of history had the effect of a 'charge of dynamite on historical science' (Hobsbawm 1984: 106).

For Marx, 'the subject-matter of history is structured and accessible to thought' (Vilar 1973: 65) and the science of society is historical for a reason that cannot be circumvented: 'all property relations in the past have continually been subject to historical change' (Marx and Engels 1848: 498). From this anti-metaphysical assumption, Marx identifies a specificity of the capitalist mode of production that is historical in a more extensive as well as more intensive sense than previous modes of production. More extensive because capital inaugurates universal history as set of conditions involving all individuals (Ricciardi 2019), unfolding at the level of the world market; more intensive not because it represents a higher degree of civilization, but because it is a structure that cannot but deconstruct itself insofar as it is characterized by radical antagonism (Negri 1991). History is therefore in a specific sense the science of capitalist society.

The link between history and the present is reinforced by the fact that Marx describes communism in its theoretical side as 'science, which is produced by the historical movement' (Marx 1847a: 178). Marx makes one clarification: the existence of the proletariat and the action of the working class offer a privileged access to history. Hence there are not simply multiple perspectives on history, but the point of view of those who exercize domination and aim to preserve it, who do not and cannot see history in the present, and the revolutionary point of view that recognizes and intensifies the movement in action by making history in the present (Balibar 1974). History is thus the history of those who are oppressed not because of a tradition of injustice and defeat, but from the subversive possibility recognized in the present misery.

Marx is attracted to the science of the rising bourgeoisie as a science produced by the historical movement. He thus recognizes that the idea of history as class struggle is not his invention. After inviting him to tell the 'democratic gents ... they should study the historical works of Thierry, Guizot, John Wade and so forth, in order to enlighten themselves as to the past "history of the classes"', Marx writes to Weydemeyer:

> I do not claim to have discovered either the existence of classes in modern society or the struggle between them. Long before me, bourgeois historians had described the historical development of this struggle between the classes, as had bourgeois economists their economic anatomy.
>
> MARX to WEYDEMEYER 3/5/1852 in MECW 39: 62

In this chapter, I focus on Marx's reading of two French historians to whom he gives credit for having identified society as the 'theatre of all history' (Marx and Engels 1845–1846: 50): Augustin Thierry and François Guizot. Clues to the study of the works of Thierry and Guizot – which probably took place in the first half of the 1840s (Perini 1976; Kaiser 1967: 81, 213) – are already present in *The German Ideology* (1845–1846). The description of the long and uneven rise of the Third Estate gives Marx a picture of a social movement that cannot be traced back to the intentions of particular individuals and to political events. His imagination is captivated by this story of human masses in movement: if Marx draws material on the changes in the division of labour in the transition from the centrality of the countryside to the city from the histories of civil society, Thierry and Guizot provide him with a reading of this transformation as an antagonistic process. Nevertheless, like the classical economists – the 'historians' of the era in which the bourgeoisie struggled against the feudal society (Marx 1847a: 176) – who believe that 'there has been history, but there is no longer any' (Marx 1847a: 174), so the bourgeois historians identify the antagonism in order to declare its end and establish a principle of government. Marx, on the contrary, intends to bring history back into the present. While the French historians aim to 'join anew the chain of time and ideas' (Thierry 1859: 7), stating that the constitutional role of the historical discipline is to mend the rift produced by the Revolution and declare the end of domination as the remnant of a past conquest, Marx uses history instead to break that chain, to indicate the persistence of domination within capitalist society, and to investigate the conditions in which the proletariat can take the lead in the historical movement.

One of the ways in which Marx brings history into the present is by constructing an analogy between the bourgeoisie's centuries-old rise against the feudal regime and the proletarian uprising. In the *Manifesto*, after describing the way in which the bourgeoisie broke the limits of feudal property relations, Marx and Engels write:

> A similar movement is going on before our own eyes. ... For many a decade past the history of industry and commerce is but the history of the revolt of modern productive forces against modern conditions of production.
>
> MARX and ENGELS 1848: 489

The process is similar, but with a leap in scale and radicality: the struggle of the proletariat against the bourgeoisie does not stop at the borders of the nation but takes its place at the level of the world market; its aim is not domination, but liberation from all enslavement.

In the 1950s this analogy disappears even at the rhetorical level. Re-immersing himself in historical research, Marx delves into the conditions that hold back what seemed to be the rapid overthrow of capitalist society. What matters is not to add a chapter to the eternal struggle between oppressed and oppressors, substituting a more truthful end of history to the end of bourgeois history. Rather, the task is to follow the history of the global conditions within which the action of the proletariat is situated (Consolati 2018). Marx and Engels thus broaden the spectrum of investigation to the internal dynamics of the world market and note that, on this scale, the upward movement of the bourgeoisie has not yet come to a halt: it 'has for the second time experienced its 16th century' (Marx to Engels 10/8/1858 in MECW 40: 346). Initially convinced that the bourgeoisie would contribute with some speed to its own decline, over the years Marx deepened the heavily destructive character of the movement of capital and the counter-revolutionary tension produced by the entry of the proletariat as a class into history (Bongiovanni 1989a). The attempt to seal a pact between the past and the present that excludes the proletariat from the political scene is the response to the European revolution of 1848, the 'nasty revolution' (Marx 1850a: 69) in the face of which the French historical school casts off its anti-feudal robes to take up arms against those who, by breaking the unity of the people, 'repudiated the past ages' (Guizot 1875: 238). The initial analogy between the struggle of the bourgeoisie against the nobility and that of the proletariat against the bourgeoisie also recedes once and for all when the bourgeoisie's deep entanglement with persistent 'remnants' of feudalism emerges in order to solidify that society which the same deployed capital increasingly threatens to ruin. Thierry and Guizot's reading allows us to show the implications and tensions of this passage.

Augustin Thierry, defined by Marx as the *'le père* of the class struggle' (Marx to Engels 7/27/1854 in MECW 39: 473), began his career working alongside Saint-Simon, from whom he distanced himself by declaring that he was more attracted by medieval disorder than by industrial order (Ducange 2015). He thus began to investigate the origins of the precarious order that had emerged from the French Revolution in order to identify in the past indications of the subject who should lead the nation as well as the constitutional order most suited to stabilising the swirling movement of history. His research culminated in *The Formation and Progress of the Tiers État* (1853), in which the initial radical opposition between the conquering Franks and the industrious Gauls was moderated through an action of progressive social levelling by the Third Estate and the monarchy (Gossman 1976; Farrer 1972). Thus, French history over the previous six centuries is understood as a 'vast movement' that eliminated all relations of personal domination 'to exhibit at length in their stead a united people, a law the same to all, a free and sovereign people' (Thierry 1859: 14).

Marx wrote to Engels that Thierry's book 'has interested me greatly', and among the *Exzerpte* there are more than seventy pages of notes. What attracts his attention is, first and foremost, the history of the antagonistic constitution of the bourgeoisie through 'this sequence of metamorphoses leading up to the domination of the class', which 'has never before been thus presented – at least so far as the material is concerned' (Marx to Engels 7/27/1854 in MECW 39: 474). According to Thierry's portrayal, in the formation of the Third Estate there are multiple stratifications and two opposing movements, one of progress, the other of decadence: beyond the original opposition between conquerors and conquered, which inaugurates history as the scene of a more or less latent conflict, the transition from the Middle Ages to the modern age is the story of a dissolution and the story of a constitution that involves the industrial class. The municipal revolution of the 18th century is the first political movement in which the hitherto dispersed and fragmented burgesses are the protagonists. The first political action of the Third Estate, from the moment it obtained a place in the Estates General, was to assert municipal rights against feudal privileges. In his notes, Marx emphasizes the insistence on the insurrectional origin of the communes and finds in them the birth of a 'law of the bourgeoisie hostile to that of the noble classes which regulates according to its principles the status of persons, the constitution of the family and the transmission of inheritance' (Marx 1853h: 521).

The recognition of the communes as the first moment of the bourgeoisie's constitution as a class is already clear in *The German Ideology*. Here, the creation of common ideas and interests among the serfs who fled the countryside is determined for Marx through 'the contradiction to the existing relations and of the mode of labour determined by this' (Marx and Engels 1845–1846: 76), well before a declared political partition that tends to make programmatic the connection between the ideas and interests of the various strata that comprise the industrial class. Marx thus emphasizes in his notes, firstly, the fact that the process of emancipation from feudal constraints cannot be traced back to a project but arose from an individual mass movement such as the flight of the serfs from the countryside. Second, he stresses that the individual subtraction was painstakingly followed by an organized opposition that was anything but linear, since the class was divided into multiple strata that were often in conflict with each other.

In the second stage, the legal production resulting from the insurrection of the communes was countered by what Thierry calls a new 'right subversive of existing rights' (Thierry 1859: 57): through the recovery of Roman law, the public law of the rising monarchy contributed to defusing both feudal and municipal constitutions. While polemicizing against those who consider sworn communities the result of royal concessions, Thierry insists on the progressive function of the monarchy in producing the conditions of political equality and administrative centralization. According to Thierry, a new society is only truly inaugurated when the Third Estate renounces the defence of municipal rights, that is, when its commercial components achieve hegemony, even by temporarily mixing, during the French Revolution and in the face of the excesses of absolutist power, with those popular strata that are irrepressible in their destructively democratic tendencies. It is now no longer the fugitive outlaws organized in sworn communities who are at the head of the antagonism, but the class of officers and the commercial bourgeoisie. In this passage, Marx notes the fact that the claim to municipal freedom is equated with feudal privilege, while the spirit of independence of the communes is replaced by an attachment 'to things purely practical and of present interest' (Marx 1853h: 527). When meticulously annotating Thierry's text, there is no place for mechanical considerations concerning the mirroring of material interests and ideas. What emerges from this reading is Marx's focus on the historical process that from fragmentation leads to the constitution of common ideas and interests against existing relations. The resulting society bears the mark of the anti-feudal struggle, that is, of the historical conditions within which its constitution was determined, including the identification of history with the progressive liberation from the domination of man over man and the related claim to have put an end to domination and thus to history itself.

While commenting on these passages, Marx highlights the basic flaw in Thierry's reconstruction, namely his desire to declare the end of the struggle and thus of history in the unity of the nation. This desire is manifested in the preface of the book, where Thierry rails against those who, in 1848, propose counter-histories that trace the origin of the conflict between the bourgeoisie and the proletariat to the distant past. In this respect, Marx notes that the

> Third Estate is not exclusively the bourgeoisie, much less bourgeoisie as a class. It is the people, insofar as the bourgeoisie, as opposed to the nobility and the clergy, represents them. The Third Estate contains the elements, which after its victory split up, but all under the leadership of the bourgeoisie. As for 'the roots in history of an antagonism born yesterday', this results from Thierry's own representation.
>
> MARX 1853h: 501

In Thierry's narrative, the Third Estate is a peculiar subject, being both author and product of the social revolution that decrees its progressive rise. The subject of history is constituted and transformed in the course of history itself and then disappears, triumphing in the unity of the nation (Thierry 1859: 215). Marx emphasizes that, in order to produce that definitive pact between past and present that puts an end to history, Thierry must resort to the representative device that allows the Third Estate and the people to overlap, and the former to make history in the name of the latter. The narrative of the rise of the bourgeoisie is thus inaugurated and punctuated by the convocation of the Estates General, in which, as Marx notes, only a small portion of the people was actually represented. This portion, however, 'considered itself charged with supporting the cause of the mass of non-nobles' (Marx 1853h: 523). For Thierry, moreover, the history of the Third Estate, and thus the antagonism, ends when the Estates General are dissolved, and the representative principle is realized in the social unity of the whole people. In the coincidence of the Third Estate and the people, Marx sees the condition for decreeing the end of history when this coincidence has no remaining obstacles deriving from the past. He then reverses this assumption: the Third Estate can only appear as 'one' as long as its struggle against the nobility and clergy lasts. Indeed, 'had Mr. Thierry read our stuff, he would know that the decisive opposition between bourgeoisie and *people* does not, of course, crystallize until the former ceases, as *tiers-état*, to oppose the *clergé* and the *noblesse*' (Marx to Engels 7/27/1854 in MECW 39: 474). If Marx already indicates the constitution of a new domination well within the history of the Third Estate – which Thierry does not grasp by glossing over the history of the guilds and the commercial bourgeoisie in a striking manner – at the same time he affirms the need to think of the formation of the class not so much from a set of interests and from ideas that reflect them, but from the combination of ideas and interests that is formed in the struggle against a specific existing situation. The bourgeoisie itself only becomes a class in its own right at the moment when it stops being a people and opposes the proletariat.

The relationship between the bourgeoisie and the proletariat thus has nothing to do with Marx's historical re-proposition of a Hegelian master-slave dialectic. In Thierry's narrative, two worlds confront each other through the historical figures of winners and losers: conquest and industry, war and labour. Once political equality has been achieved, the conflict in which the Third Estate is the protagonist can come to an end. On the contrary, it is not possible for the proletariat to 'achieve its salvation behind society's back' (Marx 1852a: 110). Antagonism is of a different quality also because it is not based on the claim to represent the whole of society, it is the antagonism of a part that does not unify different subjects in a representative sense (Battistini 2004). Thus, by rejecting the representative device that bridges the distance between social movement and political partition through a single narrative, this distance opens up as a theoretical and practical problem. Communism as a product of the historical movement is in any case not its representation, narrative or political. Marx uses history, but not as a historian.

For Guizot, more decisively than in Thierry, the recognition of the class struggle as the moving principle of history serves to place social peace as the primary goal of government (Rosanvallon 1985; Thies 2008). Guizot, like Thierry, also criticizes the idea that political legitimacy derives from a past achievement. On the contrary, real legitimacy is conferred by duration, as it is the recognisable sign of the agreement between political order and social order. Time sanctions a power that is not absolute because it is measured by the slow work of civilization, a 'silent and concealed work of centralization ... accomplished ... without premeditation or design' (Guizot 1875: 196), which constitutes 'the general and definitive fact' (Guizot 1875: 5). Political power can either favour the movement for the formation of a single society from the many struggling societies, becoming its representative and holding point, or hinder it. The anti-historical power is not only the reactionary one, but also the one that pretends – as both absolute monarchs and revolutionaries did in the 18th century – to impose untimely and arbitrary rational projects on the general fact of civilization. Compared to Thierry, Guizot is more resolute in portraying the monarchy as an anti-feudal institution, recognising in the Orleanist monarchy the power finally capable of preserving the relationship between past and present against those who want to sever it by declaring war on society. This is, moreover, the vocation that the monarchy has demonstrated throughout its history, along which it has walked 'with the same step' as that of society (Guizot 1875: 162). Together with the people, it has been the force that has opposed the feudal regime, constituting the holding point of a society that 'desires to form and regulate itself, without knowing how to do so by the free concord of individual wills'. In relation to this society it has, depending on historical events, acted to 'retard the dissolution of society' or to 'accelerate its formation', becoming the guarantor of the continuity of the history of civilization (Guizot 1875: 168). Monarchical centralization thus responded to the dissolution of community ties produced by the crisis of the feudal society and to the constitutive political instability of the communal world, first by saving its different bodies and then by intervening to produce a social and symbolic levelling. With the guilds reintroducing privilege into the communal constitution and the resulting inequality between an upper middle class and a population of day labourers, the need then arose for political control of the popular segment animated by 'a blind, unbridled and ferocious spirit of democracy' (Guizot 1875: 143). It is not unlikely that Marx is referring to Guizot when, in *Moral Criticism and Moralising Criticism* (1847), he writes:

> Modern histories have demonstrated that *absolute monarchy* appears in those transitional periods when the old feudal estates are in decline and the medieval estate of burghers is evolving into the modern bourgeois class, without one of the contending parties having as yet finally disposed of the other. The elements on which absolute monarchy is based are thus by no means its own product; they rather form its social prerequisite.
>
> MARX 1847b: 326

Marx is grappling here with the problem of German political 'backwardness' and with democrats who misread it as the eternal law of the relationship between political power and social constitution, identifying the democratic form as the solution to the social question. Denouncing the distortions of the Prussian monarchy, they fail to see that elsewhere it does not play against, but in favour of the unfolding of capitalist society. This is true according to Marx starting with the history of absolutism in its relation to capitalist accumulation. The historical talent that Marx acknowledges in Guizot consists in relating political power to the movement taking place in society (Jaeck 1988). Yet, if Guizot identifies the sign of its eternal mission in the mediating role that the monarchy has historically played, carefully distinguishing the universal principle from the accidental excesses that have nonetheless propped up its history, Marx derives from it the link between the monarchy and its 'social prerequisite', as well as in general the need to consider the modern state historically, in the many places and different forms that it has assumed. This does not mean believing that, once the social conditions have changed, the political form will adapt by itself: the apparatus that supported the claims of absolute sovereigns cannot easily be consigned to the past. Not only does it maintain its constitutional role in countries, such as Germany, where a scaffolding of social compromises continues to hold up forms of domination that appear obsolete. Elsewhere too, in fact, this apparatus

> remains for a long time afterwards in possession of a traditional power in the illusory community (state, law), which has won an existence independent of the individuals; a power which in the last resort can only be broken by a revolution.
>
> MARX and ENGELS 1845–1846: 83

A problem thus emerges in relation to politics and its history that is not resolved in the mirroring of class interests and political form but requires us to consider the historical and anti-historical character of political power in a relation, that is as constant as it is empirically varied, with the upheavals taking place in society.

These themes returned in 1850, when Marx reviewed Guizot's booklet entitled *Pourquoi la révolution d'Angleterre a-t-elle-réussi?*. The review is important because here the relationship between revolution, society, and the forms of politics is explored, shortly before Louis Bonaparte's 18 Brumaire decisively twisted this relationship. By telling the story of the English revolution, Guizot intends to show the reasons why it 'succeeded', i.e. that it resulted in a lasting order which is missing in France because there it is pursued 'in vain, amid those mysterious experiments in revolution' (Guizot 1856: 1). The English revolution broke out because 'great changes had taken place in the relative strengths of the various classes … without any anlogous change having been wrought in the government' (Guizot 1856: 38). The sequel is a disjointed attempt by the Commons and the Crown to put an end to the revolution by curbing those who aim not only to reform the political order to bring it into line with the social order, but also to destroy society. The essay concludes with a warning directed across the Channel: 'the policy which preserves states is also that alone which terminates and founds revolutions' (Guizot 1856: 78). In reviewing the pamphlet, Marx focuses on the causes that Guizot puts forward to explain the conservative character of the English revolution (Marx 1850b; Hill 1948). The problem that arises is the distinction between the revolution that perfects the state, eliminating its 'anti-historical' elements, and the revolution that destroys society (Hill 1948). Guizot justifies conservatism partly by its religious character and partly by the traditionalist tendency of parliaments, whose aim was to secure society against coming revolutions and the excesses of absolutism. In response to this, Marx points out that the parallel constructed by Guizot is 'coarse', because he does not analyse 'the entirely different position of the classes' in the two historical situations but focuses on the balance between Parliament and the Crown and on foreign policy, ignoring the relationship between these, economic policy and the rise of the financial and industrial bourgeoisie. It is remarkable, Marx writes, that

> even the most capable people of the *ancien régime*, people whose own kind of talent in the realm of history can by no means be disputed, have been brought to such a state of perplexity by the fatal events of February that they have lost all understanding of history.
>
> MARX 1850b: 251

The enigma of the conservative character of the English Revolution and its difference from the French Revolution, which Guizot fails to grasp, lies instead in the alliance between the bourgeoisie and the landowners, who in fact already hold bourgeois property, not feudal property. Here the historical pattern of the rise of the bourgeoisie takes on a specific configuration due as much to the particular evolution of the English commercial bourgeoisie as to the early emergence of manufacturing as to the transformations that had already taken place in feudal property itself. Guizot also replicates the basic flaw of his school: the coincidence between constitutional equilibrium and the end of history. 'For M. Guizot, English history ends with the consolidation of the constitutional monarchy', writes Marx (Marx 1850b: 255). He, on the contrary, reads in the English revolution a political, rather than a bourgeois, revolution (Bongiovanni 1989b: 20) which, passing through the republic, leads to the consolidation of the constitutional monarchy. It is not an end, however, but the beginning of a revolution deeper than any political revolution. With it, in fact, 'the large-scale development and transformation of bourgeois society in England began' (Marx 1850b: 255). Where Guizot sees nothing but quiet,

> the most violent conflicts, the most thoroughgoing revolutions, were actually developing ... A new, more colossal bourgeoisie arises. While the old bourgeoisie fights the French Revolution, the new one conquers the world market.
>
> MARX 1850b: 255

Against the reduction of a mass social movement to the constitutional game, Marx contrasts the gap between the violent but superficial changes in the political form and the profound social transformation, which is also brought about by the apparently stable framework of the constitutional monarchy that is all Guizot can see. While Guizot congratulates himself on the fact that England is untouched by the aberrations of socialism, he does not realize that

> class antagonisms in English society have become more acute than in any other country. Here a bourgeoisie possessed of unequalled wealth and productive forces is opposed by a proletariat whose strength and concentration are likewise unequalled.
>
> MARX 1850b: 255

Marx does not insist on the revolutionary tradition of those who, like the Levellers, first posed the social question as a problem irreducible to changes in government. He does not engage in the telling of a counter-history of the English revolution. The image of a present history that literally happens in another place than the one in which the balance between Parliament and the Crown is played out is a clear indication of the critique of politics as a sphere capable of guaranteeing and representing historical continuity.

With the *coup d'état* of Louis Bonaparte, it became clear to Marx that the bourgeoisie, the protagonist in the worldwide transformation of the conditions of production and social reproduction, was increasingly embracing counter-revolutionary positions. What are the reasons for that turning back of history? In part this is because in France the class conflict has not reached the extent and intensity that makes it a general fact: 'the struggle of the industrial wage-worker against the industrial bourgeois is in France a partial phenomenon' (Marx 1850a: 57). There is also, however, the 'anti-historical' action of the bourgeoisie in the face of the danger of proletarian revolution. In this sense, the conflicting monarchist factions, united in the party of order that dominated the representative republic after the June massacre,

> understood that to secure their united rule necessitated the uniting of the means of repression of two epochs, that the means of subjugation of the July monarchy had to be supplemented and strengthened by the means of subjugation of the Restoration.
>
> MARX 1852a: 141

It therefore combines a limitation of suffrage with a state of siege against any social ferment. The parliamentary republic itself – the most advanced political form of the modern state – is what prepares for the return of the past: the centrality of Louis Bonaparte's personal power. Forged against feudalism, the military and bureaucratic state machinery remains inextricably linked to the past: in an addition later deleted in the second edition of *The Eighteenth Brumaire*, Marx defines the bureaucracy as 'a centralization that is still afflicted with its opposite, with feudalism' (Marx 1852a: 193, note b). From here Marx will come to well-known conclusions about the necessity for the entire state apparatus to be extinguished in order to make the dissolution of society possible.

The time of bourgeois modernity turns out to be a reversible time where revolutionary gaps can be stitched up, re-establishing the agreement between past and present: in the present, 'historical' and 'anti-historical' forces, dissolving forces and preserving forces, confront each other. Bringing back the history in the present cannot be done through any analogy with the rise of the bourgeoisie: 'the social revolution of the 19th century cannot draw its poetry from the past, but only from the future' (Marx 1852a: 106). The task of the revolutionary practice of history is then not so much to introduce an instantaneous caesura into its courses and recourses, nor to affirm a project of society that is preserved from historical accidents, but to work 'until a situation has been created which makes all turning back impossible' (Marx 1852a: 107), to prevent the chain of times and ideas from being welded together by expelling history from the present. Not a single decisive moment, but a strategy of preventing historical reversibility. If the bourgeois revolution can be understood as the final act of a drama that has now reached its epilogue, the proletarian revolution is first and foremost the opening up of a field of practicability of history in the present. In this sense, it cannot be more distant from the outcome of an automatic historical dialectic. The investigation of the conditions within which history is made in the present dominated by capital is, after all, the task that Marx will set himself from now on with the critique of political economy.

CHAPTER 3

The Social Object

Marx, the Economists, the Mercantile Society

Maurizio Merlo

1 The Border Dialectics and Competition

The programmatic plan presented by Marx in the *Grundrisse* is divided into four sections. The first section is about the exchange, money, and price value. The second is on the 'internal structure of production', the third on 'its culmination in the state' and 'as the conclusion, the world market, in which production is posited as a totality and all its moments also, but in which simultaneously all contradictions are set in motion. Hence the world market is likewise both the presupposition of the totality and its bearer' (Marx 1857–1861a: 160).

At first, the world market appears as the arena of conflict between national capitals, a space for its *competition*. Its logical status, even before the historical one, is the dialectics between *obstacle* and *limit*, amplified to a global level. Any obstacle to the competition is an intrinsic limit for the previous modes of productions. According to Marx, this dialectic involves the objective mechanism of the conversion of the negative into positive, the external obstacle into internal limit. Capital

> constantly revolutionizes ... tearing down all barriers which impede the development of the productive forces, the extension of the range of needs, the differentiation of production, and the exploitation and exchange of all natural and spiritual powers.

But from the fact that capital posits every such limit as a barrier which it has ideally already overcome, it does not at all follow that capital has really overcome it; and since every such limit contradicts the determination of capital, its production is subject to contradictions which are constantly overcome but just as constantly posited (Marx 1857–1861a: 337).

The dominance of capital is not immediately evident. The mechanistic image of free competition as attraction and repulsion of capitals appears inadequate. Therefore, from this results in the distinction between a negative-historical meaning and a positive one of competition as a real condition of capital as such. The first meaning is the negation of the feudal production, the overcoming of guilds and legal regulations. The second shows capital as such, that is to say, its reference to itself as *other* capital. As a matter of fact, free competition is nothing but the free movement of capitals 'within conditions which are not part of any dissolved earlier stages but are capital's own conditions. The dominance of capital is the presupposition for free competition' (Marx 1857–1861b: 39). The exterior, *coercive* nature of the dominance law of capital on every single capital produces as effect that 'not a single category of the bourgeois economy, not even the most basic one, e.g., the determination of value, really comes into its own through free competition', since it only is the executive power of said law (Marx 1857–1861b: 39; Marx 1867a: 588; cf. Rosdolsky 1977: 40–50). The validity of the general law suppresses the supposed autonomy and independence of the single capitals and makes it essential to build the credit system. This creates the necessity to abstract from the competition to grasp the intrinsic laws of capital. The dialectics between limit and obstacle replicates itself on the world market level, to such an extent that

> private exchange produces world trade, private independence produces a complete dependence on the so-called world market, and the fragmented acts of exchange produce a banking and credit system whose accountancy at least records the balancing of private exchange.
>
> MARX 1857–1861a: 96

The dialectics between limit or border [*Grenze*] immanence and obstacle [*Schranke*] exteriority finds in the conflict between national states (each state is an obstacle for the others) the principal trait of the world market. As a crucial atmosphere of capital, in the world market the separate and rival processes of accumulation functionally reactivates orders that are not produced by the state, that appear, therefore, as *derivative* (Luporini 1978). These orders are in a state of tension with respect to the capitalistic subversion of the competitive effectiveness of the value law expressed in the national currency. The latter works as a *universal* commodity since it is, through the flow of commodities of national capitals, even if the different currencies have their traits, a mere consequence and not the content of the state organization (Marx 1857–1861a: 463–466). The world market is the only adequate sphere of circulation for capital. The different national areas relate to the world market as *particularizations of a universal*, that is to say, as national capital inside a global, unified, real, reproducing connection (Marx 1867a: 580).

The separate, competitive processes of accumulation functionally reactivate previous obstacles and presuppositions of historical-political character. The capitalistic dominance subverts the effectiveness of the law of equivalent and imposes 'the most complete subjugation of individuality to social conditions, that assume the form of objective power, or rather of overpowering objects' (Marx 1857–1861b: 39–40). The dominant characteristic of the capitalistic market is detected in the imperatives that it imposes to its agents, the maximization of profit and the accumulation of capital, long before the extraction of surplus labour stands out as a socially dominant process. The analysis of 'capital in general' needs to rely on the threshold of surplus-value *production* maintaining and surpassing the circulation sphere. For this reason, it is important to start from the '*capital of the whole society*' (Marx 1857–1861a: 272).

Marx analyses the 'contemporary history' of capital inside the dialectics between position and presupposition. Capital exhibits double historicity: on one hand, it emerges from *given* conditions that anticipate it, on the other hand, it presents itself as a capital which history is the effect of its own systematic action. A capitalist, to posit himself as capital, put into circulation values that are *not* created with past wage labour. This is a 'condition that belongs to the antediluvian capital conditions, to its *historical presuppositions* ... that, as such, belong to the past. This means that they belong to the *history of its construction*, certainly not to its *contemporary* history'. The conditions of the birth of capital, of its evolution 'disappear with the development of real capital, the capital which, setting out from its own reality, itself posits the conditions for its realization' (Marx 1857–1861a: 387-88). Thus, 'originally', the presuppositions for the transformation of money into capital are external to its birth. However, 'as soon as the capital as such emerges, it creates its own presuppositions', that is to say, the possession of the real conditions for the creation of new values *without exchange*. In the development of *Capital*, 'the conditions of direct exploitation, and those of realising it, are not identical' (Marx 1894: 243) but they are temporally, spatially, and conceptually different.

During the confrontation with Ricardo, Marx points out how he assumes the reality of bourgeois relations of production as *already given*. The reductionism of his 'partially isolated system' (Lunghini 1977: 46ff) considers the existing relations of production as a smooth space, free from intermediations and available for the development of productive forces. In Ricardo's system, the economistic apologetic identifies commodity circulation and the immediate exchange of products (Marx 1867a: 124, notes). Value, far from being determined by the market, is reduced to a production price, a simple product of an equation system that, in line with technical coefficients, is not a part of the historical trait of a mode of production anymore. Ricardo assumes the existence of unlimited competition and, therefore, can define the forms of capital movement as 'pure'. However, he *reluctantly* admits the capital's historical trait and the limited nature of competition. The *immediate* identification of capital with the social relation of production that it establishes requires that the conditions of the social use of capital (competition, equalization of the rates of profit, constant revolution of labour processes, and extraction of surplus labour) are identical with the ones needed for it to exist. Therefore, its economic relation is part of a unique relation of property of the means of production on one side and of the labour power on the other. Marx re-elaborates the *Ricardian* matrix of the analysis of capital as relations of production that requires the complete objectification of the social relations made by institutions (Grenier 1996: 85ff), developing the concept of tendency, more specifically, the tendency of capital to dominate social processes translates in the transformation of the conditions of its evolution in the results of its own existence. Said tendency produces a gap from the empirical reality of phenomena and social stratification. The 'capital society' as a result (that does not match the effective history of its construction) is part of a general logic of historical evolution according to which the epochal form of a society is the result of external and previous conditions to the specific dominance relation, before being the result of the reproduction of this relation on its own basis (Dardot and Laval 2012: 376–378).

Looking for the missing link between the unfolding of the capitalistic mode of production and the forms that precede it, Marx reinterprets, in light of Steuart's mercantilism, the Ricardian theory of the increased productivity of labour not as a mere machine for the social-organic exchange, but as a place of formation of the thirst for power of the ruling classes. Steuart differentiates 'specifically social labour' that is expressed in the exchange-value, and 'real labour' that produces use-value. The first is considered as a general equivalent that assumes the sale of the labour power and authorizes a previous homogenization of the differences between concrete labours. The second is the *industry* that creates the general equivalent without being it. The relevant information is the opposition between the sale of the labour power and the labour involved in the production of commodities that is not (yet) social labour since it is not 'posited' by the capital yet. Given its non-homogeneity, it cannot work as a general equivalent, that has to be looked for in the exchange figures. Marx finds in Steuart the lever to break the doctrinal configuration of classic political economy, detecting the faults inside his model, the omissions, and the removals of the ghost that guarded the crib of the bourgeois economy. In his mercantilist declination, far from being a mere residue of a waned era, money is presented as the 'primitive form of the basic presuppositions' of the bourgeois economy, the production of abstract wealth (Marx 1859a: 390).

The bourgeois apologetic of capital confuses the accumulation of objective conditions of labour with the process of the original establishment/

constitution of capital. It does not create such conditions but the 'monetary wealth', that in the historical process of dissolution of the ancient mode of production is able to buy the objective conditions of labour and to obtain in exchange for money the same living labour 'of the now free workers' (Marx 1857–1861a: 430). When the capital becomes a presupposition itself, that is to say, when it creates the presuppositions of its own conservation and growth, only then can the single capitals be produced by accumulation, keeping the essential condition still, that 'the hoard is transformed into capital only by the exploitation of labour' (Marx 1857–1861a: 388).

It is impossible then to interpret the dynamics of the world market based on the 'Eurocentric' and mercantile view proposed by Adam Smith, who describes *funds* accumulation as a commercialization model. The amount of accumulation as such is not, according to Marx, a constitutive element of capital. In the Smithian model, capital is simply accumulated labour as a means for new labour. However, it is 'impossible to pass directly from labour to capital'. Therefore, 'we must begin not with labour but with value, or more precisely, with the exchange value already developed in the movement of circulation' (Marx 1857–1861a: 190). Accumulation must be marked with the specificity of the social relation of capital, that is to say, the transformation of social relations based on property. On the contrary, the logic of trade is based on the exchange of mutual needs both within a community and between communities spatially far or close. The same logic is valid if the circulation of commodities is mediated by money.

From the perspective of the world market, or the *intensity* of processes, the capitalistic social process is far from having unilateral and systemic characteristics, with the empirical omni-laterality of its circulation inside the social tissue. It rather exhibits a multiplicity of forms and social relations that are irreducible to a *unicum,* and it reacts to every simplified image of the dominance relation as all-pervasive and basically inclined to the spatial expansion of its characteristics. The differences between the forms are distributed on the register of the 'objectively weak' modes of dominance and on the register of social universes in which personal relationships are mediated by objective mechanisms that ensure permanence and accumulation of profit. They also ensure the reproduction of the distributive structure of capital and, with this, dominance and dependence relations (Bourdieu 1976). The internal logic of the capitalistic process is emancipated from every merely extensive, empirical-spatial, socially related dominance denotation. It proceeds according to the *intensity* lines of the objectification process until the construction of the 'capital society' as social connection able to be historically above the other categories of the given social formation (Mezzadra and Neilson 2013: 66–75).

In its intensive aspect, the world market 'is not only the domestic market in relation to all the foreign markets existing outside it, but at the same time the domestic market of all foreign markets, as, in turn, components of the home market' (Marx 1857–1861a: 210). The structure of the world market is the totality of the connections between the various national capitals, determined on each occasion by the dominant fraction of the capital. The necessary making of the national internal market, in which perimeter there is the competition of capital as a fraction of the whole capital, is concurrent to the making of the world market as a space for the competition between national bourgeoisies in their relationship with the structures of the state.

Since 1857, the concept of social abstraction expresses, according to Marx, the simple *labour* category in the abstract sociality of labour indifferent to every determination. Marx assigns to this category a primary role since it can provide the structural coordinates of the bourgeois society. However, this *prius* is overturned in *posterius* as soon as the center of research is the relation between simple circulation and production inside the *model* of the simple mercantile economy. Since this moment on, the polarity of labour in general and abstract labour prevents the identification of a historical determination of a category with the empirical expansion of its generality. In terms of model, simple circulation shows the partial existence of a mercantile production developed at an intermediate level between the high level of capitalistic dominance on one side and a level of development that has already crossed the threshold of the stabilization of the separation between exchange and use value on the other. The determinations of abstract wage labour are not limited to the alignment to those of the simple commodity and commodities exchange. They must already be contradictorily present in the simple circulation and *hidden* at the same time. The mercantile society hypostatizes a unique element of the capitalistic society, commodity, separating it from the structure in which it is inscribed (Rancière 1973: 88–89).

It is important to take into consideration the problem regarding the articulation between mercantile and capitalistic society. The first constitutes an abstract model that makes it possible to introduce for differentiated thresholds the constitutive elements of a *model* able to integrate commodity and wage relation. The appearance of a logic and historical priority of the mercantile society compared to the capitalistic society is the inversion of the actual data. The mercantile society is a product of the capitalistic society according to a specific logic that removes the wage relation from the model. The notion of 'simple mercantile production' meets the need to set the status of commodity that hides wage labour. This notion is similar to the Smithian notion of *commercial society*. It is a logical moment of the analysis that puts on the side the wage relation that is hidden inside the analytical course of commodity. The structural effect that opens its way in the empirical reality and in the history *before* the constitution of structure itself derives from the nature of commodities that *some* products of labour have acquired or are acquiring and that leads a gradual historical process. The socialization of abstract work develops if concrete labour becomes 'a totality of different kinds of labour that embraces the world market' until the available time becomes 'true wealth' (Marx 1861–1863c 390–391). The coercion of the world market is the crucial operator of conversion of the negative of the 'absolute poverty' of the labour power into the positive of labour socialization, of the absolute poverty of the labour power under development of socialized labour.

2   Thresholds

The insufficient conceptual welding between internal and world market produces a considerable fluctuation in the passage from capital to political state. The problematic relation between civil society and state and that between structure and superstructures focuses on the difference between the concept of political from the concept of state. In *Capital,* there is not the field of mutual and asymmetrical determination between civil society and state belonging to the *Grundrisse.* Every non-empirical reference to the state surrenders to the theoretical dominance of the relation between structure and superstructure that is limited to a 'merely' political criticism of political economy. In other words, it blocks 'any potential theoretical passage to the state related to the functioning of the capitalistic mode of production' (Luporini 1978: 44). However, the analysis of money as a universal commodity underlines the problem of the national and international articulation of capital. As a matter of fact, in the analysis of money there are *economic* elements that are different by nature, origin, and effectiveness.

Through the examination of money, Marx, in *Capital,* opens a new way, different from the *ultra-dialectical* one regarding the relation between limit and obstacle described in the *Grundrisse.* This to characterize the systemic thresholds of the economical-social formations. Marx proceeds with a typification that leans on the ideal connection of 'the systems of different countries', focusing on the unitarian, unequal, antagonistic *system of systems.* The theming of the existence of a *level of development* that is common to moments of the social production distant in time or separated in space makes the concept of *social formation* indicate the *totality of social relations.* Said relations range from the means of production to the *culture* of a historical given society in which there are, in the same historical moment, more modes of production that are subject to the laws of capital as the dominant mode of production.

To the unique category of 'social formation', it is associated the non-univocal concept of 'economic-social formation' that appears in the *Preface* of *A Contribution to the Critique of Political Economy* written in 1859. This concept, even if singular, implies an *organic* plurality in which every constituent element is functional or suitable to the existence of the others. In the same historical period, coexist different modes of production that are subject to the laws of capital as the dominant mode of production and other economic-social formations found both on the historical-temporal level and on the geographical-spatial one. This constitutes the emergence of a *continuum* in which internal variations create discontinuous levels of development of social formations: an epochal discontinuity connected to a structural continuity.

The fundamental concept of *system* refers to the notion of the 'society of producers of commodities' and, therefore, to the 'world of commodities'. The construction of the theoretical field of commodity form coincides with the subject itself ('commodity') as a simple concrete concept able to build a structure. Marx relates the plural and inter-relational structure of objectivity to the problem of history (and of pre-capitalistic forms). It is directly connected to the production processes of use-values and indirectly connected to 'supersensible' objective and inter-subjective social relations. If the so-called precapitalistic forms tend to directly reproduce themselves as social forms, in the specifically capitalistic mode of production and circulation, the economic mechanism indirectly reproduces social relations in the moment in which it is reproduced as such. Categories must be able to realize the diversity of the social reproduction forms also starting from the changes of the relation between economics and politics.

The internal hierarchy of the processes of social reproduction differentiates the forms based on their level of complexity, measured by the relation with commodity as a generalized form of the product of labour. Stating this, Marx does not mean a claimed original historicity of the simple form of commodity but the systematic originality of the connection diachrony-synchrony. This connection constitutes the fundamental relation between the logic of the temporal passage between social forms that are placed along a diachronical differential scale and a logic of the passage of the relations between the forms that belong to a unique historical time. This connection is not referred to empirical, naturalistic, and chronological criteria nor to the parallelism between history and logical order. It refers to the *subsumption* of simple historicity to the dimension of the structure. As a consequence, simple determinations acquire historicity as soon as they are subsumed in a structured *totality*.

3   The Social Object: Dialectics of Value-forms

Capital uses the dialectics of the *Grundrisse* in the space between the form covered by the presuppositions that precede the genesis of capital and the new form imprinted on them by the movement of self-position of capital, starting now from the commodity form as a contradictory unit of use value and value. The study of value-forms articulates a criterion of proportionality with the forms of society on the one hand and the modes of production on the other. The procedures to represent the value-form considered in their historical evolution are connected both with the political sphere and with the determinations of the reflection intended as an act of 'posing' and 'presupposing' that is far from being reduced to a mere speculative process.

In the chessboard of value-forms, the equivalent first presents itself as a general value-form only to then occupy the threshold of *systematic* transition to money form. The simple or accidental form of commodity appears as a germ of the money form and, simultaneously, as a hieroglyph that has to be deciphered. Its simplicity exists only in appearance since the equivalent is completely unstable. It is born and dies 'with the momentary social acts' (Marx 1867a: 99) and does not crystallize into a lasting social bond in money form. As a material expression of the value of the other commodity intended as a given quantity of a 'thing', the equivalent form does not contain any quantitative determination of value but has, by nature, the form of it (Marx 1867a: 67). In the simple form of value unfolds the opposition between relative form and equivalent form of value. The first expresses its being-value as something that differs from its body, while the second applies the inverse principle, a body of commodity, 'the material commodity itself – the coat – just as it is, expresses value, and is endowed naturally with the form of value' (Marx 1867a: 67, modified English translation). Although this concept applies only within the value relation, within the formal space of exchange, the properties of something do not derive from said relation; they only act within it. The equivalent-form appears as a material expression of the value of the other commodity, intended as a given quantity of a thing that in its natural tangible form represents value, that is sensible and suprasensible at the same time. In the value dimension, objects are posited in *forms* that are determined by the structure of the space of formal operations (representation and expression) by which 'within the relation of value with linen, the coat itself has a higher value than outside said relation'. The coat represents the 'support' [*Träger*] of the abstraction of the 'supernatural' value (Marx 1867a: 62). In other words, exchanges take place within the *systems* that give commodities an exchange-value that is different from the one with which it would be possible to determine their use-value. (White 1975: 287–288).

The shift of objectivity from a material, physical, to a social standpoint identifies basically relations of values and relations of things. In those cases, in which the equivalent-form already seems able to activate relations of value, the relations among things simultaneously appear as relations among values. This oscillation and equivocation cease as soon as the threshold of analysis of the general form of equivalent is crossed. As a matter of fact, said form first appears as a generic form of value to then shift through the systematic development of the money form. The condition of circulation is therefore the existence of a specific kind of commodities that are capable of socially reproduce themselves as such and of shifting to the socially valid value-form as the *natural* form of the money-commodity. Money is, therefore, the primordial form of capital, the incunabulum of the capitalist form of production and reproduction of the process.

Since the chain of value equations extends indefinitely, the expression of relative value is incomplete and produces equivalent fragmentary forms that exclude each other from said equation. In the absence of a single equivalent and in the proliferation of rival ones that exclude each other, the total value-form is defective. In the absence of a general equivalent, simple products or use-values face each other instead of commodities (Spivak 1999: 100–101). Therefore, it is only in the general value-form that is socially valid and institutionalized that the commodities express their values in relation to a single commodity. The inversion of the simple form does not produce the same relation, but a dissymmetry between traders since one of the two terms will always be in a situation of dominance with respect to the other. To define the relative value-form, Marx resorts to the concept of a sovereignty relation, using an analogy: the value of a commodity is expressed in the use-value of another. This also means that individual A cannot behave with individual B in the same way he would in presence of the majesty: said majesty has to become for A, at the same time, the physical form of B. Therefore, B is not the equivalent of A, but he is the equivalent of the majesty *in corpore* (Marx 1867a: 62).

The moment in which this thing stabilizes in a definitive way is represented by the endpoint of the intertwining of a natural form with the general and social equivalent-form. The stabilization of the congruence between the natural properties of gold and the social function can be expressed with the following formula: gold and silver are not money by nature, but money is 'naturally' gold and silver, that is, an object whose physical properties are consistent with the presupposition of value. This formula underlines how a natural form of a specific commodity becomes the socially valid equivalent-form. This dynamic identification, the simultaneous growth in the excluded commodity of natural form and social objectivity: this leads to the analysis of the significant oscillation of the status of objectivity itself. This is intended as a metonymic manifestation of the structure or of the social-phantom existence of the sensible and suprasensible at the same time.

Magic, aura, *Zauberwirkung*: money functions as a sort of mystic supplement of power, in addition to its role of measurement of values and means of circulation. This is intended as an excess of power-potential that money exerts on imagination and social representation. The processes of materialization, dematerialization, and re-materialization of money circumscribe the framework of the vicissitudes of national states such as institutions *of* the world market intended as the arena of the conflict for all the various currencies. Given the impossibility of a world-state, the commodity society 'does not identify itself *neither* with the universal trading republic, *nor* with a space that is purely national, but with the *articulation* of state sovereignty within the world market' (Balibar 2011: 335).

The crystallization of the general equivalent in money-form is marked by the transition from the phenomenological to the paradigmatic axis. This process shows obvious precedents in the 'formal living' found in Hegel during his Jena period and in the Kantian *possessio noumenon*. (Drach 2004). Unlike the Hegelian concrete universal that includes its own particularizations and is their inner essence, for Marx the universal of value exists 'close to and beyond' commodities. It *really* exists outside of them (Arthur 2009). The *gold* commodity, without equivalent, can only be external to the trading community in which it occupies the place of the sovereign. It collaterally exists outside of the realm of commodities and, exceptionally, it makes rules and establishes the place of social normativity. The conceptual difference of money as the measure of value on one side and as price scale on the other results in the fact that the only commodity is 'value' and yet not the immediate incarnation of the universal. This precisely because it is value by means of the price-form. In the general form or money-form, all commodities express their value through a unique equivalent, social expression of the world of commodities.

The institution of the general equivalent is intended by Marx as a process of exclusion of a specific commodity that incorporates immediate social value. This exceeds the theoretical foundation of commodity as a product of concrete labour. In other words, as a general equivalent gold-money is excluded from the labour processes that are part of society since its production cannot be compared to a general process of common labour. Different concrete labours find their universal expression as human labour in general, employed in the production of gold or silver.

The salient point regarding the concept of excluded commodity that represents the general equivalent stands in the specific social function that it has as money. Said function, as stated by Marx, is the product of the 'social action of all the commodities'. This expression underlines the problematic nature of society intended as a collection of relations (legal-contractual and more). Individual commodities have relations with each other since they are 'animated things'.

> The relations connecting the labour of one individual with that of the rest appear, not as direct social relations between individuals at work, but as what they really are, material relations between persons and social relations between things.
>
> MARX 1867a: 84

The two aspects consist of 'the social contract of commodities' (Balibar 2011: 327).

In order that these objects may enter into relation with each other as commodities, their guardians must place themselves in relation to one another, as persons whose will resides in those objects, and must behave in such a way that each does not appropriate the commodity of the other, and part with his own, except by means of an act done by mutual consent. They must, therefore, mutually recognize in each other the rights of private proprietors. This juridical relation, which thus expresses itself in a contract, whether such contract be part of a developed legal system or not, is a relation between two wills, and is but the reflex of the real economic relation between the two. It is this economic relation that determines the subject matter comprised in each such juridical act (Marx 1867a: 95).

The act of exchanging the 'useful thing' form is made up of the 'thing of value' that exists behind the traders' back but also in front of them, because it is the aim of their actions. The mechanism of exchange seems to be controlled by 'crossing structures': the owner of the commodities wants to alienate his commodity with another that for him is value of use. On the other side, he wants to realize his commodity as value 'whether his own commodity has or do not have a use-value for the owner of the other commodity'. Where money is not used, commodities are 'an equivalent for those who do not possess it ... only if it is value of use for the latter'.

Hence, in the trading process, there is an opposition between 'the only individual and at the same time only generally social' trait of exchange. This means that what is true for the individual trader cannot be true at the same time for all the subjects involved. This contradiction finds its systematic solution only in the money-form since the act of exchanging intended as a specific act of traders that recognize each other is an intrinsically contradictory process. The same problem echoes in Hegel's '*Tun aller und jeder*' and in Hobbes's '*act both of himself, and of all the rest*'. In the imputation 'social action of all commodities', the Proudhonian idea of society-person is rejected. Society is the collection of relations and practices of different individuals that in a non-intentional manner satisfy the needs of their existence, giving life to a system with an omnilateral material dependence. Instead of creating an actual 'community', they create a collection of relations of mutual estrangement and dependence. The solution to the contradiction between individual and social processes stands in its systematic dislocation of the equivalent form. Commodity owners

> cannot bring their commodities into relation as values, and therefore as commodities, except by comparing them [*gegensätzlich*, by opposition] with some one other commodity as the universal equivalent ... But a particular commodity cannot become the universal equivalent except by a social act.
>
> MARX 1867a: 97

As a matter of fact, if the acts of will of those who take part in the exchange comply with the value-form, the juxtaposition of value-form and exchange structure finds the *embarrassment* of the subjects as a result. This implies a systematic void that may not ever be filled by resorting to money as a convention, or to the conscious nature of the voluntary act of exchange. From intersubjective relations of those traders who are owners of commodities, there could never arise a general equivalent-form. Money-form does not have its genesis in the contract, and it cannot be intended as only 'contract subject-matter' since it expresses the connection everyone has with those who take part in the exchange and not only with their interpersonal relations. The operations of 'sale without purchase' and of 'purchase without sale' that may lead to a crisis, appear to be intrinsically contradictory if carried out on a general scale.

The equivalent must already possess the traits of a separate corporeity for the owners of commodities to operate following the value terms. Value is a given abstraction in front of the owners of commodities and, once the money-form is assumed, it structures the actions and intentions of the subjects. The act of exchange presents itself as systematically and juridically overdetermined. The action goes at the same time through the thing, the sensible, and the supersensible substrate of a complex system of relations, otherwise abstract. It is in this specific juridic meaning that the notion of fetishism should be reconsidered. It formally occupies the dialectical place of a reflection on subjectivity,

or rather on the representations, produced by different *Träger*, that are inter-
posed as necessary middle term between individuals and the not immediately
perceived social trait of their activities.

4   Commodities and Money

The social action of all commodities excludes a specific commodity as a general equivalent and thus presides over the establishment of a normativity that
becomes the 'socially validated form that acquires social authenticity'. The
general equivalent commodity is excluded since the labour that produces
it is immediately social. This means that it is an immediate materialization
of general labour time as a representation of what is intended common to
the money commodity and to commodities in general. 'These objects, gold,
and silver, just as they come out of the bowels of the earth, are forthwith the
direct incarnation of all human labour. Hence the magic of money' (Marx
1867a: 103).

Marx takes charge of this magical element when analysing the splitting of
the expression of commodities and their value on one side and on the other
the representation this has in the general equivalent as a representation of
a determined social totality that includes different components (otherwise
classified as 'irrational', such as trust). These components are distributed on
the doble register of symbolization and expression, of the phenomenal form
in its particularity, and of money as a manifestation of the universal in the
phenomenal sphere: a thing in its commodity form exhibits its ideality as the
expression of what is invisible. Thus, gold starts as a mere means of circulation
and ascends to the status of sovereign executioner of commodities, the representation overdetermines the expression of value. 'Is no longer money that
represents the commodity, but it is the commodity that represents money'. The
sovereignty of money is a process of 'transubstantiation':

> from its status of servitude, in which it appears as a mere means of cir-
> culation, money suddenly becomes the ruler and god in the world of
> commodities. It represents the celestial existence of commodities, while
> these represent its earthly existence.
>
> MARX 1857–1861a. 154

The non-realization of a commodity in money leads to an *only* imaginative
trait of its price, which persists in the social representation and becomes
autonomous from the matter of the general equivalent.

Money only circulates commodities which have already been ideally transformed into money, not only in the mind of the individual but in the representation [*Vorstellung*] of society. The ideal transformation into money on the one side and the real one on the other, are not governed by the same laws at all. The relation between them must be investigated' (Marx 1857–1861a: 122–23; modified English translation).

The social representation precedes the real exchange and money makes property deeds circulate instead of the commodities on which said deeds apply. In other words, money has command over future labour. The ideal price is the form of the social since it is exterior from separate subjects and the condition of circulation intended as a social totality. The genesis of the money-form and the institutionalization of its function show the hidden face of sovereignty and, at the same time, the centrifugal trait of the monetary representation from the national space of state representation. The individual acts of exchange cannot depict the anatomy of the commodity society, what they do is giving the monetary expression of the social, of the separation of the trade subjects, and of their omnilateral material dependence. Circulation is not the sum of individual acts of exchange but a '*circuit* of exchanges, a *totality* of them, in a constant flow, extended more or less on the whole surface of society; a system of acts of exchange'. Circulation makes exchange values circulate as prices and 'the concept of price must therefore be developed *before* that of circulation'. Circulation realizes the prices (Marx 1857–1861a: 122). The concept of social totality sheds light on the fact that the monetary social bond presupposes a subordination of inter-individual power relations to a collective principle of authority. Money is the expression of said principle and the state is a component of this. In more general terms, the coining of the social is not expressed in the operations of value creation (which pertain to private producers) but in the operations of the authority that are external to the production processes and that can impose alone the sign through which the values of use can circulate. Circulation is therefore the first category of social totality and also the first in which the work of the abstraction from the places of production of exchanged commodities can be seen. If in the secret laboratory of the production process capital presents itself as an owner and *master*, in the field of circulation it presents itself as 'dependent and determined by the social nexus' (Marx 1857–1861b: 27), in which society in the form of general, dominating determinations mediates between production and consumption through money. Only circulation breaks the time, space, and individual barriers of the exchange and 'these effects by splitting up, into the antithesis of a sale and a purchase, the direct identity that in barter does exist between the alienation of one's own and the acquisition of some other man's product' (Marx 1867a: 123).

Capital and labour can only be opposite as foreign and autonomous figures. Before the start of the production process, there is the facing of the owner of the money as capitalist *in pectore* on one hand, and the free labour power on the other. What separates them is not (yet) property, but the access to the general equivalent as a condition of the expression of value quantities itself. The conditions that make the labour power a commodity – the deprivation of the means of production and the subsequent exclusion of workers from the social division of labour – exclude it from commodity relations. The movement of circulation refers beyond itself to the labour power as a transit link to the genesis of an abstract sociality. If money is the link between a commodities society and a capitalist society, their presupposition about it is different. The owner of the labour power is intended as a direct seller of living labour and not of commodities. The reciprocal class relation between capitalist and worker represents now the prerequisite of the 'purely money relation' between the simple owner of capital as a buyer and the simple seller of living labour. '(James Mill admits that) the determination of the value of commodities by labour time is false because the value of the most important commodity, labour itself, contradicts this law of value of commodities' (Marx 1861–1863c: 285). The subsumption is monetary, subordination is born within capital, from the determined content of sale. In other words, it is determined from the specific relation of dependence and not from former forms of subordination,

> it is not any kind of political and socially fixed relation of dominance and subordination ... To be sure, the relation of production itself creates a new relation of dominance and subordination (and this also produces political, etc., expressions of itself).
>
> MARX 1861–1863a: 431

CHAPTER 4

The Artificial Nature and the Genetic History of Capital

Marx and the Modern Theory of Colonization

Paola Rudan

Only when and where wage labour is its basis does commodity production impose itself upon society as a whole; but only then and there also does it unfold all its hidden potentialities.

MARX 1982: 733

∙ ∙ ∙

To accumulate is to conquer the world of social wealth, to increase the mass of human beings exploited by him, and thus to extend both the direct and the indirect sway of the capitalist.

MARX 1867a: 588

∙ ∙
∙

Marx's analysis of the modern theory of colonization is intimately linked to that of 'so-called primitive accumulation' [*Ursprüngliche Akkumulation*]. Since he considers colonialism as one of the moments of primitive accumulation – i.e., of 'the historical process of divorcing the producer from the means of production' (Marx 1867a: 705–706) – it might be argued that this link has an explanatory function. In this section of *Capital*, however, Marx does not deal with colonialism as a historical phenomenon, but rather discusses the theory of colonization proposed by Edward Gibbons Wakefield in his *England and America* (Wakefield 1833). This theory allows Marx not so much to show how primitive accumulation took place historically, but rather to bring to light an essential element of that process, which consists in the role the state plays in the overcoming of pre-capitalist forms of property. The separation of the producer from the means of production, in other words, is the artifice lying beneath the natural laws of the capitalist mode of production.

This reading also allows for a clarification of the connection between space and history in Marx's discourse. As we shall see, in fact, Marx finds in Wakefield's theory a 'critical' capacity that depends on the shift in perspective from the motherland to the colonies, from a situation in which capitalist relations are fully developed to one in which their conditions of existence have yet to be 'produced'. However, this shift in perspective must be complemented by a return movement, whereby the specific colonial condition allows us to shed light on the 'truth as to the conditions of capitalist production in the mother country' (Marx 1867a: 752–753), that is, on their artificial and violent origin. Primitive accumulation can therefore be understood as the actual 'pre-historic stage of capital and of the mode of production corresponding with it' (Marx 1867a: 706) not because it precedes capital chronologically along an evolutionary or progressive line, but because it defines the preconditions of its existence, which can only be grasped retrospectively. History, then, is not merely the chronological succession of events, but results from their logical arrangement. Just as 'the anatomy of man is a key to the anatomy of the ape' (Marx 1857–1861a: 42), so also is it possible to identify the conditions of its affirmation from the deployed capital relations. The history of the capitalist mode of production is realized as a 'totality' at the moment when it achieves a fully global dimension. This process takes place not so much through imperialistic expansion, but rather through the qualitative definition of space and its subjection to the logic of capital, which thus becomes the author of its own history.

1   The Definition of the Field

Marx accepts the definition of 'colonies' as 'virgin soil, colonized by free immigrants' offered by Wakefield and agrees with him in stating that 'the United States are, speaking economically, still only a colony of Europe' (Marx 1867a: 751, n. 21; Wakefield 1833, vol. ii: 109). As Wakefield explains, in fact, 'it is not dependence that constitutes a colony', but rather two different factors. First, it requires the existence of 'waste land, that is, land not yet the property of individual property, but liable to become so through the intervention of government'. Second, a colony involves the migration of people either from an old country to a new one, or from a part of a new, already settled country to the waste lands of that same country. Colonization, therefore, does not coincide with imperialistic expansion but with the 'removal of people from an old to a new country and the settlement of people on the waste land of the new country'. For Wakefield, then, colonization is 'an art rather than a science', a 'performance' (Wakefield 1833, vol. ii: 74–75) whose end is that of governing the mobility of people to vacant lands and their capacity for appropriation.[1] The setting of the problem explains why, for Marx, Wakefield's theory is 'immensely important' for a 'correct understanding' not of colonialism as a historical phenomenon, but of 'modern landed property' and, therefore, of the conditions of existence of the capitalist mode of production (Marx 1857–1861a: 208).

Wakefield discusses these conditions when he asks about the 'means to be employed' to achieve colonization from the identification of its ends. These vary depending on whether one considers the interests of the 'old' or the 'new' society, although they tend to coincide. England needs to extend the market in order to dispose of its 'surplus produce'; to relieve itself from its surplus population; to 'enlarge the field for employing capital'. Three goals that can be reduced to one, 'namely, an enlargement of the field for employing capital and labour'. In contrast, the United States needs 'more capital and labour for cultivating an unlimited field'. The interests of the two societies converge because England must decompress an excess of competition between capitalists, which produces their 'uneasiness', and between workers, which produces their misery, while the US needs workers to employ the capital at their disposal. Thus, a double meaning of the term 'field' emerges from Wakefield's analysis: it refers to the open and not yet occupied space as a precondition for the production of wealth, and then to the land as a means of production. The absence of a spatial limit therefore constitutes a possibility for the expansion of production itself. This limitlessness, however, also defines the limits 'of the field of production and of the market in which to dispose of the surplus produce', because it determines the lack of free labour to which to give employment: 'from whatever point of view we look at this subject', Wakefield concludes, 'it appears that the great want of colonies is Labour, the original purchase-money of all things' (Wakefield 1833, vol. II: 75, 83–84, 110–111, 102–103n., 112, 118).[2]

---

1   Wakefield had published anonymously, with the same intention, a *Sketch of a Proposal for Colonization Australasia* already in 1829 (Semmel 1961). The distinction between science and art is taken from Bentham 1830: 204.

2   Wakefield admits the validity of Bentham's principle that calculates 'the limitation of production and trade by the limitation of capital' (Bentham 1830: 230) only insofar as we speak of capital for which there is employment. In this respect, he refers to Adam Smith, according to whom the limitation of labour mobility is a limitation of capital, 'the quantity of stock which can be employed in any branch of business depending very much upon that of labour which can be employed in it'. Smith was also the first who observed that 'there is a continual complaint of the scarcity of hands in North America' (Smith 1838: 169, 86) and thus who recognized that, beyond the limits of capital, there are limits to its ability to employ labour due to the absence of a field of production. Wakefield's importance in classical political economy's reflection on colonization is thus that it considers colonization as offering an answer to both the problem of overpopulation and that of overproduction (Winch 1963 and Winch 1966).

For Wakefield, this lack can be explained by the fact that, by purchasing land, US workers can become landowners or capitalists, 'master[s] of other labourers':

> It is the extreme cheapness of new land which causes this minute division of labour. At all events, calculate the *squatter*, I must work by myself ... If the price of the new land was such as to keep the people together, so that they might combine their labour, ... the motive of the *squatter* would entirely cease.
>
> WAKEFIELD 1833, vol. II: 178, 182

As long as workers are able to escape the wage-labour relationship by buying land at a cheap price – or, like squatters, by appropriating it through occupation and use – the presence of an 'unlimited field' will be the main limit to the use of capital. The accessibility of land and its availability for occupation and use must therefore be limited through a '*redemptioner* system'. The American capitalist would have to pay to import the poor from England, i.e., those who have no resources to bear the costs of travel but who, at the same time, constitute 'the class of people whose immigration into a colony it would be most useful to promote' in order to replace workers who have become capitalists and landowners (Wakefield 1833, vol. II: 183–184). By itself, however, this measure would be insufficient, for there is nothing to prevent the poor from appropriating the remaining available land upon arrival in the colonies (Wakefield 1833, vol. II: 188). Therefore, for Wakefield, it is necessary to institute 'some kind of slavery' that forces workers to remain as such, ensuring a constant supply of labour regulated by demand: workers must work to redeem themselves, i.e., to repay the costs of travel, and they must work 'in combination', i.e., in relation to the capitalist (Wakefield 1833, vol. II: 185, 191–192). Slavery in the strict sense, which Wakefield considers not a resource but an obstacle to the production of wealth (Wakefield 1833, vol. II: 112), must be replaced by 'some kind of slavery' that is the necessary condition of existence of 'free labour'. In order to ensure the continuity of combined labour and to ensure that the absence of a spatial limitation does not become a limitation on the production of wealth, government intervention is therefore essential (Kittrell 1973: 89):

> Land to be an element of colonization, must not only be waste, but it must be public property, liable to be converted into private property for the end in view. In the art of colonization, therefore, the first rule is of a negative kind: it is, that governments, having power over waste land, and seeking to promote the removal of people, should never throw away any

of that power; should never dispose of waste land except for the object in view, for the removal of people, for the greatest progress of colonization.

WAKEFIELD 1833, vol. II: 125

This passage allows us to explain why Wakefield's theory is 'immensely important' for Marx. It demonstrates the fundamental difference between individual ownership of the means of production – whose precondition is the existence of waste land owned by the community, available for occupation and use by the worker – and private capitalist ownership – which instead presupposes a public ownership of the land and thus the government's power to regulate the process of appropriation (Marx 1857–1861a: 389ff; Anderson 2010: 157ff.). According to Marx, insofar as he grasps this difference, Wakefield is able to unravel the 'secret' of the colonies' resistance to the settlement of capital, namely the fact that there the land is 'still the property of the people' [*Volkseigentum*] so that each settler can appropriate it to make it an individual means of production. This very fact makes impossible the separation of agriculture from industry, the destruction of rural domestic industry and, with it, the formation of an internal market for capital, as well as the field of 'abstinence' for the capitalist. The labourers, in other words, 'decline to allow the capitalist to abstain from the payment for the greater part of their labour' (Marx 1867a: 755–757)[3]. It thus becomes clear why

> if, within a society, the modern relations of production, i.e. capital, are developed in their totality, and this society now takes possession of a new terrain, as e.g. in the colonies, it finds, more especially its representative the capitalist finds, that his capital ceases to be capital without wage labour, and that one of the premisses of wage labour is not only landed property in general but modern landed property; landed property which, as capitalized rent, is expensive and as such excludes the direct utilization of the soil by individuals. Therefore, Wakefield's theory of colonization, followed in practice by the English government in Australia.
>
> MARX 1857–1861a: 208

While giving voice to the complaint of the American capitalist, unable to 'retain' the worker (Wakefield 1833, vol. II: 191), Wakefield demonstrates that

---

3 Even in his discussion of the 'differential rent', Marx makes it clear that an 'illimited [*sic*] field of action' prevents the constitution of a class of capitalists, and that one can speak of capitalist production. His 'definition of the field' means that the term 'field' should be taken to mean the 'field of action' of capital (Marx 1861–1863b: 515).

capital 'is not a thing, but a social relation between persons established by the instrumentality of things' (Marx 1867a: 753).

2   The Artificial Origin of Capital

Although he gives Wakefield credit for discovering in the colonies 'the truth as to the conditions of capitalist production in the mother country', Marx considers him guilty of the same sin of mystification committed by the classical political economist who – turning his gaze from the colonies to Western Europe, where 'the process of primitive accumulation is more or less accomplished', – 'applies the notions of law and of property inherited from a pre-capitalistic world with all the more anxious zeal and all the greater unction, the more loudly the facts cry out in the face of his ideology' (Marx 1867a: 752). Wakefield's argument is in fact marked by a fundamental contradiction. He recognizes that individual ownership of the means of production that is based on the appropriation of waste land prevents the establishment of wage labour and therefore calls for government intervention to regulate the appropriation process. However, Wakefield does not question the Lockean identity between labour and property as the foundation of appropriation and instead argues – echoing Adam Smith – that 'labour creates capital before capital employs labour' (Wakefield 1833, vol. II: 110). On this basis, he believes that 'for promoting the accumulation of capital' mankind has 'divided themselves into owners of capital and owners of labour':

> But this division was, in fact, the result of concert or combination. The capitals of all being equal, one man saves *because* he expects to find others willing to work for him; other men spend *because* they expect to find some man ready to employ them; and if it were not for this readiness to co-operate, to act in concert or combination, the division of the industrious classes into capitalists and labourers could not be maintained.
>
> WAKEFIELD 1833, vol. I: 26

For Locke, the self-ownership that legitimizes the appropriation of the common land through labour is the presupposition of the contract that establishes political society by consensus. For Wakefield, the identity between labour and property lies at the foundation of accumulation, which occurs on the basis of an agreement motivated by mutual interest. The sin of mystification that Marx imputes to Wakefield consists precisely in this account of the origin, in the description of this '*contrat social*' of a quite original kind in virtue of which the mass of mankind, moved by an 'instinct of self-denying fanaticism', would have 'expropriated itself in honor of the accumulation of capital'. One would expect, Marx continues, that precisely in the colonies this social contract would pass from the realm of dreams into the realm of reality, 'but what is the purpose, then, of "systematic colonization" in antithesis to "spontaneous, unregulated colonization"'? (Marx 1867a: 754). By positing this antithesis, in fact, Wakefield

> proves how the development of the social productive power of labour, co-operation, division of labour, use of machinery on a large scale, &c, are impossible without the expropriation of the labourers, and the corresponding transformation of their means of production into capital. In the interest of the so-called national wealth, he seeks for artificial means to ensure the poverty of the people.
>
> MARX 1867a: 752

Wakefield's theory thus sheds light on the process of systematization of poverty that took place in England in the 18th century, when the term 'poor' began to be used no longer to refer to individuals dependent on benefits, but to those who could live only by their own labour. This is a fundamental historical and semantic shift – fully theorized by Bentham but also present in the more famous work of Eden (Bentham 2001: 3; Eden 1797) – that Marx points out in the chapter devoted to so-called primitive accumulation (Marx 1867a: 747, n. a) and that allows the specific difference between 'ancient civilized countries', where 'the labourer, though free, is by a law of Nature dependent on capitalists', and the colonies, where 'this dependence must be created by artificial means', to be recorded. With this comparison, Marx does not simply look at the colonies from the point of view of Western Europe, as Wakefield does, but shifts his gaze from the colonies to Western Europe to bring to light the artificial origin of those natural laws even where they are fully operative. In the colonies the 'pretty fancy' of the 'free contract between ... equally independent owners of commodities' passed off 'by the smug political economist' in the motherland is shattered. Looking at Europe from the colonies it is possible to see that the 'great beauty of capitalist production' consists in the continuous reproduction of the absolute 'social dependence of the labourer on the capitalist' (Marx 1867a: 756–757; Harvey 1981: 6).

It is clear then why, in reading Wakefield, Marx is not interested in the situation of the colonies, but in telling – from modern theory of colonization – 'the truth as to the conditions of capitalist production in the mother country'. Wakefield's systematic colonization is not so much important insofar as it was actually carried out – something that only 'for a time' England tried to 'enforce by Acts of Parliament'[4] – but because it allows us to understand the historical significance of processes that have already taken place in Europe – such as the 'system of protection at its origin' that 'attempted to manufacture capitalists artificially in the mother country' – from conditions that have not yet fully developed, such as those requiring the 'manufacture of wage workers in the Colonies' (Marx 1867a: 753). In the movement from the motherland to the colonies and back to the motherland, through the modern theory of colonization Marx is able to show what the secret of that 'manufacturing' consists in, and what the 'artificial means' necessary to bring about the 'so-called primitive accumulation' are. These are not the consensualistic artifice of the contract, but a process of 'fearful and painful expropriation of the mass of the people' that 'forms the prelude to the history of capital' (Marx 1867a: 749), entirely put in place through the intervention of the state (Pappe 1951: 50, Tronti 1977: 212, Mezzadra 2008: 137; Read 2003: 25):

> The different moments of primitive accumulation distribute themselves now, more or less in chronological order, particularly over Spain, Portugal, Holland, France, and England. In England at the end of the 17th century, they arrive at a systematical combination, embracing the colonies, the national debt, the modern mode of taxation, and the protectionist system. These methods depend in part on brute force, e.g., the colonial system. But they all employ the power of the state, the concentrated and organized force of society, to hasten, hothouse fashion, the process of transformation of the feudal mode of production into the capitalist mode, and to shorten the transition. Force is the midwife of every old society pregnant with a new one. It is itself an economic power.
>
> MARX 1867a: 739

Just as the colonization proposed by Wakefield envisaged legislation capable of governing the process of land appropriation by immigrants by requiring them to pay the capitalist a 'ransom ... for leave to retire from the wage labour market to the land' (Marx 1867a: 759), so during the 18th century in England, with the Bills of Inclosures of Commons, the same law had become 'the instrument of the theft of the people's land' and a 'parliamentary *coup d'état*' had been enacted to transform common property into private property

---

4   The first 'assisted migration' initiatives were put in place by the British government between 1819 and 1827, to be followed by two subsequent reforms in 1836 and 1839, also driven by Wakefield's theories (Broeze 1982).

(Marx 1867a: 715). It is the intervention of the state that allows the different moments of the primitive accumulation to be considered as systems. The intervention of the state – which sweeps away customary legislation by centralizing (and positivizing) the production of law – is what makes it possible to get rid of the 'anti-capitalistic cancer of the colonies' (Marx 1867a: 758) by establishing the capitalist's right 'to appropriate the unpaid labour of others' and by putting the worker in the 'impossibility ... of appropriating his own product'. In this way, 'the separation of property from labour has become the necessary consequence of a law that apparently originated in their identity' (Marx 1867a: 583). The need for centralization of control over the processes of appropriation is determined by the fact that, as long as the reproduction of the wage labourer 'as a wage labourer' (Marx 1867a: 571) and the production of a workers' surplus population are hindered by the survival of precapitalist forms of producer ownership, not only is the sense of exploitation reduced but also the sense of dependence on the capitalist devoted to abstinence. This process therefore needs, in order to constitute itself, 'the power of the state to *regulate* wages, i.e., to force them within the limits suitable for making surplus value, to lengthen the working day and to keep the labourer himself in the normal degree of dependence'. It is, precisely, an artifice, a violent acceleration, which becomes less and less necessary the more 'the organization of the capitalist process of production, once fully developed, breaks down all resistance' and 'the constant generation of a relative surplus population keeps the law of supply and demand of labour, and therefore keeps wages, in a rut that corresponds with the wants of capital'[5]. The more, in short, 'the labourer can be left to the *natural laws of production*, i.e., to his dependence on capital' (Marx 1867a: 726).

---

5 For Marx, 'the law of capitalist production, that is at the bottom of the pretended *natural law of population*' simply consists of the correlation 'between the unpaid and the paid labour of the same labouring population'. This law is necessary for the price of labour to remain 'confined within limits that not only leave intact the foundations of the capitalist system, but also secure its reproduction on a progressive scale'. Hence, 'capitalist accumulation itself constantly produces, and produces in the direct ration of its own energy and extent, a relatively redundant population of labourers, i.e., a population of greater extent than suffices for the average needs of the self expansion of capital, and therefore a surplus population' (Marx 1867a: 615–616, 624, Harvey 1981: 6). From the late 1820s onwards, the question of systematic colonization is discussed in close relation to the Malthusian principle of population. Malthus himself was involved in the evaluation of the plan proposed by Wilmot-Horton's Emigration Committee in 1827 (Kittrel 1965).

3   The Genetic History of Capital

> What is called historical development rests, in general, on the fact that
> the latest form regards the earlier ones as stages leading towards itself
> and always conceives them in a one-sided manner, since only rarely, and
> under quite definite conditions, is it capable of self-criticism.
>
> MARX 1857–1861a: 42–43

With these words Marx introduces in the *Grundrisse* some fundamental passages concerning the historicity of economic categories and, in particular,
land ownership and rent. Against the classical political economists, who 'who
obliterate all historical differences and see in all forms of society the bourgeois
forms' (Marx 1857–1861a: 42), he states that capital 'must form both the point of
departure and the conclusion' (Marx 1857–1861a: 44): this means that the economic categories should not be presented 'successively in the order in which
they played the determining role in history' but according to 'their mutual relation in modern bourgeois society, and this is quite the reverse of what appears
to be their natural relation' (Marx 1857–1861a: 44). The example of this is given
landed property (Rosdolsky 1977: 35ff):

> In all forms in which landed property rules supreme, the nature relation-
> ship still predominates; in the forms in which capital rules supreme, the
> social, historically evolved element predominates. Rent cannot be under-
> stood without capital, but capital can be understood without rent.
>
> MARX 1857–1861a: 44

This argument is particularly relevant for understanding Marx's critique of
Wakefield. Not only because, as we have seen, his theory of colonization is
important for the exact understanding of capitalist landed property but also
because, according to Marx, Wakefield makes the same mistake as the classical political economists by calling 'capital' the means of production which
are 'the individual property of many independent labourers', even though in
reality 'they are its exact opposite ... It is with as with the feudal jurist. The
latter stuck on to pure monetary relations the labels supplied by feudal laws'
(Marx 1867a: 753–754). The analysis of the modern theory of colonization,
therefore, is central to understanding how Marx conceives the historicity of
capital.

It should be clarified that making capital the point of departure and the
conclusion of the analysis does not mean identifying a linear historical movement that leads to capital in a way that is as natural as it is inescapable. This

is – if anything – the outcome of the 'evolutionary history' of Wakefield and the classical political economists, whose retrospective gaze establishes 'the continuing present of an origin homogeneous with the current process' (Balibar 1970: 277). Although there are 'general determinations of production' – such as property, legal relations or forms of government – which are defined as 'general conditions of all productions' (Marx 1857–1861a: 24), they do not allow us to grasp any 'of the actual historical stages of production itself' (Marx 1857–1861a: 26). Thus, for example, it is evident that 'all production is appropriation of nature by the individual', but 'it is ridiculous to make a leap from this to a definite form of property, e.g. private property ... History shows, on the contrary, that common property ... is the earlier form, a form which in the shape of communal property continues to play a significant role for a long time' (Marx 1857–1861a: 25; Il'enkov 1982: ch. 4). For Marx, then, history is not determined by continuity, but on the contrary by the specific difference in which the 'general conditions of all productions' manifest themselves. From this it also follows that history is not defined by a unilinear and necessary succession: looking at the colonies from the motherland, as Wakefield does, it is possible to understand what the former lack in order for the capitalist mode of production to take hold, to grasp precisely their specific difference. However, this does not mean that the capitalist mode of production is the necessary destiny, determined according to a natural evolutionary path, of the colonies. There is no evolutionary necessity in the transition from pre-capitalist forms of property to capitalist private property. The primitive accumulation – the expropriation realized through the social violence of the state – is therefore presented as the 'dissolution' of an antithesis, as 'a total revolution ... of material production' (Marx 1857–1861a: 431, 207). By showing the artificial origin of the natural laws of capital, the modern theory of colonization allows precisely to shed light on a violent rupture from which capital can begin to write its own history.

Recognising that capital is not a spontaneous order (Neocleous 2011: 507) does not mean that the laws of capital are any less 'natural'. On the contrary, Marx believes that the completion of the work of accumulation is achieved through a double movement of centralization and extension of scale that can be considered precisely as an 'immanent law' of the capitalist mode of production (Marx 1867a: 621ff, 588):

> Hand in hand with this centralization, or this expropriation of many capitalists by few, develop, on an ever-extending scale, the co-operative form of the labour process, the conscious technical application of science, the methodical cultivation of the soil, the transformation of the instruments

of labour into instruments of labour only usable in common, the econo-
mizing of all means of production by their use as the means of production of combined, socialized labour, the entanglement of all peoples in
the net of the world market, and with this, the international character of
the capitalistic regime.

MARX 1867a: 750

This double movement is the basis of the Malthusian 'natural law of population' whose 'nature', according to Marx, coincides entirely with its being 'peculiar to the capitalist mode of production', that is, 'historically valid'. Capital,
in fact, needs a worker population that exceeds the needs of valorization in
order to exercize its command over labour, to reproduce itself by guaranteeing the production of the wage labourer as a wage labourer while maintaining
its social dependence (Marx 1867a: 626ff; Rosdolsky 1977: 250ff; Meek 1953).
Marx himself makes it clear that precisely this naturally capitalist demographic regime has in fact rendered Wakefield's proposal obsolete, since more
emigrants from Europe flowed into the US than could move to the frontier,
but also because the civil war produced a very rapid centralization of capital
and the governance of appropriation processes, so that 'the great republic has
... ceased to be the promised land for emigrant labourers' (Marx 1867a: 760).
Once the natural laws of capital are in place, the state is called upon to guarantee their maintenance. When

> Adverse circumstances prevent the creation of an industrial reserve
> army and, with it, the absolute dependence of the working class upon
> the capitalist class, capital, along with its commonplace Sancho Panza,
> rebel against the 'sacred' law of supply and demand and tries to check its
> inconvenient action by forcible means and state interference.
>
> MARX 1867a: 634

This is, however, a different function from that which the state performs in the
process of primitive accumulation: 'The conditions and presuppositions of the
becoming, the *emergence*, of capital imply precisely that it is not yet in being
but is only *becoming*. Hence, they disappear with the development of real capital' (Marx 1857–1861a: 387–88). The state is placed precisely in this gap between
the becoming and the real existence of capital because it violently 'dissolves'
the antithesis that is produced by virtue of an objective movement, immanent
to pre-capitalist relations of production (Balibar 1970: 306).

Once that antithesis is dissolved, the state 'disappears' in the sense that
its action is redefined by the 'real', i.e., accomplished, capitalist relations. The

coercion that is applied to straighten out the natural laws of the capitalist mode of production is qualitatively different from that which characterizes the so-called primitive accumulation; because the violence of the state is now historicized, it is entirely subdued to 'the economic power that dominates everything in bourgeois society' (Marx 1857–1861a: 44). In this passage from the becoming of capital to the existence of capital, in other words, the state ceases to be the 'presupposition' and is transformed into the result of the capitalist mode of production, at least if we admit that the result is not such by virtue of a chronological succession – something that comes after capital affirmation – but a moment that changes in meaning once capital has assigned its 'organs' their determined function (Il'enkov 1960: ch. 4). As Marx makes clear in the *Grundrisse*, explicitly referring to Wakefield and the colonies:

> If in the fully developed bourgeois system each economic relationship presupposes the other in a bourgeois-economic form, and everything posited is thus also a premiss, that is the case with every organic system. This organic system itself has its premisses as a totality, and its development into a totality consists precisely in subordinating all elements of society to itself, or in creating out of it the organs it still lacks. This is historically how it becomes a totality.
>
> MARX 1857–1861a: 208

The combined reading of chapters on the so-called primitive accumulation and on the modern theory of colonization from the first volume of *Capital* allows us to reconstruct what might be called its 'genetic history':

> the exchange as it takes place between value and living labour, presupposes an *historical process* ... is the history of the emergence [*Entstehungsgeschichte*] of both capital and wage labour. In other words, the *extra-economic origin* of property means nothing but the *historical origin* of the bourgeois economy.
>
> MARX 1857–1861a: 412–13

This genetic history is the reversal of evolutionary history because it allows us to show that the capitalist social relation is historical precisely because it is unnecessary, because its origin is extra-economic, i.e., artificial. The realization of this process corresponds to the movement of capital's expansion throughout space, to a colonization that is not so much imperial domination as a definition of the field, the affirmation of '*wage labour* in its *classical* form, as permeating the whole extent of society, and making itself in lieu of the soil the ground on which society rests' (Marx 1857–1861a: 207). This does not imply a homogenization of the conditions of different points in space or a single trajectory of development. If capital is a power that dominates the whole of society, this domination also extends to those relations that appear residual but are, nevertheless, subject to its logic (Anderson 2010; Harootunian 2015). It is this qualification of space, the globalization of capital (Neocleous 2011: 507), that accomplishes its development as a 'historical totality'.

CHAPTER 5

The Feminine Ferment
Marx and the Critique of Patriarchy

Eleonora Cappuccilli and Roberta Ferrari

1   For a Critique of Patriarchal History

In Marx's work there is no organic discussion of patriarchy. Yet the problem of patriarchy, its subjects, effects and historical forms, cannot be seen simply as an appendage to the alleged (and disproven) libertinism of Karl Marx as a man in his relationship with women (Carver 2005). Despite the disinterest attributed to him, the problem of patriarchy in fact runs through his entire oeuvre, although in fragments that must be reconstructed. These fragments of a critique of patriarchal discourse make up the trajectory of a problem that he follows throughout his life and that he unsurprisingly takes up towards the end of his life in an in-depth study aiming to trace its origins and changes. Far from constituting a secondary piece of reasoning on the origin of the state (Iacono 1988), he sees the structure of patriarchy and the relations established by it as a crucial question, in which the global scope of capital and its all-pervasive and transformative nature are implicated, as well as its tendency to both make its own structures and preserve those that are not immediately capitalist.

So far, no systematic study of the conceptualization of patriarchy in Marx has been produced – although there have been a few fruitful attempts in this direction (Brown 2012; Carver 2013) – and debates on the relationship between Marxism and feminism have only partly touched on this point (see Vogel 1983; Hartmann 1979; Holmstrom 2002; Delphy 1984; Barrett 1980). Although we will not attempt to recompose Marxian thought on patriarchy into a coherent whole, we intend to set out the terms of the problem by starting from a perceived insufficiency in the questions so far posed of Marx's work on this issue.

Marx observes women's double work, both inside and outside the family sphere, and the changes that work undergoes with their entry into the factory. He thus considers the family regime as central to male domination. However, what receives less attention or remains implicit in Marxian analysis is the way in which this domination changes shape. Since he does not use refined semantic differentiations to identify the various patriarchal forms, using concepts such as 'the patriarchal industries of a peasant family' (Marx 1867a: 89; Marx

1857–1861a: 407. Cf. Folbre 1987: 332; Brunner 1968: 103–127), 'parental oppres-sion', 'paternal power', 'patria potestas' and 'paternal authority', for both ancient and capitalist societies, it is necessary to politically and historically distinguish between two different ideas in his reflections on patriarchy. We will therefore distinguish between patriarchalism, based on paternal authority and charac-terized by the equivalence (and later the analogy) between political power and the power of the father, and patriarchy as a social form within capitalism, in which power is transformed into male domination, both socio-symbolic and material (Irigaray 1985), and in which the subordination of women becomes central to social reproduction. This is the transition from the paternal power of peasant and communitarian patriarchalism to the 'social-sexual pact' that underpins modern patriarchy and the capital relationship (see Pateman 2018). The hypothesis we intend to discuss, therefore, is that while patriarchal-ism constitutes a form of domination and a mode of production in the pre-capitalist era, it does not die out, but is transformed into modern patriarchy, i.e., the hidden content of capitalist production and ideology.

Finally, we will develop our reflection along two axes that are not always separable from each other: on the one hand, the political problem of patriar-chy underlying global capital; on the other hand, the scientific problem, i.e., the unresolved questions that Marx explores by calling into question common sense, especially historical-anthropological common sense, to reveal patriar-chy as a battleground and not as an eternal and universal power structure. That is, he challenges not only the idea that the power of the father is the founda-tion of the social order, but also the very idea that personal power is necessary to maintaining that order.

In analysing the critique of patriarchy in Marx, we are principally interested in examining the relationship between production and reproduction, in an attempt to question the presumed undervaluation of the reproductive moment in the Marxian theoretical framework (cf. James and Dalla Costa 1972). The analysis of the nexus between production and reproduction reveals patriar-chy as an implicit and hidden relation in the capital relation and shows how both take part in a general dialectical process (Marx 1867a: 565–566), although their functions remain distinct. In this process, Marx captures the centrality of women as active social subjects and as a peculiar commodity that not only produces value in the factory and reproduces itself at minimal cost, but also reproduces the labour force and the conditions of production. In other words, he notes that, through women and their labour, the factory enters the home and the home, i.e. the patriarchal order of the family, enters the factory, where it reproduces a hierarchically divided labour force to ensure the reproduction of its regime.

Secondly, the problem of patriarchy allows for the emergence of a tension between homogenization and differentiation that permeates capital: as a hierarchical system, patriarchy acts on the whole of society as an institution of stratification and discipline. Starting from the observation of the coexistence of domestic industry, domestic work and the sexual division of labour in the factory, Marx shows the impossible homogeneity of the capital relation and its capacity to exploit differences and hierarchies, which it constantly produces and reinvents.

Thirdly, in connection with the problem of the tension between homogenization, permanence and the exploitation of differences, we address the question of the subjects of patriarchy. It is precisely the irreducible capitalist heterogeneity that allows patriarchy to affect different subjects, namely women and girls as the object of male domination as well as children, wives, servants and slaves as subjects of the *pater familias*. Patriarchal power is defined both as the father's 'power of life and death over his sons and descendants as well as over slaves and servants' and as '*deminutio capitis*', i.e., the loss of the wife's rights of gentility at the time of marriage, which deprives her of the capacity to inherit (Marx 1880–1882: 119; cf. Anderson 2002). Patriarchy both persists in capitalism as paternal and parental power and also becomes the specific oppression of women. However, for Marx, women are not simply the object of oppression but are also a political subject, an indispensable 'ferment' of the overthrow of not only the patriarchal relation but also the capital relation (Marx 1857–1861a: 424–425; contra Federici 2017).

The Marxian critique of patriarchy is also related to the role of the state in capital's valorization and in exploitation. This role implies that the state assumes a patriarchal disciplining function previously entrusted to the family. Patriarchal power establishes a political link between the state and the family.

In delineating these different axes of analysis, we will not follow the progression of Marxian works chronologically but reconstruct the political importance that Marx accords to the problem of patriarchy in the light of the social and material relations of the capitalist present rather than in some mythical patriarchal pre-capitalist genesis. Patriarchalism is understood from the present of patriarchy (Marx 1857–1861a: 17–18): he thus only studies its origins towards the end of his life, when he has already reflected on its present. Women are presented as agents of transformation and as unforeseen subjects of the revolutionary process, who 'played a noble and prominent part' in the workers' movement (Marx 1869a: 77). In order to truly overthrow the relations of domination, Marx asserts that the whole of society must change, starting with the family. It is a question of recognising a force of insubordination in the 'feminine ferment' that is not just about women, nor exclusively about overthrowing the capitalist system, but about the radical transformation of society.

2   **Patriarchy, Community and Family in the Pre-capitalist Era**

In the German Ideology, Marx and Engels identify the family as the primary location for the division of labour, private property and the subordination of women:

> The division of labour in which all these contradictions are implicit, and which in its turn is based on the natural division of labour in the family and the separation of society into individual families opposed to one another, simultaneously implies the distribution, and indeed the unequal distribution, both quantitative and qualitative, of labour and its products, hence property, the nucleus, the first form of which lies in the family, where wife and children are the slaves of the husband.
>   MARX and ENGELS 1845–1846: 46

Social organization emerges as an extension of the family, to which a specific type of property corresponds:

> The first form of property is tribal property [*Stammeigentum*]. It corresponds to the undeveloped stage of production, at which a people lives by hunting and fishing, by cattle-raising or, at most, by agriculture ... The division of labour is at this stage still very elementary and is confined to a further extension of the natural division of labour existing in the family. The social structure is, therefore, limited to an extension of the family: patriarchal chieftains, below them the members of the tribe, finally slaves. The slavery latent in the family only develops gradually with the increase of population, the growth of wants, and with the extension of external intercourse, both of war and of barter.
>   MARX and ENGELS 1845–1846 in MECW 5: 33

Thus, according to the Marxian reconstruction, the organization of the tribal community closely depends on the mode of production, the form of tribal property and the division of labour, which is presented as an extension of that which takes place in the family. These reflections are part of an attempt to trace 'the extra-economic origin of property', which 'means nothing but the historical origin of the bourgeois economy' (Marx 1857–1861a: 413; cf. Wood

2008). In this framework, patriarchalism thus appears as one of the objective conditions of the historical origin of the bourgeois economy.

When dealing with pre-capitalist forms of property in the *Grundrisse,* Marx returns to the relationship between community, the individual and the division of labour, but with an emphasis on the progressive separation of the subject from the conditions of their reproduction. He does not long for a return to pre-capitalist communities, because within them the individual lives an existence predetermined by the objective conditions of nature. There is no free and full development of either the individual or society, and this is linked to the fact that the purpose of such communities is not the production of wealth (Marx 1857–1861a: 411), but the maintenance of the individual proprietor, the family and the community itself. It neither allows for the emergence of individual nor of collective freedom:

> The object of all these communities is preservation, i.e. the reproduction of their individual members as proprietors, i.e. in the same objective mode of existence, which also constitutes the relationship of the members to each other, and therefore constitutes the community itself.
>
> MARX 1857–1861a: 417

However, increases in population destroy the natural conditions of existence of the producer instead of reproducing them (Marx 1857–1861a: 417–418). The reproduction of the community is thus 'at the same time necessarily new production and the destruction of the old form', until, ultimately, the community decays in the process of transforming itself (Marx 1857–1861a: 417). The demise of the community is the dawn of the individual. In spite of their continued function in reproduction and in the denial of their individuality in modern society, it is women, by marrying and thus leaving the original consanguineous family, who promote this change, leading to the disintegration of the community. However, despite undergoing constant changes, the family resists the dissolution of blood ties.

In the final years of his life, through his reading of Austin, Maine, Morgan, Lubbock, Niebuhr and Mommsen, Marx returned to the family as the link between the individual and the community in its various forms. The result of this reflection is a series of notes that Engels would later systematize and develop in *The Origins of the Family, Private Property and the State,* in which he declares that 'the first-class oppression [coincides] with [the oppression] of the female sex by the male' (Engels 1884: 173) and argues that with the birth of the family come private property, exploitation, class division and the state. Marx takes from Morgan the reconstruction of the historical succession of family forms: consanguineous, Punaluan, Syndiasmian, patriarchal and monogamous (Marx 1880–1882: 102). Commenting on Morgan's Ancient Society, Marx states that:

> The modern family contains the germ not only of servitus (slavery) but also serfdom, since it contains from the beginning a relation to services for agriculture. It contains in miniature all the antagonisms within itself which are later broadly developed in society and its state. In the Syndyasmian family there are the seeds of paternal authority *in nuce*; they developed as the family assumed monogamous characters. When property began to be created in masses and the desire for its transmission to children had changed descent from the female line to the male, the first real foundation for paternal power was posed.
>
> MARX 1880–1882: 120

Paternal authority has its origin in the family, but it is only with the spread of private property that paternal power can extend beyond the family circle and become political power. However, this reconstruction does not always apply: the monogamous family is not the result of a necessary succession of family forms.

Because of its intrinsic historical dynamism, the family contains in miniature all the antagonisms of society, which will fully unfold in the state. At the same time, the family gives rise to the space of freedom that allows for the emergence of the individual, a fundamental premise of wage labour. In order to trace this history of emancipation and the parallel oppression of women and children, Marx must start from the crisis of previous forms of community: the development of the monogamous family takes place antagonistically and in parallel with the dissolution of old blood ties (Marx 1880–1882: 120). The patriarchal family thus appears as a moment of transition from the consanguineous to the monogamous form. Typical of ancient Roman and Greek societies, and sporadically observable in some dispersed Indian communities, the patriarchal family – technically defined as a 'property-making organization' that involves servants and slaves (Marx 1880–1882: 135) – is clearly distinguished from the monogamous family and the bourgeois family. With the patriarchal family, the subordination of women becomes a precondition of the social order.

It is a priority for Marx to historicize not only capital, in its historical and transitory character, but also the family in both its bourgeois and patriarchal forms – hence the polemic with Maine who, on the contrary, follows the 'fashion' of 'making the patriarchal family ... the typical family of primitive society'

(Marx 1880–1882: 119; cf. Anderson 2010: 201). Despite being aware that 'modern society reposes upon the Monogamian family' (Marx 1880–1882: 126), Marx finds it mystifying to turn this family into a model:

> It is, of course, just as absurd to hold the Teutonic-Christian form of the family to be absolute and final as it would be to apply that character to the ancient Roman, the ancient Greek, or the Eastern forms which, moreover, taken together form a series in historical development.
>
> MARX 1867a: 492

While 'Maine and his consorts' say that in primitive societies the authority of the patriarch or the *pater familias* over the family is 'the element or germ out of which all permanent power of man over man has been gradually developed' (Marx 1880–1882: 333), for Marx paternity cannot be the foundation and model of sovereignty since the private family is not the basis from which the tribe and, later, society develops (Krader 1974: 40).

While denying patriarchy as the universal model of any primitive society, Marx does not allow himself to be dazzled by the myth of matriarchy, i.e., (the female origin of supreme state power) (Bachofen 1870: VIII). Unlike Bachofen, Marx does not believe that, with the passage from matrilineal to patrilineal descent, there has been, once and for all, a 'world-historic defeat of the female sex' (Engels 1884: 165). On the contrary, he acknowledges that matrilineality is also a patriarchal structure, as evidenced by the fact that women still enjoyed a lower degree of sexual freedom than men (Marx 1880–1882: 117). However, this does not imply that they are passive objects of male domination. In the Roman family, for example:

> Materfamilias was mistress of the family; went into the streets freely without restraint by her husband, frequented with the men the theatres and festive banquets; in the house not confined to particular apartments, nor excluded from the table of the men. Roman females had more personal dignity and independence than the Greek ones; but marriage gave them *in manum viri*; war = daughter des husband; he had the power of correction and of life and death in case of adultery.
>
> MARX 1880–1882: 121

By highlighting the elements of continuity – such as the conflict between men and women and between social groups, or women's unwillingness to submit silently to male domination – Marx emphasizes the moments of rupture that mark the development of patriarchal social relations, up to the point where capital transfigures them, assuming their hierarchical traits. The entry of women into the factory marks a moment of a crucial transformation of the patriarchal power in capitalism: the exit of women from the domestic sphere entails 'the dissolution, under the capitalist system, of the old family ties', opening up a space for the constitution of new social forms and relations (Marx 1867a: 492).

This means that, even if the family appears in different historical epochs, it does not remain the same, but embraces the possibilities of action of its members and their claim to freedom (contra Iacono 1988: 763). When Marx and Engels state that 'the bourgeoisie has torn away from the family its sentimental veil, and has reduced the family relation to a mere money relation' (Marx and Engels 1848: 487), they are arguing that although the family has not always been a space for the valorization of capital, it has always been a structure of order, in which there is only a veil separating the economy of power from sentiment. With the rise of the bourgeoisie, the family became the terrain on which capital exercized its power to intensify the extraction of surplus value, through a modification of the family structure that would allow for the valorization of the work of all its members, the devaluation of women's work and thus the maintenance of its socially reproductive function. If, on the one hand, women, men and children are treated equally in the factory, because 'capital is by nature a leveller, since it exacts in every sphere of production equality in the conditions of the exploitation of labour' (Marx 1867a: 401), on the other hand 'women and young girls' are specially chosen for 'one of the most shameful, dirtiest and worst paid jobs', namely 'sorting rags', a carrier for 'the spread of smallpox and other infectious diseases, and they themselves are the first victims' (Marx 1867a: 466; cf. Brown 2012: 82–83).

But if the bourgeois family is not immutable, there is nothing to protect it from the threat of dissolution:

> In its completely developed form this family exists only among the bourgeoisie. But this state of things finds its complement in the practical absence of the family among the proletarians, and in public prostitution. The bourgeois family will vanish as a matter of course when its complement vanishes, and both will vanish with the vanishing of capital.
>
> MARX and ENGELS 1848: 501

The different forms of oppression do not follow one another chronologically. Modern patriarchy is not a secondary contradiction to be corrected after the abolition of the present state of affairs, but part of the 'genetic history' of capital: the dissolution of the bourgeois family in which the oppression of women lurks is necessary for the downfall of capitalism, as the family is the 'organ' of capital itself (Marx 1857–1861a: 412). At the same time, Marx observes the relationship that capitalism disrupts and exploits between the sexes and consequently between family members and identifies it as mutable and as not having an eternal nature. Its nature is in fact always political.

3   The Vampire of Patriarchy: Towards a Critique of Patriarchal Society

In 1844 Marx writes that nature 'taken abstractly ... is nothing for man' (Marx 1844a: 345). In this way, he introduces the relationship between the sexes as a historical and social relationship that becomes natural and, as a result, political:

> In the approach to woman as the spoil and handmaid of communal lust is expressed the infinite degradation in which man exists for himself, for the secret of this approach has its unambiguous, decisive, plain and undisguised expression in the relation of man to woman and in the manner in which the direct and natural species-relationship is conceived.
>
> MARX 1844a: 295

Since for Marx there is no nature as essence, but 'historically specific forms of human nature' (Holmstrom 1984: 459), patriarchy is not the residue of an archaic social form, but the way in which domination in society is articulated from sexual difference, exceeding and reinforcing class antagonism.

In articles published in the *New York Tribune* between 1849 and 1862, Marx deals with the condition of women in very different contexts, including the Preston strike of 1853, the abduction of young women for forced labour in factories and the 'Bulwer scandal' (Marx 1858a: 596). Lady Bulwer became famous for freely expressing her opinion about her ex-husband Edward Bulwer, a Tory writer and politician, who had long mistreated her and continued to discredit her. During his electoral campaign, Lady Bulwer interrupted a rally and publicly denounced his abuse against her (Marx 1858a). The consequence of this act was her forced hospitalization in an asylum, orchestrated by her ex-husband and son with the support of doctors and public officials. Marx observed that the much-vaunted British freedom was based on the freedom of some to oppress others: he believed internment in asylums was the neutralization of insubordination by medical authorities who exploited alleged and manipulated 'madness' to their own advantage: 'British law requires nothing beyond the declaration in writing of a relative, countersigned by two medical men, with whom fees and personal influence may go a great length in directing their opinions. The surest way of rendering a person mad is to take him to the madhouse'. Behind Lady Bulwer's insubordination Marx saw the despotism of a society in which the ruling class was a class of men. He did not consider her to be a victim of capitalist oppression in the economic sense, but a subject who refused to subordinate herself and to accept her 'abuses', i.e., a subject that took more than the freedom that patriarchal society was willing to allow her.

Marx's attention to the social condition of women as women and to the oppression perpetuated by men inside and outside the family is also evident in his review of Jacques Peuchet's book *Mémoires tirés des archives de la police de Paris*. From these memoirs, Marx extracts a number of cases of oppression through 'parental authority', with men driving women from different social backgrounds to suicide, including a young woman ostracized by her family and community for violating her pre-marital chastity obligation, another forced to suffer the violence of a jealous husband and a girl who was denied an abortion. Commenting on these cases, Marx attacks bourgeois morality as a patriarchal institution, which survived even the French revolution, making paternal authority an absolute power over women (Marx 1846: 597). The critique of bourgeois morality emerges particularly clearly in *The Holy Family*, where Marx and Engels discuss the case of the prostitute Fleur de Marie (Sue 1844).

> We meet Marie surrounded by criminals, as a prostitute in bondage to the proprietress of the criminals' tavern. In this debasement she preserves a human nobleness of soul ... We must observe Fleur de Marie attentively from her first appearance in order to be able to compare her original form with her Critical transformation. In spite of her frailty, Fleur de Marie at once gives proof of vitality, energy, cheerfulness, resilience of character – qualities which alone explain her human development in her inhuman situation. When Chourineur ill-treats her, she defends herself with her scissors. That is the situation in which we first find her. *She does not appear as a defenceless lamb who surrenders without any resistance to overwhelming brutality; she is a girl who can vindicate her rights and put up a fight.*
>
> MARX and ENGELS 1845: 168, italics ours

Fleur de Marie's freedom and integrity make her a subject of struggle. In the following passage, Marx overturns the bourgeois conception of good and evil, contrasting it not only with the material conditions it produces, but above all with Fleur's 'natural' autonomy, which fights against an 'unnatural' fate. The 'essential nature' he refers to here is not some alleged feminine authenticity, but the conquest of her own subjective individuality:

> Good and *evil*, as Marie conceives them, are not the *moral abstractions* of good and evil. She ... is *good* because she is still *young*, full of hope and vitality. Her situation is *not good*, because it puts an unnatural constraint on her, because ... it is not the fulfilment of her human desires; because it is full of torment and without joy. She measures her situation in life by her *own individuality*, her *essential nature*, not by the *ideal of what is good*. In *natural* surroundings, where the chains of bourgeois life fall ... she herself is neither good nor bad, but *human*.
>
> MARX and ENGELS 1845: 169–170

Not only does Marx attack morality as the ideological translation of an abstract conception of nature, but he also unmasks the patriarchal power of society that manifests itself in it. His critique of bourgeois morality is also a critique of sexual discipline as a social code. That is why he emphasizes Marie's free individuality against the social order; it is in her rejection of that order that we find her humanity and desire for freedom.

Marx describes the condition of women as a struggle against society and against the male and patriarchal claim to possess women, at the root of which is private property understood as paternal domination:

> The relationship of private property ... finds expression in the brutish form of opposing to *marriage* (certainly a *form of exclusive private property*) the *community of women*, in which a woman becomes a piece of *communal* and *common* property. ... This type of communism – since it negates the *personality* of man in every sphere – is but the logical expression of private property, which is this negation.
>
> MARX 1844a: 294–295

The discourse of the common ownership of women, used by the bourgeoisie to discredit communism, is in reality, according to Marx, a mystification of the bourgeois form of the relations between the sexes. The social form of sexual relations based on the reduction of women to commodities sums up the essence of private property. In order to make woman a possession, an attempt is made to console her for her civil misery by making her an object of rhetorical worship as a mother, 'a stupid rustic idyll' (Marx and Engels 1850: 244). She can be possessed or worshipped, but she cannot act autonomously. The Marxian critique of patriarchy is part of his larger critique of society: women are a subject that is internal to capitalist organization, whilst also differing from the male subject. There are two reasons for this difference. Firstly because, 'in the family ... the wife represents the proletariat ... The administration of the household lost its public character. It was no longer the concern of society. It became a private service. The wife became the first domestic servant, pushed out of participation in social production' (Engels 1884: 181). And, secondly, because women work within and outside of the domestic sphere and in and out of production (Ferrari 2017).

Albeit implicitly, Marx clearly recognizes the home as a site of production, in terms of both home-based work [*Verlagssystem*] connected to the factory, and of that kind of work which capital considers 'unproductive'. The 'unproductive women' (Marx 1867a: 449) are a part of the 'productivity of modern industry', based on the exploitation of 'other spheres of production' and reproducing a class of servants and serfs:

> The extraordinary productiveness of modern industry, accompanied as it is by both a more extensive and a more intense exploitation of labour power in all other spheres of production, allows of the unproductive employment of a larger and larger part of the working class, and the consequent reproduction, on a constantly extending scale, of the ancient domestic slaves under the name of a servant class, including men-servants, women-servants, lackeys, &c.
>
> MARX 1867a: 449

Exploitation does not only concern labour that is immediately productive for capital. The work of servants and that in the family circle is unproductive from the point of view of capital, though no less necessary for its reproduction (Luxemburg 1971 [1912]). At the same time, women's entry into the factory is an opportunity for freedom: outside the home, 'the woman has thus become an active agent in our social production' and this, also thanks to 'the deployment of machines, leads to the disintegration of all formerly existing social and family relations' (Marx 1868a: 384).

By leaving the home to enter the factory, women escape the control of fathers and husbands, but find themselves under the command of the factory bell. For the capitalist, the women workers who pass from the slavery of the *Verlagssystem* to the factory are docile and malleable material (Marx 1867a: 464–465), because they are prepared for the worst degree of exploitation. Women's labour is already devalued, at the price of an overall devaluation of the whole family: 'four days' labour takes the place of one' (Marx 1867a: 398–399). Jobs considered typically feminine and domestic quickly became wage labour. However, it is with the introduction of machines that female labour, along with child labour, becomes predominant and remains in specific sectors so for most of the 18th and 19th centuries (Foster and Clark 2018). This shift transforms both the capitalist mode of production and social reproduction. Women are removed, at least in part, from their reproductive role, which nevertheless, as Marx notices, returns in the 'abominable' conditions in which they are put to work outside the home as well (Marx 1868a: 383). Society reorganizes itself through relying on the more intense exploitation of women workers and reducing the cost of reproduction, which is limited to guaranteeing the survival – or also the replacement – of the labour force. The machine allows each member of the family to be put to work and the family to be valued on the basis of the sexual division of labour, so as to determine the 'absolute contradiction' of capital:

> If modern industry, by its very nature, therefore necessitates variation of labour, fluency of function, universal mobility of the labourer, on the other hand, in its capitalistic form, it reproduces the old division of labour *with its ossified particularizations*. We have seen how this *absolute contradiction* between the technical necessities of modern industry, and the social character inherent in its capitalistic form, dispels all fixity and security in the situation of the labourer; how it constantly threatens, by taking away the instruments of labour, to snatch from his hands his means of subsistence, and, by suppressing his detail-function, to make him superfluous.
>
> MARX 1867a: 489–490, italics added

The state responds to this anarchy with factory legislation, which nevertheless only corrects the contradiction enough to prevent the dissolution of the family and the sexual division of labour. The state has to safeguard itself from the war between capitalists and workers and, at the same time, guarantee the continuity of the inequalities necessary for social reproduction and patriarchal power relations:

> So long as factory legislation is confined to regulating the labour in factories, manufactories, &c, it is regarded as a mere interference with the exploiting rights of capital. But when it comes to regulating the so-called 'home-labour', it is immediately viewed as a direct attack on the *patria potestas,* on parental authority. The tender-hearted English Parliament long affected to shrink from taking this step. The force of facts, however, compelled it at last to acknowledge that modern industry, in overturning

the economic foundation on which was based the traditional family, and the family labour corresponding to it, had also unloosened all traditional family ties. The rights of the children had to be proclaimed.

MARX 1867a: 491–492

Capital breaks through the walls of the home by rearticulating parental domination to its advantage, so much so that the state defends child labour in the name of 'the rights of the children'. In turn, *patriarchal power lives in capitalist society as a vampire*. The partial replacement of sweatshop exploitation by factory exploitation does not result in the neutralization of the sexual division of labour, which corresponds to the 'division of labour in society' (Marx 1867a: 356). On the contrary, machines allow patriarchy to be concretely and broadly valorized:

> The labour of women and children was, therefore, the first thing sought for by capitalists who used machinery! That mighty substitute for labour and labourers was forthwith changed into a means for *increasing the number of wage labourers* by enrolling, under the direct sway of capital, every member of the workman's family, without distinction of age or sex. ... *Forced labour for the capitalist has usurped the place not only of childish play, but of free labour in the domestic circle.*
>
> MARX 1867a: 529, italics added

The factory enters the home, imposing a double command on women, reducing their freedom to a minimum, and splitting up the family by basing it on relations of enmity. Here we see a relationship between capital and patriarchy in which the latter exceeds the form and immediate interests of the former, while making it its condition of existence and development (hooks 1981: 9off).

Patriarchy is never subsumed in its entirety by capital, nor does it simply present itself as its effect, but is a heterogeneous factor that capital 'finds' and uses differently each time (Spivak 1981: 150ff). Thus, while mechanization destroys a precise male image of the workforce, apparently producing indifference and interchangeability, capital enhances sexual difference by making it an instrument of domination. In the factory, capital is accompanied by the vampire of patriarchy, which acts not only at the expense of women, but of the entire workforce.

But there is a further contradiction within the process of social production:

> However terrible and disgusting the dissolution, under the capitalist system, of the old family ties may appear, nevertheless, modern industry, by

assigning as it does an important part in the process of production, outside the domestic sphere, to women, to young persons, and to children of
both sexes, creates a new economic foundation for a higher form of the
family and of the relations between the sexes.

MARX 1867a: 492

Not only does capitalism nourish patriarchy but tends to do so to the point of
questioning it, developing its contradictions, and producing the subject that
will create and organize its explosion. Marx sees in the expropriation of property the opportunity for liberation from the family and recognizes women as
the 'decisive' subject of change. For this reason, in addition to the abolition of
the articles of the Napoleonic Code that sanctioned the inferiority of women,
he included equal pay and the 'socialized' responsibility for reproduction in
the programme of the Parti Ouvrier.

The question of reproduction is absolutely central to Marx's critique
of patriarchy, although the connection is not made explicit in Chapter 21
of *Capital*. Here Marx criticizes classical political economy and its definition of
production, stating that the conditions of production are at the same time the
conditions of reproduction:

Capitalist production, therefore, under its aspect of a continuous connected process, of a process of reproduction, produces not only commodities, not only surplus value, but it also produces and reproduces the
capitalist relation; on the one side the capitalist, on the other the wage
labourer.

MARX 1867a: 577

If labour that does not produce commodities is for Marx 'social labour', then
reproduction is that broader process of the reproduction of the social and
political conditions of life and production that takes place within a relation of
domination that cannot be compensated or monetized: no amount of money
can compensate for sexual subordination. As a relationship that establishes
sexual subordination, it can only be overturned. In other words, reproduction
cannot be reformed, but must be subverted.

The sexual division of labour is thus the internal structure of the relationship between production and reproduction. In this sense, it is not only women's
reproductive labour that reaffirms patriarchy, but also the capitalist production of which it is a part. For Marx, social reproduction reveals the contradiction between the levelling off effect of capital and its hierarchical dominium,
and thus constitutes a crucial point in the process of capitalist valorization,
crucial also for its potential power to obstruct capitalism.

The Marxian analysis of patriarchy moves the critique of capitalism a step further. The struggle against the patriarchal family becomes the struggle of the working class to transform society.

4   Conclusions

Against Maine's 'thick head', Marx criticizes the ancestral triumph of patriarchy, observing the dynamic relationship of patriarchy with capitalism by starting from its historical conditions. By going back to its external earlier roots, Marx sees patriarchy as the genetic social relationship of capital, i.e., as its concealed political condition. He does not, therefore, delineate a dual system, but rather notes the coexistence of interconnected social formations (Folbre 1987), never quite separable but also specific in their constitution and effects. Recognising this connection also allows him to see women as decisive political subjects and to indicate in their oppression a crucial point of capitalist domination.

In 1868, Marx writes that 'German women should begin by driving their husbands to self-emancipation' (Marx to Kugelmann 5/12/1868 in MECW 43: 175), and in the report of the congress of the First International in 1869 he enthusiastically comments on the strike of the women silk-winders in Lyon (Marx 1869a: 77). Thus, Marx's studies of patriarchy in the *Anthropological Notebooks* came after he had already recognized women as a central subject for the overthrow of capitalism.

Marx recognizes the 'feminine ferment' as an essential revolutionary ferment in the struggle against the bourgeoisie and patriarchal capitalism. Acknowledging the focus of Marxian analysis on heterogeneous modes of social production and on the patriarchal reproduction of society allows us to use Marx's thought as a political weapon. This weapon is useful within the framework of a neoliberal order in which patriarchy and capitalism renew their nuptials, and in which the subsumption of reproductive labour changes the terms and meaning of social reproduction in a broad sense, providing patriarchy with a continuous and violent actuality and a new legitimation. The Marxian analysis of patriarchy thus poses questions about capitalist exploitation during neoliberalism and its crisis, outside the paradigm of the white wage labourer and from the partial but central condition of women. From this analysis, the destruction of patriarchy emerges as the laboratory of all social and political radical change. It is for this reason that Marx's thought continues to fuel the polemical flame of feminist discourse.

CHAPTER 6

The City as a Time-Machine
Marx and Urban Transformations

Niccolò Cuppini

> Intercourse between nations has spread across the whole globe to
> such an extent that one could say all the world has virtually become
> a single city in which a permanent fair of all commodities is taking
> place, so that everyone, without leaving his home, can, by means
> of money, obtain and enjoy everything produced by the earth, the
> animals, and human industry. A marvelous invention!
>
> MONTANARI 1804: 40

∴

Numerous texts have been written on 'Marxism and the city' but, as far as this
writer knows, there are none on 'Marx and the city'. In fact, there is a tendency
to see this as a major gap in his thought. Why, we might ask, is there no city
in Marx? Let's be clear from the outset: it is the question that is wrong. In this
chapter, I will try to rethink the way that this subject is posed. The city is a
recurring theme in his early work, but over the course of his life it progressively
thins out, dissolves or at least transmutes. If it is very significant in *The German
Ideology* and, as a political element, in *The Class Struggles in France* and *The
Eighteenth Brumaire* (and, in part, in *The Manifesto*), but it is dealt with in only
a few passages in his most famous work, *Capital*. Why is this? Let anticipate the
answer: because in Marx the city is a historical category, and so is abandoned
when he writes about current issues. It is, moreover, a historical category that
cannot be taken in isolation, but needs to be accompanied by its dialectical
reference, the countryside. In fact, Marx identifies, in the separation between
the city and the countryside, the first cause of the division developed and
mediated through the exchange of goods and the opposition between manual
and intellectual labour, as well as between those who hold capital and those
who sell their labour power. It is therefore the relationship between town and
country that Marx frames historically, and it is precisely that relationship that

he sees disappearing at the time. In front of Marx's eyes, the city and the countryside vanish as historical relations, overcome by new antagonisms developed
in modern industry on a global level.

I will now investigate Marx's reconstruction of this disappearance by analysing his texts, aiming to investigate the hypothesis that it is on the ruins of the
city (and the countryside) that a new figure emerges, which we could call the
metropolis. More precisely, this new figure is what Marx was looking for: a new
antagonistic dynamic that historically was given as an opposition between the
city and the countryside, and that is now determined as an unprecedented
class conflict between new social subjectivities, articulated within a market
that was becoming global and a territory that was becoming an infrastructure,
meaning it was becoming urbanized. Marx thought in terms of processes, and
at the time the forces that constituted the commodity form established the
city-industry as a scenario of new contradictions that went beyond the city
as such. Thus, when commenting on Engels's studies on Manchester, Marx
argued that Engels perfectly understood 'the spirit of the capitalist mode of
production', clearly showing how the urban problematic had to be dislocated
onto a new level.

1   The Historical City in Marx

The process which precedes the formation of the capitalist relationship is analysed in the *Grundrisse* and is taken up again in *Capital* under the title 'Original
Accumulation'. Marx claims that '[a]ncient classical history is the history of
cities, but cities based on landed property and agriculture ... modern [history]
is the urbanization of the countryside, not, as in ancient times, the ruralization of the city' (Marx 1857–1861a: 406). The work of historical reconstruction
that he lays out in *The German Ideology*, and that can also be found in the
Manuscripts and later on in the *Grundrisse*, is here iconically gathered. It is
necessary to return to *The German Ideology* in order to deepen our understanding of his historical analysis of the city, which is framed as a form of division
between labour and private property. The citations below provide a brief sum-
mary of his argument.

> The most important division of material and mental labour is the sepa-
> ration of town and country. The contradiction between town and coun-
> try begins with the transition from barbarism to civilization ... and runs
> through the whole history of civilization to the present day.
>
> MARX and ENGELS 1845–1846: 64

He then adds:

> The advent of the town implies, at the same time, the necessity of administration, police, taxes, etc., in short of the municipality [*des Gemeindewesens*], and thus of politics in general'.
>
> MARX and ENGELS 1845–1846: 64

He follows this with his first description of the division of the population into two great classes based on the division of labour and instruments of production appears for the first time:

> The town is in actual fact already the concentration of the population, of the instruments of production, of capital, of pleasures, of needs, while the country demonstrates just the opposite fact, isolation and separation. The contradiction between town and country can only exist within the framework of private property.
>
> IBID

This antagonism expresses the subsumption of the individual to a certain activity imposed on them. A subjection which makes one man into a restricted town-animal, another into a restricted country-animal, and daily creates anew the conflict between their interests. Labour is here again the chief thing, power over individuals, and as long as this power exists, private property must exist.

Marx proposes a historical succession in which a series of different forms of property are defined through the changing city-countryside relationship, starting from tribal property and moving on to the history of classical antiquity, which is a history of cities based on land ownership and agriculture. Looking historically at society within the city-countryside relationship, we observe a process of the 'ruralization of the city' (Lefebvre 2016: 160). The third form of property is feudal, which arose in the face of the destruction of previous productive forces. The feudal system was a limited social universe, in which the land was personalized in its lord and the serf was a mere accessory of the land. In this period, it was the countryside that shaped society, in which

> industry (town life) develops over and against landed property (aristocratic feudal life) and itself continues to bear the feudal character of its opposite in the form of monopoly, craft, guild, corporation, etc., within which labour still has a seemingly social significance, still the significance of the real community, and has not yet reached the stage of indifference to its content, of complete being-for-self, i.e., of abstraction from all other being, and hence has not yet become liberated capital.
>
> MARX 1844a: 286

But it was precisely within this unprecedented scenario that the city-country antithesis was developing, with new socio-economic conditions leading to the separation of capital (based on work and exchange) from land ownership. If the European Middle Ages arose from the countryside, it was the tipping of the scales towards the urban environment that determined the 'starting point' of a new history. As Marx wrote: 'From the serfs of the Middle Ages sprang the chartered burghers of the earliest towns. From the burgesses the first elements of the bourgeoisie were developed' (Marx and Engels 1848: 485). With the expansion of this social force the city usurped aristocratic power and founded a new political organization in the Commune, in which

> Capital was a naturally evolved capital, consisting of a house, the tools of the craft, and the natural, hereditary customers; and not being realizable, on account of the backwardness of intercourse and the lack of circulation, it had to be handed down from father to son. Unlike modern capital, which can be assessed in money, and which may be indifferently invested in this thing or that, this capital was directly connected with the particular work of the owner, inseparable from it and to this extent estate capital.
>
> MARX and ENGELS 1845–1846: 66

The commercial city, in which mobile capital prevailed, began to emerge from the medieval city. The commercial city snatched weaving from the countryside, making it into a manufacturing industry, enlarging its commercial networks and giving birth to new social subjects (such as merchants and weavers).

> The next extension of the division of labour was the separation of production and intercourse, the formation of a special class of merchants ... With intercourse vested in a particular class, with the extension of trade ... there immediately appears a reciprocal action between production and intercourse. The towns enter into relations with one another ... and the separation between production and intercourse soon calls forth a new division of production between the individual towns ... The local restrictions of earlier times begin gradually to be broken down.
>
> MARX and ENGELS 1845–1846: 67

This was a trans-urban phenomenon in which the same social dynamics were reproduced at different levels: the citizens united against the nobility of the countryside, commerce expanded, and from the numerous local bourgeoisies of the individual cities, a bourgeois class very gradually arose. The bourgeoisie had created these conditions because they had freed themselves from feudal ties, and because they were in opposition to that system. With the establishment of connections between individual cities, these common conditions developed into class conditions.

With the concentration of population and capital, the division of labour between cities, and the consequent emergence of manufacturing, weaving changed from being an activity carried out in the countryside to being a new, more developed activity, transforming even 'villages and commercial hamlets, which gradually became cities and even, very soon, the most dominant cities in each country'. There was a decisive shift towards the capital relationship, in parallel with the opening up of a new global dimension:

> In the guilds the patriarchal relations between journeyman and master continued to exist; in manufacture their place was taken by the monetary relations between worker and capitalist ... Manufacture and the movement of production in general received an enormous impetus through the extension of intercourse which came with the discovery of America and the sea-route to the East Indies.
>
> MARX and ENGELS 1845–1846: 69

Within this broad historical context, reconstructed here through the words of Marx, the commercial cities emerged, which, particularly in England, encouraged the concentration of trade and manufacturing. Faced with an expanding world market and growing demand, large scale industry was born, giving rise to the third period of private property since the Middle Ages. Universalised competition established the means of communication and the modern world market, subjected trade to itself and transformed all capital into industrial capital, thus generating rapid circulation (the perfection of the financial system) and the centralization of capital. With universal competition it forced all individuals to the extreme limits of their energy.

> It produced world history for the first time ... In the place of naturally grown towns it created the modern, large industrial cities which have sprung up overnight ... It completed the victory of the town over the country ... large-scale industry created a class which in all nations has the same interest and for which nationality is already dead.
>
> MARX and ENGELS 1845–1846: 73

The preceding genealogical reconstruction can be summarized in this way: ancient society perishes without producing a new society, because the ancient city is a closed system, which dominates the countryside, and in which the social contradictions remain within the city. In the Middle Ages, on the other hand, a conflict between city and country gradually emerged, becoming critical when the urban system was no longer able to close it on itself and thus started to break with the feudal system, and from this clash came industry and new commerce (economic), movable property and new social subjectivities (social) and the state (political). This was the result of the first great class struggle, which expressed itself through social forms: bourgeoisie *vs.* feudalism, city *vs.* countryside, movable property *vs.* land. It could be said that in the period in which Marx lived the city had subsumed the countryside, making the industrial city the new historical scenario and thus what we might expect him to focus on. However, although he is aware of and also discusses issues relating to the industrial city – when, for example, following Engels, he writes about worker alienation and housing in the industrial city – the industrial city *as such* is not part of his reflection. Marx's point actually seems to be that the division of labour and, therefore, the division into classes, feeds a conflict of a new kind. This new conflict goes beyond the city-countryside division and is thus not expressed in a dialectic between the industrial city and its 'other'. Marx's search for the contradiction that could determine new historical differences was determined within the 'industrial city', which drastically changed what the city meant historically. For example, the industrial city could not be understood without global commerce and the urbanization of the countryside. But on this new geographical dimension to speak of 'the city' in a historical sense becomes paradoxical: the contradiction that Marx sought was to be found in a new scenario that could not be encompassed 'in the city'.

Let's try to analyse this argument by going through *The Manifesto* and *Capital*, and then looking at the explosion of the city-country dichotomy that Marx witnessed. As is well known, Marx praised the revolutionary character of the bourgeoisie, which

> has subjected the country to the rule of the towns. It has created enormous cities, has greatly increased the urban population as compared with the rural, and has thus rescued a considerable part of the population from the idiocy of rural life ... It has agglomerated population, centralized means of production, and has concentrated property in a few hands.
> MARX and ENGELS 1848: 488

However, he reminds us shortly afterwards that

> The means of production and of exchange, on whose foundation the bourgeoise built itself up, were generated in feudal society. At a certain

stage in the development of these means of production and of exchange
... the feudal relations of property became no longer compatible with the
already developed productive forces; they became so many fetters. They
had to be burst asunder; they were burst asunder.

MARX and ENGELS 1848: 489

It is evident that this historical reference lays the basis for Marx's present problem, and in *Capital* we find further confirmation of this:

In the sphere of agriculture, modern industry has a more revolutionary
effect than elsewhere, for this reason, that it annihilates the peasant, that
bulwark of the old society, and replaces him by the wage labourer. Thus,
the desire for social changes, and the class antagonisms are brought to
the same level in the country as in the towns.

MARX 1867a: 506

It was precisely this equality between city and country (with the relative disappearance of its typical subjects, the peasant and the citizen) that meant it
made no sense in Marx's theoretical framework to focus on the city as such. He
reiterates shortly afterwards:

Capitalist production completely tears asunder the old bond of union
which held together agriculture and manufacture in their infancy. But at
the same time, it creates the material conditions for a higher synthesis in
the future, viz., the union of agriculture and industry on the basis of the
more perfected forms they have each acquired during their temporary
separation ...

... This union clearly did not indicate a smooth and homogeneous plan
but announced a common condition of exploitation: 'By this action it
destroys at the same time the health of the town labourer and the intellectual life of the rural labourer'.

MARX 1867a: 507

2   The 'City' of Marx

We have now arrived at the historical threshold within which Marx lived and
acted. The overcoming of the city/country relationship as a historical engine
was redefining the coordinates within a new paradigm in which big industry

and modern agriculture were united within the capitalist system of production. If in ancient times the countryside was the territory of the city, now new social subjectivities within the world market were moving on a territory that was urbanizing, while at the same time the centres were becoming more rural, with the migration of populations from the countryside and the logic of land ownership being introduced into the city. Before analysing this new scenario, it is worth pointing out some further general contextual factors that made it possible, which can be traced back to questions of geographical extension, new forms of power, and technological novelty. All of these in their own way overlap with the emergence of the 'new city'.

In order to reach the moment when 'all the wealth of society first goes into the possession of the capitalist' we should grasp the fully global extension of the new system:

> The discovery of gold and silver in America, the extirpation, enslavement and entombment in mines of the aborigenal population, the beginning of the conquest and looting of the East Indies, the turning of Africa into a warren for the commercial hunting of black-skins, signalised the rosy dawn of the era of capitalist production. These idyllic proceedings are the chief momenta of primitive accumulation. On their heels treads the commercial war of the European nations, with the globe for a theatre.
>
> MARX 1867a: 739

To reach the 19th century capitalist mode of production, not only a global extensive move, but also an 'intensive' move was required, in which a special economic force was at work, which was decisive in order to determine capitalist 'methods':

> These methods depend in part on brute force, e. g., the colonial system. But they all imply the power of the state, the concentrated and organized force of society, to hasten, hothouse fashion, the process of transformation of the feudal mode of production into the capitalist mode, and to shorten the transition. Force is the midwife of every old society pregnant with a new one. It is itself an economic power.
>
> MARX 1867a: 739

But these two moments would not have been sufficient had they not been integrated by technological innovation, initially the steam engine, which connected the city, country and colony in a continuum, thus breaking down any clear borders between them. Marx echoes this comment by Alexander

Redgrave: 'the steam engine is the mother of industrial cities [transplanting] factories away from the falls of the country, into the middle of the towns' (Marx 1867a: 560). And recalling John Fielden, Marx writes:

> In places, far from the cities, [where] thousands of arms were suddenly required', which are hired through 'the custom of procuring apprentices (!) from the different workhouses ... It was customary for the master (i.e. the boy-stealer) to dress and feed his apprentices and to lodge them in an apprentice house near the factory'.
>
> MARX 1867a: 746

And notes elsewhere:

> Whilst the cotton industry introduced child slavery in England, it gave the United States a stimulus to the transformation of the earlier, more or less patriarchal slavery, into a system of commercial exploitation. In fact, the veiled slavery of the wage workers in Europe needed, for its pedestal, slavery pure and simple in the new world.
>
> MARX 1867a: 747

This was the new system of interconnections that was established by creating new cities or distorting old ones. 'Liverpool waxed fat on the slave trade. This was its method of primitive accumulation' (Marx 1867a: 747). This new system was transforming the countryside and 'distant' lands, resulting in the mutation of

> at one pole, the social means of production and subsistence into capital, at the opposite pole, the mass of the population into waged labourers, into *free labouring poor*, that artificial product of modern society.
>
> MARX 1867a: 747

The new system has won, now it was a matter of observing the territorial phenomenology and the forms through which the new social relations expressed themselves.

The more production was based on exchange, the more crucial communication and transport systems became. The large-scale production of these systems was necessary for the realization of the value of the commodity on the market, bringing to the fore the spatial conditioning of the circulation of capital, or rather the problem of the speed of transport. As Marx says, there is a 'spatial moment' connected with the expansion of the market:

The reduction of the costs of this real circulation (in space) is part of the development of the productive forces carried out by capital ... The quantity of products which can be produced ... depends on the speed of circulation ... Thus, while capital must strive on the one hand to tear down every local barrier to traffic, i.e. to exchange, and to conquer the whole world as its market, it strives on the other hand to annihilate space by means of time, i.e. to reduce to a minimum the time required for the movement [of products] from one place to another. The more capital has been developed, and the greater therefore the expansion of the market in which it circulates, which constitutes the spatial path of its circulation, the more it goes on to strive for an even greater spatial expansion of the market and for a more complete annihilation of space by means of time.

MARX 1857–1861: 462–463

This passage from the *Grundrisse* encapsulates the transformation that has taken place in which historical forms give way to a new actuality – that of Marx's time and our own. In fact, these words have a series of implications that are crucial for understanding the dynamics that guide metropolitan development and define the always shifting urbanized territory. The territorial propagation of capital not only signals the antagonism between city and country, but the generalization of the structures of production and the capitalist market. The forms of the past dissolve within a metropolitan texture that progressively establishes new productive centres and infrastructural networks. Rivers, seas, roads and railways become indispensable for the circulation and propagation of capital, engulfing the previous landscape. Marx believed that the 'city' in which he lived was this emerging construction, in which the state and capital itself took charge of establishing the infrastructures that colonized the territory, making the separation between the city and the countryside obsolete.

We have said that the city and the countryside became subject to the same laws, leading to the radical rupture of previous equilibriums. Inside the old word 'city' there was, therefore, something new that could not be grasp by using the same word. In Chapter 23 of *Capital* Marx claims that the law of worker overpopulation is one of the conditions of existence of the capitalist mode of production and in Chapter 24 he analyses the 'cause' of this dynamic as rural expropriation and expulsion from the land. Other relevant passages are found scattered throughout the first and third books. The housing condition in particular (of the big cities and of the countryside) is seen as an indicator of growing misery, and he notes that 'in order to clarify fully the laws of accumulation it is necessary to examine also the situation of the worker outside the factory'. In Chapter 23, Marx traces numerous examples in the English context. The dynamic that leads to this new condition is clear: 'the greater the centralization of the means of production, the greater is the corresponding heaping together of the labourers, within a given space; that therefore the swifter capitalistic accumulation, the more miserable are the dwellings of the working people' (Marx 1867a: 651). The second half of the 19th century was also the period in which, especially in response to the workers' and urban insurgency of 1848, urban centres were hit by portentous processes of restructuring, which Walter Benjamin would later locate in nineteenth-century capital Paris, but which unfolded far beyond the French capital:

> *Improvements* of towns, accompanying the increase of wealth, by the demolition of badly built quarters, the erection of palaces for banks, warehouses, &c., the widening of streets for business traffic, for the carriages of luxury, and for the introduction of tramways, &c., drive away the poor into even worse and more crowded hiding places.
> MARX 1867a: 651

In order to describe this process Marx once again resorts to a metaphor that, by placing the definition of the new metropolitan dynamics on a planetary scale, links the metropolis and the colony:

> The dearness of dwellings is in inverse ratio to their excellence, and that the mines of misery are exploited by house speculators with more profit or less cost than ever were the mines of Potosi. The antagonistic character of capitalist accumulation, and therefore of the capitalistic relations of property generally, is here so evident.
> MARX 1867a: 651

'The sources from which all wealth flows: the land and the worker', thus linked the Bolivian mines to the extraction of value from the backs of the English workers in English cities. What was defined as the *malady* now gripping English cities had proceeded hand in hand with the development of industry, the accumulation of capital and the increase and 'embellishment of cities'. The recourse to a colonial lexicon was also adopted by government statistics: 'There are about 20 large colonies in London, of about 10,000 persons each, whose miserable condition exceeds almost anything who has seen elsewhere in England' (Marx 1867a: 652).

Just as Marx sensed the development of capitalist territorial articulation on a large scale (extensive urbanization), so he seemed to grasp the urban dynamics that it induced in the 'centres' (intensive urbanization):

Except London, there was at the beginning of the 19th century no single town in England of 100,000 inhabitants. Only five had more than 50,000. Now there are 28 towns with more than 50,000 inhabitants. 'The result of this change is not only that the class of town people is enormously increased, but the old close-packed little towns are now centres, built round on every side, open nowhere to air, and being no longer agreeable to the rich are abandoned by them for the pleasanter outskirts'... The more rapidly capital accumulates in an industrial or commercial town, the more rapidly flows the stream of exploitable human material, the more miserable are the improvised dwellings of the labourers.

MARX 1867a: 654–655

3   The City beyond the City

Cities, or rather, at this point, areas of intensive urbanization, were the places of maximum exploitation in which a certain relationship of production materialized, but they were also where the proletariat was forged and where a historical project of emancipation took shape and was concentrated. When Marx analyses the city there is a certain tension toward determinism and a staging approach that can certainly be problematized. At times he seems to look backwards at the city/country division, and when focusing on the industrial city he basically believes that the categories of political economy are sufficient to interpret this new urban space. Perhaps something is missing here in Marx's elaboration. What in the German debate was called the *Großstadt* begins to take on peculiarities that exceed and escape an analytical grid exclusively based on (the critique of) political economy. The new emerging urban landscapes were the bearers of a series of contradictions of their own. For example, Marx anticipates Simmel by arguing that the nineteenth-century metropolis was the place where money reigned. However, it was precisely money that opened up a path of liberation from feudal constraints that was a prelude to the potential subsequent overcoming of the wage relationship. In short, the bourgeois-industrial city was a 'pre-history' with its own peculiarities in which it was already possible to grasp the tendency towards a completely different condition of life and social organization. The bourgeois city contained the seeds of its own overthrow. But Marx does not stress the liberating potential of that city. However, by starting from his general theoretical position, it is possible to tie up the threads of his reflections in order to guide our research today;

rather than starting from the 'gaps' left by Marx, we can start from the methods and perspectives that we have sketched out above.

Marx was not looking for that thing called 'the city', which was the bourgeois domain and the ideological theatre of social peace; he was looking for division. If you really want to look for 'the city', philosophically, in Marx, you must highlight an aspect that has always been inherent to the city: stasis, the civil war. Thus, to grasp the city in Marx, it is necessary to frame it as the historical form of a specific and transient configuration of the division of labour and property and of the conflict that results. With the affirmation of the capitalist mode of production, with capital as the dominant social relationship, and with the invasion of the whole territory by this new dynamic that overcomes the city/ countryside dichotomy, the previous forms of codification of the social relationship are lost; all that is solid dissolves into air. If already in Marx the social relationship was no longer defined within the historical categories of city and countryside, there is a need today to describe it in new terms. This is not to say that this has never been attempted before. Many thinkers, from Lefebvre to more recent theorizations by Neil Brenner and Andy Merrifield, amongst others, have attempted to do this by adopting the category of 'urban/urbanization' as a new analytical framework. It is beyond the scope of this text to propose alternative models, but it would be helpful to problematize this assumption and to point out a need for the politicization of urban studies. In order to do this, we will take up some of the points mentioned in this chapter.

We have seen how Marx speaks of the industrial city as the new project of his epoch. The crux of his argument, however, is that this city is not bounded, it is not an identifiable unit, it is not a geographical concept, but is economic-political. For example, Marx gives Manchester as an example of an industrial city but argues that can only be understood as a plexus of relations on a planetary scale. It cannot be understood by only looking at its smokestacks or its neighbourhoods. Echoing W.E.B. Du Bois, we might say that to understand it we also have to look at the plantations on the other side of the Atlantic, at the processes of colonization in Ireland, and at mass urbanization and the great coal-mining territories of central England. This is the industrial city, its extent, its size, its subjects. In the same way, we cannot understand the Paris at the time, and its political and economic centrality, without understanding that in the second half of the 19th century the French city was the crucial junction of all the nascent infrastructures of the European territory, the barycentre of the continental railways which anthropized the landscape, redeveloped and broke up the urban-rural connections, and wound upwards into the grandiose symbol of the Eiffel Tower, which was nothing more than a tangle of tracks. The industrial city, Marx's city, was an expanding process within which new lines of social division were being drawn.

There has been too long a tendency to distinguish the process of industrialization from that of urbanization, but it could be argued that industrialization and urbanization are two sides of the same coin. The former cannot exist without the urbanization of the territory (in the political and geographical sense), and the latter cannot exist without the industrial production of the urban and the industrialization of the countryside. In other words, urbanization/industrialization indicates a new antagonism that structures society, in which the plebs of the medieval commune emerged as the proletariat, as a potential class, becoming the expression of a social relationship that was no longer played out on an 'outside' (e.g. the countryside with respect to the city, or vice versa) but 'inside' urbanization/industrialization – where inside, however, increasingly designates a planetary dimension, composed of a series of lines of power and division. A historical time accelerated by the new class relations becomes a vortex in space, and, from then on, the city as a spatial form constantly changes, until the *forma Urbis* completely disappears. It is no coincidence that within a few decades (end of the 19th century – beginning of the 20th century) the city walls, which marked the historic city/countryside border would be demolished.

Secondly, if with industry the city ceases to be the 'subject' of the historical process, this new condition does not eliminate 'the political problem of the city', that is, that of the subject. The city/country dialectic is decomposed and dislocated globally and runs along the lines of new class profiles. Antagonistic social relations, the engines of historical movement, take on new forms, composed of changing assemblages of lines of power and fracture, of differences and commonalities. The class hypothesis that Marx puts forward is therefore the search for a new form, capable of practicing a power (which Max Weber would call 'illegitimate') adequate to the new passage of capital as a social relation and the scenario produced by the capitalist mode of production. Evidently this 'form' is something that emerges and is implicated within a series of other 'forms' – for example, the commodity form and the money form, which with their power of abstraction have made the world into a single city.

Today it is therefore a question of abandoning the city as a romantic vision linked to the past, now emptied of heuristic value. The recourse to the idea of the 'urban' and to a new series of categories has played an important role in describing and thinking politically about the struggles and conflicts that took place in the 1960s and 1970s. But are we sure that it is still useful today to attempt to re-actualize the Marxian problem of antagonism in historical processes? From the 1970s to the present, the focus of critical urban thought has been on 'space', which has been a productive source of theoretical renewal. However, we should return to a previously mentioned quote: cancelling space through time.

Of the two terms raised by the quotation ('annihilation of space by means of time', Marx 1857–1861: 463), the most under-examined, is that relating to time. Could it be time to think in urban terms about the production of time and the revolution of temporality induced by capitalism today? This question has yet to be answered by research, but it is necessary to start reflecting on how the city works as a temporal device, a time machine. The city synchronizes and organizes social time and is a stratified deposit of living history. We are used to imagining contemporary metropolises by starting from their landscapes, but it is just as necessary to try to trace their chronoscapes and the complex gene-alogical origins that make up their structure. Here then is a further question. How can we go 'beyond the city', while avoiding the "spatial trap" and thinking about forms of antagonism from a temporal point of view? Could this be a use-ful key to interpreting new struggles and conflicts? The framework of 'urban struggles' has been used as an analytical lens to describe many mobilizations – whether in terms of the periphery, the peri-urban, or the occupations of central squares etc. – from the *banlieue* riots to those in the Anglo-Saxon world, and from the cycle of uprisings in 2011–2013 to the mobilization of the *gilets jaunes*. Although this framework is not wrong, it has become self-evident and risks forgetting the other aspect of the process – industrialization, that is, posing the problem of the city from the point of view of labour. Thus, the search for new interpretative matrices and new lines of antagonism today seems more necessary than ever and could give rise to a new phase in urban studies that adopts new analytical tools.

To do this, there is an urgent need to forge a new political urban lens, and to do so we must inevitably engage with the Commune in Marx, and particu-larly with the political document *The Civil War in France* in which he explic-itly discusses it. Completed just two days after the massacre that extinguished the revolutionary experience, the writing follows *The Class Struggles in France from 1848 to 1850* and *The 18th Brumaire of Louis Bonaparte*. The Commune is the first historical realization of that 'Social Republic' in the name of which the Parisian proletariat had risen up in February 1848. The civil war, a typical figure of the city from ancient Greece to the present, is 'inscribed in that secular war which in the struggle for the limitation of the working day has its culminating moment in the reconfiguration of power' (Ricciardi 2019: 74). The experience of the Commune cannot be simply compared to the civil war linked to the class struggle but represents the coming into being of an organized and polit-ical form of the class struggle itself; it is the emergence of a partisan power, a counter-power, which has Paris not as its background nor as its stage, but as its battleground.

While the distinction between the city and the countryside was still very much in evidence in the 1848 analysis, it was unsurprisingly much more blurred. Paris was 'the central seat of the old governmental power and, at the same time, the social fortress of the French working class', Marx tells us, when he discusses how the Commune presented itself as in direct opposition to the Empire. But it is in the process of its potential political development that we see the gap beyond the city/country dichotomy.

> The Paris Commune was, of course, to serve as a model to all the great industrial centres of France. The communal régime once established in Paris and the secondary centres, the old, centralized Government would in the provinces, too, have to give way to the self-government of the producers. In a rough sketch of national organization which the Commune had no time to develop, it states clearly that the Commune was to be the political form of even the smallest country hamlet.
>
> MARX 1871: 332

The categories Marx uses here are industrial centres, secondary centres, provinces and hamlets, no longer cities and the countryside, and he put emphasis on the Commune as a political form. Furthermore, he argues:

> It is generally the fate of completely new historical creations to be mistaken for the counterpart of older and even defunct forms of social life, to which they may bear a certain likeness. Thus, this new Commune, which breaks the modern state power, has been mistaken for a reproduction of the mediaeval Communes ... The communal constitution has been mistaken for an attempt to break up into a federation of small states ... that unity of great nations which, if originally brought about by political force, has now become a powerful coefficient of social production. The antagonism of the Commune against the state power has been mistaken for an exaggerated form of the ancient struggle against over-centralization.
>
> MARX 1871: 333

On the one hand, defunct forms of social life cannot explain the historical novelty represented by the Commune, and, on the other hand, the antagonism between the Commune and the state is not a struggle against centralization nor the glorifying of small local homelands, but a new dynamic of class struggle:

The multiplicity of interpretations to which the Commune has been subjected, and the multiplicity of interests which construed it in their favour,
show that it was a thoroughly expansive political form, while all previous
forms of government had been emphatically repressive. Its true secret
was this. It was essentially ... the produce of the struggle of the producing against the appropriating class, the political form at last discovered
under which to work out the economical emancipation of Labour.

MARX 1871: 334

This is where we come to Marx's central point: the Commune represented the
discovery of a new expansive political form adequate to the expression of the
class project which had been incubated for decades, which found here its first
materialization. For Marx, this new form was the product of the class struggle and its movement, and therefore couldn't be stabilized, a form that at that
precise time produced a reversal of power relations. It did not institutional-
ize communism but was a prelude to its structuring as a counter-power with
a capacity for enduring power. This raises another question about where to
look for a functional analogue of the form-Commune today. Following Marx,
we might say it is a question about the 'impossible possible'. The Commune
wanted to transform 'the means of production, land and capital, now chiefly
the means of enslaving and exploiting labour, into mere instruments of free
and associated labour. But this is Communism, *impossible* Communism!' It
intended to supplant the capitalist system with co-operative production.
'What else, gentlemen, would it be but Communism, *possible* Communism?'
(Marx 1871: 335).

CHAPTER 7

Marx and Darwin

Technology and Anthropology

Fabio Raimondi

The purpose of this essay[1] is to formulate a hypothesis to clarify what Marx meant by the wording 'critical history of technology' and what relationship it had with Darwin's *Origin of Species* (Marx 1867a: 375 n. 2).

Marx's interest in technology is indebted to some Engelsian observations which appeared in 1844 *Outlines of a Critique of Political Economy* (Engels 1844: 442–443) and then developed in *The Condition of the Working Class in England* of 1845:

> The history of the proletariat in England begins with the second half of the last century, with the invention of the steam-engine and of machinery for working cotton, [and] while the industrial proletariat was thus developing with the first ... machine, the same machine gave rise to the agricultural proletariat ... The proletariat was called into existence by the introduction of machinery.
>
> ENGELS 1845: 307, 311, 321

The wording 'critical history of technology' appears in a note from *Capital* in which Marx, referring to John Wyatt's invention of the spinning machine, writes:

> A critical history of technology would show how little any of the inventions of the 18th century are the work of a single individual. Hitherto there is no such book. Darwin has interested us in the history of Nature's Technology, i.e., in the formation of the organs of plants and animals, which organs serve as instruments of production for sustaining life. Does not the history of the productive organs of man, of organs that are the material basis of all social organization, deserve equal attention? And

1 A broader Italian version is available at the following address http://www.sifp.it/articoli-libri-e-interviste-articles-books-and-interviews/marx-darwin-e-la-storia-critica-della-tecnologia. Thanks to S., as usual.

would not such a history be easier to compile, since, as Vico says, human history differs from natural history in this, that we have made the former, but not the latter? Technology discloses man's mode of dealing with Nature, the process of production by which, he sustains his life, and thereby also lays bare the mode of formation of his social relations, and of the mental conceptions that flow from them. Every history of religion, even, that fails to take account of this material basis, is uncritical.

MARX 1867a: 375 n. 2

This history should have been social and critical, both because the social man is the man organized in society to extending production (Rabinbach 1990: 73) and because this history must not abstract from technology as the material basis to produce man's life, his social relations, and his ideas (Marx 1867a: 187–195). The parallelism with Darwin is built on the analogy between natural technology and the productive organs of the social man as if Marx's aim were an evolutionary history of the natural production by social man of his artificial organs. In this way, Marx places his own investigation in the wake of Darwin's 'technological view of evolution' (Cornell 1984: 313), dealing with how the artificial and productive organs of social man are grafted onto natural history (Vadée 1998: 375, 378–379) and interact with it in the perspective of 'a technological interpretation of the history of life that makes nature both an external agent itself in the image of man and at the same time a product of external forces like the organisms under man's control' (Cornell 1984: 320). The hypothesis is supported both by the fact that Darwin's idea of what Marx called natural technology derived from the study of breeding techniques and by the fact that the latter is related to the problem of 'accumulation' (see at least Darwin 1859: 4, 30–32).

Marx tried to insert himself into the Darwinian perspective (perhaps to complete it) through the hypothesis of tracing a critical history of technology. Referring to the fact that Hodgskin in his *Labour defended against the claims of capital* (1825) had not sufficiently highlighted 'the stage of the development of the productive power of labour', Marx specifies that this power 'comprises not only the skill and capacity of the worker, but likewise the objective organs which this labour has created for itself and which it daily renews', and then he continues:

This is really the primary factor, the point of departure and it is the result of a process of development. Accumulation [*Aufhäufung*] in this context means assimilation, continual preservation and at the same time transformation of what has already been handed over and realized. In this way

Darwin makes accumulation through inheritance the driving principle in the formation of all organic things, of plants and animals; thus the various organisms themselves are formed as a result of *accumulation* [*Häufung*] and are only *inventions*, gradually accumulated inventions of living beings. But this is not the only prerequisite of production. Such a prerequisite in the case of animals and plants is external nature, that is both inorganic nature and their relationship with other animals and plants. Man, who produces in society, likewise faces an already modified nature (and in particular natural factors which have been transformed into means of his own activity) and definite relations existing between the producers. This accumulation [*Akkumulation*] is in part the result of the historical process, in part, as far as the individual worker is concerned, transmission of skill.

> MARX 1861–1863c: 427–428

The distinction between *Aufhäufung* and *Akkumulation* is due to the fact that man has to do both with the same nature with which plants and animals have to do, and with the nature transformed by the organs of his own activity and formed from the whole of these organs and from the relationships among the producers that they involve. *Akkumulation* indicates the properly human accumulation, that is the result of the historical process and of the transfer of skills. History enters inside *Aufhäufung* (natural accumulation) via *Akkumulation* (accumulation produced by humans), that exists only thanks to selection. History is the overall accumulation both of natural selection and of human artificial selection, as occurs, for example, in crossbreeding by farmers and breeders. The *Akkumulation* is always aimed at specific purposes, while the *Aufhäufung* has no purpose. The wording 'critical history of technology' assimilates the Darwinian concept of natural selection and applies it, by analogy, to the productive organs of social man, that is, to the artificial aspect of a wider natural technology. According to Marx 'natural history comes to subsume human history under itself, in the same way that human history comes to subsume natural history' (cf. Krader 1978: 213, and Schmidt 1971). This process, rather than alienation (as Krader argues), is 'the progressive objectification or externalization of knowledge, memory and gesture into artefacts that makes the real subsumption of work possible' (cf. Bradley 2011: 33–34). If human history is part of nature, Darwin's theory must be completed with the study of the evolution that humans cause to nature through the techniques that transform it.

The last long quoted passage is also relevant for another series of reasons. The development of the productive forces also depends on 'objective organs', which work has created and daily renews, but not only on them. The presence of these organs is the primary factor which is, at the same time, the starting point and the result of an evolution that is not identified only with the products of the technique. Here 'evolution' is not used in the Darwinian sense which appears only in the sixth edition of the *Origin* (1872; cf. Desmond and Moore 1991: chap. 39), which Marx never read because he only read the first, but in 'vernacular' sense: 'the appearance in orderly succession of a long train of events' i.e., a 'progressive development – an orderly unfolding from simple to complex' (Gould 1977: chap. 3). These organs are used to produce in society, and they are the result of the relationship between humans and what they find in front of them: the nature already changed. Therefore, they are not only specific technical objects, but also specific relationships among producers; relationships that configure more complex 'objective organs' (such as, for example, the society itself or the relations of production) with respect to the technical tools of work. Finally, 'objective organs' are the primary factor as they are produced by 'accumulation through inheritance'. *Aufhäufung* is assimilation: conservation and remaking of what has already been handed down, and realized, such as in the reproduction of artificial crossings between plants and animals, which have proved useful in cultivation or breeding.

A specificity distinguishes humans from plants and animals: *Akkumulation* is both a historical process and, for the single worker, the transfer of skills, implying a selection that is both casual and conscious, but not necessarily better, because the results of the combination of techniques and nature are often unpredictable (Foster 2000: 201).

In the 'manufacture', which 'coincides strictly with the resolution of a handicraft into its successive manual operations' the 'individual workman' is the craftsman transformed into 'detailed labourer' (Marx 1867a: 343–344).

The *Akkumulation* that produces the 'objective organs' is produced by a historical process and by a transfer of skills: in this specific case, from the 'individual workman' to the 'detailed labourer'. The transfer is crucial, because without 'accumulation through inheritance' of skills, there is no reproduction of the 'objective organs': without the contribution of work in creating and renewing these organs daily, there would be no evolution (i.e., progress). If the 'individual workman' could not transfer his skills to others and could not transform himself into a 'detailed labourer', the 'manufacture' itself would not exist, since the factors external to living labour alone would not be sufficient to give rise to it.

The onus of conservation and renovation does not lie on the shoulders of a single 'detailed labourer', but on the entire social labour power organized for production. The reproduction is the result of a collective process, marked here and there by individual inventions, but always tested by the daily experience of labour that has the task of producing, applying, and refining them directly.

Such a broad work of 'differentiation, specialization and simplification of the instruments of labour' corresponds to what Darwin himself says about the 'specialization and differentiation in the organs of living beings' (Marx 1861–1863d: 388), in which individuals of all species and the species as such are involved. In the transition from the 'individual workman' to 'detailed labourer', 'accumulation through inheritance' is at work:

> Manufacture, in fact, produces the skill of the detail labourer, by repro-ducing, and systematically driving to an extreme within the workshop, the naturally developed differentiation of trades which it found ready to hand in society at large. On the other hand, the conversion of fractional work into the life-calling of one man, corresponds to the tendency shown by earlier societies, to make trades hereditary; either to petrify them into castes, or whenever definite historical conditions beget in the individual a tendency to vary in a manner incompatible with the nature of castes, to ossify them into guilds. Castes and guilds arise from the action of the same natural law, that regulates the differentiation of plants and animals into species and varieties, except that, when a certain degree of devel-opment has been reached, the heredity of castes and the exclusiveness of guilds are ordained as a law of society ... It is only the special skill accumulated from generation to generation, and transmitted from father to son, that gives to the Hindu, as it does to the spider, this proficiency.
>
> MARX 1867a: 344–345

Although not quoted, Darwin is present (cf. Darwin 1859: 143–150), even if Marx points out that the economic-political analysis must not take Darwin's words literally: in fact, there is a specific difference in the analogy, whose clue is the reference to the 'law of society'. The content of what is hereditary in nature is decreed law only in the human world, where the variations, selected, accu-mulated, and transmitted by inheritance, tend to become laws, sometimes unavoidable, that society takes care of defending, conserving, and reproduc-ing. This is immanence, which is as ideological as transcendence, because it is the hypostatization of a historical trend in law of the history. In fact, at a 'certain degree of development' of the 'objective organs' a political dynamic comes into play, with the aim of governing 'accumulation through inheritance'. Organization of production and politics are, in the human world, the factors that, together with the natural and technical ones, determine the variation, the selection, the accumulation, and the inheritance. This shows that politics, albeit rooted in the biological structure of the human beings, has its own laws, which do not imply its total autonomy, but only a relative autonomy.

Furthermore, these factors are decisive in the production of scientific knowledge (cf. Corbellini 2013: 23 and 121), as emerges when one tries to establish the criterion of producing variations:

> It happens that once a kind of labour – rather the different forms of labour which work together to create a particular product, a specific commodity – has been divided up, the ease with which it can be performed depends on particular modifications of the instruments which formerly served different purposes. The direction taken by these alterations is determined by experience and by the specific difficulties put in the way by the unchanged form.
>
> MARX 1861–1863d: 388

An idea reaffirmed and deepened in the *Capital*:

> The productiveness of labour depends not only on the proficiency of the workman, but on the perfection of his tools. Tools of the same kind, such as knives, drills, gimlets, hammers, &c, may be employed in different processes; and the same tool may serve various purposes in a single process. But so soon as the different operations of a labour process are disconnected the one from the other, and each fractional operation acquires in the hands of the detail labourer a suitable and peculiar form, alterations become necessary in the implements that previously served more than one purpose. The direction taken by this change is determined by the difficulties experienced in consequence of the unchanged form of the implement.
>
> MARX 1867a: 346

Specified that in manufacturing, contrary to what happens in the factory, the instruments of labour 'petrify' themselves, once they have reached the 'form … settled by experience' and that this form can be transmitted unaltered for 'thousands of years' (cf. Marx 1867a: 488–489), Marx points out that the passage from one form of production to another involves the evolution of the tools of labour:

> A differentiation whereby implements of a given sort acquire fixed shapes, adapted to each particular application, and by the specialization

of those instruments, giving to each special implement its full play only in the hands of a specific detail labourer. In Birmingham alone [5]00 varieties of hammers are produced, and not only is each adapted to one particular process, but several varieties often serve exclusively for the different operations in one and the same process. The manufacturing period simplifies, improves, and multiplies the implements of labour, by adapting them to the exclusively special functions of each detail labourer. It thus creates at the same time one of the material conditions for the existence of machinery, which consists of a combination of simple instruments.

MARX 1867a: 346

Also, in the human world variation takes place with consequent selection and 'accumulation through inheritance', with the passage from one form of production to another, but each form has its specific characteristics transferred and adapted, and therefore preserved and transformed: in the passage some forms remain, others undergo slight adaptations, others disappear and still others are born for the first time, but not for an intrinsic finalism of the objects. The variation occurs through differentiation, specialization, and simplification. Using Darwin's words:

So long as one and the same organ has different kinds of work to perform, a ground for its changeability may possibly be found in this, that natural selection preserves or suppresses each small variation of form less carefully than if that organ were destined for one special purpose alone. Thus, knives that are adapted to cut all sorts of things, may, on the whole, be of one shape; but an implement destined to be used exclusively in one way must have a different shape for every different use.

[Ch. Darwin, *On the Origin of Species* ..., London, 1859: 149] MARX 1867a: 346 n. 31[2]

For this reason, Marx can affirm that 'this differentiation, specialization, and simplification of the means of labour therefore originates spontaneously with the division of labour itself' (Marx 1861–1863d: 388). With the words of the

---

2   In fact, this is the original text of Darwin's 'epoch-making work' (Marx 1867a: 346 n. 31): 'as long as the same part has to perform diversified work, we can perhaps see why it should remain variable, that is, why natural selection should have preserved or rejected each little deviation of form less carefully than when the part has to serve for one special purpose alone. In the same way that a knife which has to cut all sorts of things may be of almost any shape; whilst a tool for some particular object had better be of some particular shape' (Darwin 1859: 149).

second book of *Capital*: 'when production by means of wage labour becomes universal', this kind of production

> carries in its wake an ever-increasing division of social labour, that is to say an ever-growing differentiation of the products which are produced in the form of commodities by a definite capitalist, ever greater division of complementary processes of production into independent processes.
>
> MARX 1885: 41

What changes with the 'transition to the factory system, which ... makes its appearance so soon as the human muscles are replaced, for the purpose of driving the machines, by a mechanical motive power, such as steam or water' (Marx 1867a: 463)?

In manufacture, the revolution in the mode of production begins with the labour power, in modern industry it begins with the instruments of labour. Our first inquiry then is, how the instruments of labour are converted from tools into machines, or what is the difference between a machine and the implements of a handicraft? We are only concerned here with striking and general characteristics; for epochs in the history of society are no more separated from each other by hard and fast lines of demarcation, than are geological epochs (Marx 1867a: 374).

Even if 'the machine does not represent a particular moment in the history of technology, its creation as a technical form of production constitutes ... the moment of rupture' (Cazzaniga 2004: 2). The difference between the craftsman's machines and tools is significant:

> All fully developed machinery consists of three essentially different parts, the motor mechanism, the transmitting mechanism, and finally the tool or working machine. The motor mechanism is that which puts the whole in motion. It either generates its own motive power, like the steam-engine, the caloric engine, the electromagnetic machine, &c., or it receives its impulse from some already existing natural force, like the water-wheel from a head of water, the wind-mill from wind, &c. The transmitting mechanism, composed of fly-wheels, shafting, toothed wheels, pullies, straps, ropes, bands, pinions, and gearing of the most varied kinds, regulates the motion, changes its form where necessary, as for instance, from linear to circular, and divides and distributes it among the working machines. These two first parts of the whole mechanism are there, solely for putting the working machines in motion, by means of which motion the subject of labour is seized upon and modified as desired. The tool or

working machine is that part of the machinery with which the industrial revolution of the 18th century started. And to this day it constantly
serves as such a starting-point, whenever a handicraft, or a manufacture,
is turned into an industry carried on by machinery.

MARX 1867a: 376

The 'machine, which is the starting-point of the industrial revolution, super-
sedes the workman, who handles a single tool, by a mechanism operating with
a number of similar tools, and set in motion by a single motive power, whatever
the form of that power may be' (Marx 1867a: 379): 'To those who are merely
mathematicians, these questions are of no moment, but they assume great
importance when it comes to establishing a connection between human social
relations and the development of these material modes of production' (Marx
to Engels 1/28/1863 in MECW 41: 450), because in the industrial revolution

we have again the co-operation by division of labour that characterizes manufacture; only now, it is a combination of detail machines ...
An essential difference at once manifests itself. In manufacture it is the
workmen who, with their manual implements, must, either singly or in
groups, carry on each particular detail process. If, on the one hand, the
workman becomes adapted to the process, on the other, the process was
previously made suitable to the workman. This subjective principle of
the division of labour no longer exists in production by machinery. Here,
the process as a whole is examined objectively, in itself, that is to say,
without regard to the question of its execution by human hands, it is analyzed into its constituent phases; and the problem, how to execute each
detail process, and bind them all into a whole, is solved by the aid of
machines, chemistry, &c. But, of course, in this case also, theory must be
perfected by accumulated experience on a large scale.

MARX 1867a: 382–383

The disappearance of the subjective dimension of worker labour in favour of
the objective dimension of the machine system means that 'in manufacture the
isolation of each detail process is a condition imposed by the nature of division
of labour, but in the fully developed factory the continuity of those processes
is, on the contrary, imperative' (Marx 1867a: 384). The 'huge automaton' (Marx
1867a: 384 and Marx 1847a: 188), produces a qualitative leap in production and
in the relations of production. It was the invention of the 'steam-engines' that
allowed a selection to be made within the 'machinery' produced by manufacture, creating a new 'basis' to be reproduced (Marx 1867a: 385). In fact, 'the

steam-engine ... did not give rise to any industrial revolution. It was, on the contrary, the invention of [tools or working] machines that made a revolution in the form of steam-engine necessary': these machines are what transform man into their 'motive power' making him replaceable by other natural forces such as, for example, 'wind, water or steam' (Marx 1867a: 378; see also Vadée 1998: 380–385). The Darwinian process is also present here, because 'a radical change in the mode of production in one sphere of industry involves a similar change in other spheres' (Marx 1867a: 386), in analogy with the Darwinian 'correlation of development' (cf. Darwin 1859: 11–12, 43); thus, for example, 'the revolution in the modes of production of industry and agriculture made necessary a revolution in the general conditions of the social process of production, i.e., in the means of communication and of transport' (Marx 1867a: 387). Likewise,

> in simple co-operation, and even in that founded on division of labour, the suppression of the isolated, by the collective workman still appears to be more or less accidental. Machinery ... operates only by means of associated labour, or labour in common. Hence the co-operative character of the labour process is ... a technical necessity dictated by the instrument of labour itself.
>
> MARX 1867a: 389

The 'co-operation ever constitutes the fundamental form of the capitalist mode of production' (Marx 1867a: 340), but if, on the one hand, the introduction of machines exploits even more the worker and the land, on the other hand, the system of machines should allow the worker to work less and enjoy a greater or at least equal quantity of products. For this to happen, however, technology cannot be managed by capitalists, but must pass into the hands of producers (workers and peasants), which means worker/peasant government of techniques and sciences, which must be used to feed everyone and reduce working hours.

The political order of capital, whoever represents it, consists in not giving way to the potential offered by the sciences and techniques to bend them and submit them to the economic interests of capital. Freeing the sciences and techniques from capital does not mean getting rid of them just as it is not enough to remove the capital. The techniques, subsumed by capital through the enslavement of the sciences and scientists, are, like the earth and the workers, exploited and, therefore, reduced to a condition far from their potential. There can be no emancipation of the human, the animal, the vegetable, and the terrestrial in general without the emancipation of the sciences and techniques from capital. When this happens, the sciences and techniques will be different, just as the worker freed from the slavery of wages will be different: at least no longer in chains.

The 'critical history of technology' is not the history of technology traced in the notes partially used in the *Capital*, but it is something else. If technology, evoked in analogy with the natural one studied by Darwin, is the human capacity to transform the criteria of natural selection through technological selection criteria, it does not concern only the transformations of work tools, because it also incorporates 'the productive organs of [the social] man ... that are the material basis of all social organization' (Marx 1867a: 375 n. 2).

Inviting us to read in the technological forms the 'factory secrets' (cf. Marx 1867a: 367), i.e., the social relations from which the factory is constituted, Marx suggests that a 'critical history of technology' is not even just a history of the modes of production in general, but it is a history that reveals the political dynamics of the organizational forms of work, because each of them brings with it a social dimension and, therefore, a political dimension.

The relationship between technology and politics is unavoidable because technical development is not individual and is only partly spontaneous or random because is the result of selection. If, in manufacture, the detail work operations obtained from the decomposition of the artisan work process become exclusive and specific functions of the 'detailed labourer', because 'each workman becomes exclusively assigned to a partial function, and that for the rest of his life, his labour power is turned into the organ of this detail function' (Marx 1867a: 343–344), this means that 'only some of the natural and acquired dispositions are strengthened in a unilateral way' (De Palma 1971: 262). Manufacture, by dividing, classifying, and grouping workers 'according to their predominating qualities ... develops a hierarchy of labour powers, to which there corresponds a scale of wages' (Marx 1867a: 354). By doing so, 'the technical laws that govern the decomposition and reorganization of work are imposed on the worker as an authoritarian plan', since 'the specialization of functions increases the constraint of the worker to sell his own labour power' and therefore 'not only [he] does have to subordinate himself to authoritarian leadership because he does not have the means of work, but he is forced to do so because he has lost the ability to exercise a full job' (De Palma 1971: 267–268). Marx concludes that

> division of labour within the workshop implies the undisputed authority of the capitalist over men, that are but parts of a mechanism that belongs to him. The division of labour within the society brings into contact independent commodity producers, who acknowledge no other authority

but that of competition, of the coercion exerted by the pressure of their mutual interests; just as in the animal kingdom, the *bellum omnium contra omnes* more or less preserves the conditions of existence of every species.

MARX 1867a: 361

The same argument, *mutatis mutandis*, can be made for the 'modern industry', because 'we have again the co-operation by division of labour that characterizes manufacture; only now, it is a combination of detail machines' (Marx 1867a: 382):

Modern industry ... sweeps away by technical means the manufacturing division of labour ... At the same time, the capitalistic form of that industry reproduces this same division of labour in a still more monstrous shape; in the factory proper, by converting the workman into a living appendage of the machine.

MARX 1867a: 486–487

A 'critical history of technology', then, is not even just a 'science of technology', which studies the problems associated with the application of machines to the factory production process (see Marx 1867a: 489): technology, therefore, does not totally coincide with the 'productive forces' (as claimed, for example, by Adler 1990: 789; MacKenzie 1984: 474–477; Smith and Marx 1994; and Shaw 1979), because these are also structured by specific class production relations.

Without retrace the Marxian analysis (cf. De Palma 1971: 269–295, and Fallot 1966) let us dwell on command, since 'the modern [industry], which is based on the application of machinery, is a social production relation, an economic category' (Marx 1847a: 183, and see Marx 1867a: chap. 14, sections 4–9). The mechanization of production requires greater coordination in worker-machine movements and, therefore, a higher degree of subordination of the worker to the rhythms of the machine and a more rigid (and scientific) direction of the integration between worker and machine; this production also requires a particular type of governance of the factory, since it generates the 'tendency to equalize and reduce to one and the same level every kind of work that has to be done by the minders of the machines' (Marx 1867a: 423).

That the workers are interchangeable (the only difference is linked to 'age and sex': Marx 1867a: 423) produces: 1) 'a barrack discipline, which is elaborated into a complete system in the factory'; discipline that finds its logical fulfilment in the factory code, in which capital formulates, like a private legislator, and at his own good will, his autocracy over his workpeople, unaccompanied by that division of responsibility, in other matters so much approved of by the bourgeoisie, and unaccompanied by the still more approved representative system'.

MARX 1867a: 426–427

2) a confusion between the 'organization of the work process [and] the social relations of cooperation' (De Palma 1971: 284), between organizational forms of cooperation and its political-social forms. The former concern a 'co-operation on a great scale, and in the employment in common, of instruments of labour and especially of machinery'; the latter, in which the 'book of penalties' replaces the 'slave-driver's lash' (see Marx 1867a: 427), indicate the capitalistic use of machinery, so that the political form that capital imposes (see Marx 1867a: 241, and Marx 1894: 805–807) on the management of factory cooperation is not the only possible one, even if 'it took both time and experience before the workpeople learnt to distinguish between machinery and its employment by capital, and to direct their attacks, not against the material instruments of production, but against the [social] mode in which they are used' (Marx 1867a: 432); a statement supported by the consideration that 'human labour power is by nature no more capital than are the means of production' (Marx 1885: 43). The workers should not indulge in acts of Luddism, but take back the machines and their management in a collective form, because the machines are

the material means and embryonic conditions, making it possible in a higher form of society to combine this surplus labour with a greater reduction of time devoted to material labour in general ... Freedom ... consist in socialized man, the associated producers, rationally regulating their interchange with Nature, bringing it under their common control, instead of being ruled by it as by the blind forces of Nature; and achieving this with the least expenditure of energy and under conditions most favorable to, and worthy of, their human nature ... The shortening of the working day is its basic prerequisite.

MARX 1894: 806–807

Machines are a long-term chance (see Raimondi 2018) because their collective management will abolish exploitation through an inversely proportional relationship between hours of the working day and productivity. Only 'when the labourer co-operates systematically with others, he strips off the fetters of his individuality, and develops the capabilities of his species' (Marx 1867a: 334).

Machines are productive forces that transmit precise production relationships. These relations are determined by the production and the organization of work in 'modern industry'. Factory discipline is intrinsically political because it is technological. And Marx elects the politics of which the technological relations of production are imbued as the object of investigation of a 'critical history of technology'. The 'accumulation through inheritance' also transmits political variations in addition to the technological variations obtained from a certain mode of production.

A 'critical history of technology', then, cannot even be a 'history of industrial technology' (Cohen 1978: 99), but only a political history (on the part of the workers) of technology; a history that is 'critical' because 'technology discloses man's mode of dealing with Nature, the process of production by which, he sustains his life, and thereby also lays bare the mode of formation of his social relations, and of the mental conceptions that flow from them' (Marx 1867a: 375 n. 2).

A political history of the technical, that is, social organization of work in the factory – a critical history because it is produced from the point of view of the working class – it is neither a history of management nor a political history of management, but it is a political history of management produced by the working-class point of view, which highlights 'the link between the *technological* element and the organizational-political element of power in the capitalist production process, [because] the class level expresses itself ... as the construction of a completely new rationality opposed to the rationality practiced by capitalism'; a rationality capable of 'managing the political and economic power of the company and, through it, of society' (Panzieri 1961: 60). It is a question of exposing a workers' point of view, from which a practice of autonomous subjectivation can be born.

A history of the interrelation between the level of techniques and the technological-political level that critically focuses (from a political working-class point of view) the relationship between formation, development and functioning of the productive forces, and their political nature (relations of production) in the capitalistic mode of production. An analysis that highlights how the transformations at the level of productive forces affect the relations of production and vice versa, but also how the means of production bring within themselves precise relations of production, only partially imposed, and governed by those who uses them (Vadée 1998: 385).

It is not a question of considering technology, as it is never a neutral set of production tools and relations, necessarily unbalanced in favour of the owners of the means of production, but that techniques are never neutral because they structurally involve production relations that can be hierarchical or egalitarians: and this depends, above all, on their nature. Their non-neutrality is always partial, because on the one hand it allows for production relationships that benefit a certain class, but on the other it opens to various possible evolutions. A working class's politics must push techniques to evolve in a direction that is congruent with their own class interests. The productive forces are intimately marked by relations of production, which are not their external effects or consequences, nor are they external to them, because they are what really structures them.

PART 2

Spaces and World: States, Revolutions, Social Movement

..

CHAPTER 8

Germany as an Anachronism

Marx, Social Science and the State

Maurizio Ricciardi

On the 20th February 1866,[1] Marx confessed to his *dear fellow* Friedrich Engels that for his work to be properly conceived, he cannot go into depth into every single detail. But – he adds – the composition, the structure, is a triumph of German scholarship [*deutsche Wissenschaft*], which an individual German may confess to, since it is *in no way* his merit but rather belongs to the nation. Which is all the more gratifying, as it is otherwise the *silliest nation* under the sun!

Marx considers science the most significant product to emerge from Germany, a fact which is made evident by his genuine enthusiasm for the experimentations of Christian Friedrich Schönbein and Justus von Liebig, namely, the intersection of chemistry and agronomy. Marx concludes: '*I feel proud of the Germans. It is our duty to emancipate this 'deep' people*' (Marx to Engels 2/20/1866 in MECW 42: 232). One could read the shift here, from German to English, as intended to establish a certain ironic distance from the ambition expressed within the statement. Throughout the torturous writing-process of *Capital*, it was the thought of Liebig and Schönbein in particular which had a significant impact on Marx, such as to elicit his declaration that they were 'more important for this matter than all the economists put together' (Marx to Engels 2/13/1866 in MECW 42: 227). Yet in spite of their 'depth' it was understood that the Germans were nevertheless difficult to emancipate, given the extent to which they had been hypnotized by '[their] own Christian-Germanic brand of bad luck' (Marx 1847b: 332) and one which provided an irreducibly German way of thinking about society and the state. Therefore, Marxian enthusiasm reserves itself not to all the branches of German science, but almost exclusively for the experimental sciences (Guerraggio and Vidoni 1982): this includes geology, whose vocabulary can be found in the Marxian concepts of 'social formation' and 'ideal average' (Haug 2013: 41–45), chemistry, agronomy (Marx 1878), mathematics (Marx 1983). This is without forgetting

---

1   The author wants to thank Alice Figes for her help in reviewing the English translation.

the importance of the cameralistics for the development of the Marxian concept of technology (Marx 1981). Indeed, science and technology are themselves revolutionary forces because they change the material conditions of the production of existence. As Marx proclaimed during an event at the Chartists' *The People Paper*, the daily newspaper: 'Steam, electricity, and the self-acting mule were revolutionists of a rather more dangerous character than even citizens Barbès, Raspail and Blanqui' (Marx 1856b: 655).

The entanglement of science's revolutionary character with the conditions of German society was for Marx, an anachronism, and for him, this was exemplified in the case of the response to the revolution of 1848. Germany failed to erase the aristocratic estates' feudal rule resulting in 'a parody of the French revolution of 1789' (Marx 1848f: 294). For German society, the past continues to dominate.

> Whereas 1648 and 1789 gained boundless self-confidence from being at the apex of creation, it was the ambition of the Berlin revolution of 1848 to constitute an anachronism. Its light was like that of the stars which reaches us, the inhabitants of the Earth, only after the bodies from which it emanated have been extinct for a hundred thousand years. The March revolution in Prussia was, on a small scale – just as it was on a small scale in everything – such a star for Europe. Its light was that of the corpse of a society which had long ago decayed.
>
> MARX 1848e: 162

It was the Prussian bourgeoisie to be held responsible. After 1848, the bourgeoisie managed to find itself at the head of the state thanks to what had effectively been a 'passive revolution' in the Gramscian sense: they had transitioned the contents of the old world into the new world. The bourgeoisie behaved like an estate in a class-society; it opposed the people and was prepared to compromise with the monarchy; it represented 'renewed interests within an obsolete society' (Marx 1848e: 162). It was this archaic and historical domination over the elements of the 'new', which Marx came to define as 'anachronism' across several of his works (Marx 1867a: 75). Rather than being demonstrative of an ineluctably fallen past, anachronism underscores the extent to which the past continues to exert a bind over the present. As a result, even the very possibility of constructing one's own history is dependent on the capacity to free oneself from the 'tradition of all the dead generations [which] weighs like a nightmare on the brain of the living' (Marx 1852a: 103). Thus, for Marx the logic of history is not progressive – 'in spite of the pretensions of *Progress*, continual retrogressions and circular movements occur' (Marx and Engels 1845: 83). Rather, history is determined by the need to extricate itself from the constantly resurfacing past (Ricciardi 2019). It is precisely this understanding of History which establishes the specific closure of the future that characterizes Marx's work. Not by chance, the greatest example of anachronism Marx identified was that of 'dead labour', the control of capital over living labour. Anachronism is thus not a 'figure' within the philosophy of history as such, but a determining element of the very environment in which historical action takes place. For this reason, there is no dominant teleology in Marx, granting meaning from the outside to individual and collective actions.

> *History* does *nothing*, it 'possesses *no* immense wealth', it 'wages *no* battles'. It is *man*, real, living man who does all that, who possesses and fights; 'history' is not, as it were, a person apart, using man as a means to achieve *its own* aims; history is *nothing but* the activity of man pursuing his aims.
> MARX and ENGELS 1845: 93; see also BENSAÏD 2004

Only from such a reading of history can one understand Marx's attitude towards the social sciences of his time. Indeed, as evident in the *Manifesto*, it was a form of knowledge which engendered no particular enthusiasm, not even in a naive sense, on the part of Marx and Engels. They were even sceptical of the syntagm 'social science' as employed by Saint-Simon, Fouret and Owen which, for them, was formed by the need to discover inevitable laws of society's development. 'Social science' is a science of society [*gesellschaftliche Wissenschaft*] and society is the true and only subject of history. Society with its class conflict, with its backward relationships, with its evolutionary tendencies, becomes the object of a science which does not contemplate 'any historical initiative or any independent political movement' on the part of the proletariat.

Indeed, social science, and Saint Simonian science in particular which 'glorified in dithyrambs the productive power of industry' (Marx 1845: 282), considers capitalist society as the fulfilment of history, affirming it as a necessary and definitive order, which, for this very reason, can only be perfected. Social scientists and socialists therefore conceive the evolution of society as dependent upon their theories. 'They therefore search after a new social science [*soziale Wissenschaft*], after new social laws [*soziale Gesetze*], that are to create these conditions'. It is for this reason that they cannot accept the autonomy of the proletariat, which for Marx, is the effective negation of existing society. 'Future history resolves itself, in their eyes, into the propaganda and the practical carrying out of their social plans' (Marx and Engels 1848: 515). Insistence on the current initiative and refusal to accept the possibility of societal planning are at the basis of the Marxian conception of action itself. The voluntaristic trait is in fact never absolutized, by virtue of the fact that it is confronted with a set of unintentional forms of action which constitute society. For this reason, Marx conceives 'the evolution of the economic formation of society ... as a process of natural history' which 'make[s] the individual responsible for relations whose creature he socially remains, however much he may subjectively raise himself above them' (Marx 1867a: 10).

Now that for Marx the domain of human activity has assumed the name and exclusive form of society, it is the latter which we must consider in order to understand anachronism's political effects. For Marx, Germany is not simply a 'late-comer' nation, but rather the society that most clearly demonstrates the overall potency that the past can exert. The same semantics of society that emerged in Germany during the 1840s is for Marx characterized by the need to eradicate forms of the past, as bequeathed by that society. This process of discursive societal development refers to the definition of a complex semantic field in which terms such as work, property, socialism and communism converge in a plethora of contradictory modalities. This occurs amidst daily political controversy, in which criticism serves to mark out a distance, to literally establish partisanship. Here however the party struggle cannot be understood as a clash between factions or even as the strategic use of knowledge to obtain a position of power (so Lacascade 2002: 163ff). The theoretical move carried out by Marx in the 1840s went beyond merely the internal, conflictual relations of the heterogeneous socialist universe, one which he knew and frequented, but aimed to redefine the very language which would give political character to the social phenomena in question. This set of semantic innovations carried out in the *Manifesto* (Koselleck 2004: 90) would not have been possible without those conflicts, which are nevertheless incorporated and summarised explicitly within the text. The histories of society, which in Germany became common and widespread literature, confirmed an expectation of change directed towards the 'social' – not simply the adjective of society – but a term destined to mean what exceeds it, contradicts it, what can develop it or at the same time deny its structure. As Karl Grün writes, the language of society has passed from the cultured circles of the capital-city to the wider public, 'which ravenously pounces on everything that bears the word 'social' on its forehead, because a sure instinct tells him what secrets of the future are hidden in this little word' (Grün 1845: 123).

This consideration is part of review of the Theodor Mundt's history of society who, together with Lorenz von Stein, undoubtedly represents one of the greatest propagators of social and societal vocabulary. Differently from Stein, he situates socialism and communism within a history, not as yet part of an opening born by the epochal contradictions of capitalism, but which together

with the impact of an inexhaustible research of happiness and liberty, finds
through work his only possible satisfaction. The 'concept of society is essentially the idea of free personality itself' (Mundt 1844: 179). Only a property
obtained by work could be the guarantee of a free personality. The inseparable
link between property and work, as also affirmed by Stein albeit on a much
more concrete level, necessitates defence against communism which has
carved out the role of *'advocatus diaboli* of society' (Mundt 1844: 427), while
socialism recognizes the state's ability to constantly re-establish the dynamics
of the societal order.

Marx recognizes the value of these innovations within political semantics.
In a letter to Feuerbach, he acknowledges that he discovered society through
the critique of theology. 'The unity of man with man, which is based on the real
differences between men, the concept of the human species brought down
from the heaven of abstraction to the real earth, what is this but the concept of
society!' (Marx to Feuerbach 8/11/1844 in MECW 3: 354). With respect to Hegel,
there would be the 'establishment of *true materialism* and of *real science*', given
that Feuerbach makes the 'the social relationship [*gesellschaftliches Verhältnis*]
of 'man to man' the basic principle of the theory' (Marx 1844a: 328). The critique
of theology not only serves the critique of politics that Marx himself assigned
as a task in those years, but also leads to the discovery of society. Seen from
such a perspective, the same reckoning with the Hegelian left reveals itself to
be more than a battle over the current effectiveness of philosophical categories. For Marx, it is a question of affirming the conflictual character of society,
which is not simply a new plan of mediation between equal individuals, but
the loci in which relations of power and domination are established. This is
clear in Marx's review of Friedrich List's *Das nationale System der politischen
Ökonomie,* which, in addition to being a decisive criticism of the national possibility of accumulation, marks the refusal of giving ethical as well as economic
meaning to work. Consequently, he identifies the fundamental dynamics of
society within the connections and oppositions between work and property.
With respect to List, Marx grapples with the specific ethical conception of
work, which in Germany dominated in a multiplicity of forms throughout the
19th century. Work thus comes to be considered as the necessary basis of private property, not only as a condition of possibility, but as a process of appropriation which determines the dynamics of society.

> If it is desired to strike a mortal blow at private property, one must attack
> it not only as a material state of affairs, but also as activity, as labour. It
> is one of the greatest misapprehensions to speak of free, human, social
> [*gesellschaftlich*] labour, of labour without private property. 'Labour' by

its very nature is unfree, unhuman, unsocial [*ungesellschaftlich*] activity, determined by private property and creating private property. Hence the abolition of private property will become a reality only when it is conceived as the abolition of 'labour' (an abolition which, of course, has become possible only as a result of labour itself, that is to say, has become possible as a result of the material activity of society and which should on no account be conceived as the replacement of one category by another).

MARX 1845: 278–279

If work is not the ethical foundation of society but a condition of submission and domination, namely society's asocial nucleus, society therefore cannot be founded on the mysticism of the productive forces as inaugurated by Saint-Simonism, which in the following decades will come to have an increasingly decisive influence in Germany. Thanks to such a mysticism of society, the 'bourgeois sees in the proletarian not a *human being,* but a *force* capable of creating wealth', a force that is literally separated from the very individuals who endure it. Instead, they are compared with other forces, and in case of necessity, they can be replaced with alternatives. Only as a functional equivalent, in fact, the proletarian 'has (enjoys) the honour of figuring as a *productive force*' (Marx 1845: 286). Thus, it is the rupture that Marx establishes between work and property which is what irremediably distances his discourse on society from that of the social sciences and socialists. For Marx, society is not a system of order that finds its fulfilment in the state. Socialists like Hermann Semmig argue instead that Communism should be the 'completion of the rule of law, not its dissolution' (Semmig 1845: 168), because it should aim to moderate the negative effects of property, not to abolish it. If not, it ends up opposing the overall property [*Gesamteigentum*] of the individual, producing despotic effects capable of annihilating individuality. Socialism, on the other hand, would be a process of the rationalization of existence, society according to its true order. However, this order is not immediately evident and cannot be affirmed without the support of science, specifically German science, entrusted with the task of resolving the contradictions of the societal relations and of continually re-establishing the conditions for its reproduction. Indeed, it is precisely because science becomes the most important aspect of the social order, which elicits Marx to comment that:

'German science' here, therefore, presents a social order [*Ordnung der Gesellschaft*], in fact 'the most reasonable social order'; '*in the shape of* socialism'. Socialism is reduced to a branch of that omnipotent, omniscient, all-embracing German science which is even able to set up a society.

MARX and ENGELS 1845–46: 458

Socialism would be nothing more than a society that is scientifically governed thanks to an ostensibly neutral structure, which becomes the instrument
for the resolution of conflict. Marx's own distancing from such an approach
emerges first in the confrontation with Bruno Bauer who in his self-critique of
his *Jewish Question*, admits that he should not have spoken 'of the form of the
state, but of society, which excludes no one, but from which only those who
do not wish to participate in its development are excluded' (Bauer 1844: 15; see
also Tomba 2002). Society thus results in representing a non-political space,
because it establishes voluntary criteria of belonging; it does not express the
series of constraints that can be traced back to the state, particularly in its
German constitutional form. As Gabriel Riesser points out, criticizing Bauer's
positions, the link between society and constitution allows 'an accommoda-
tion between the claims of reason and what is historically given, and anyone
wishing to build a social order on rational principles could not achieve the fic-
tions and balances of the constitutional structure' (Riesser 1843: 30). Critique
alone is therefore not sufficient to resolve the problem of the state, not even
if one thinks, as Bauer does, of being able to build a 'shape of the world' on a
basis that is not 'merely legal, but societal [*gesellschaftlich*]'. In this respect,
philosophical criticism not only claims to establish the shape of the world, but
also conceives the shape of the world to be a society, understood as a subject that produces itself and without the need for the violence of state power.
Precisely against this conception of society, Marx objects that societal normativity produces hierarchies and exclusions unknown to the state organization
of power alone. 'Society behaves just as exclusively as the state, only in a more
polite form: it does not throw you out, but it makes it so uncomfortable for you
that you go out of your own will' (Marx and Engels 1845: 96). It is thus impossible for Marx to think of state and society as distinct. The state and its form are
a problem of society. 'Only *political superstition* still imagines today that civil
life must be held together by the state, whereas in reality, on the contrary, the
state is held together by civil life' (Marx and Engels 1845: 121).

The analysis of society for Marx therefore provides proof of the structural
dependence of the state on a life that is civil because it is societal. In this way,
the history of the state is reconfigured, which can no longer be considered
independent. Indeed, when it claims to be, it results in disclosing the state as a
necessary anachronism of society. Indeed, Lorenz von Stein already speaks of
a 'state moment [*staatliches Moment*]' within the 'science of industry'. While
Marx considers these statements imprecise, he credits Stein with having understood that 'the history of the state is intimately connected with the history of
national economy' (Marx and Engels 1845–1846: 503). For Stein, however, the
'state moment' is a decisive one for the societal order, because it produces the

only mediation in a domain that would otherwise be irremediably at prey to conflict. For Marx, on the other hand, the state does not express (and therefore equally cannot represent) an autonomous and superior entity with respect to social struggles. Society can therefore be understood to directly express its political character. Yet it is one which does not consist in the production of 'unity' as such, but rather, alone consists in the radical split through which it is constituted (Ricciardi 2001: 143–152).

The German *Nationalökonomie* fails to recognize the substantive character of this split. It is for this reason that Marx generally does not consider it even worthwhile to critique the thought of its exponents. Only in 1881, when discussing Adolf Wagner's criticisms of *Capital*, did Marx explicitly highlight their diverging conceptions of history. For Marx, political economy is not a historical science given that it restores the meaning of the historical process from its methodological basis. It investigates and criticizes the relationships of a given period, showing their transitory and contingent character. Marx can affirm from this that his '*analytic* method, which does not proceed from *man* but from a given economic period of society, has nothing in common with the German-professorial association-of-concepts method' (Marx 1881–1882: 547). Furthermore, when criticizing the contrast between the 'logical' and the 'historical' as conceived by Rodbertus, Marx argues that history presents a coherence which can be discovered and described as a result of scientific method. Yet he is not conceiving of science as something which precedes and remains superior to the relations of society. Rather, he is positing that within a given 'social formation' some phenomena obtain a certain legitimacy which makes them 'as the *concrete* character of the *thing*, as a character appertaining essentially to *the thing itself,* although this objectivity does *not* appear in its natural form' (Marx 1881–1882: 551). Until historical and political conditions similar to those in France or England arose, political economy in Germany, rather than being seen as a science of social objectivity, was still considered a 'foreign science'. Indeed, for Marx, when those conditions are finally fulfilled economic science loses all explanatory capacity.

> Political Economy remains within that horizon (sc. a bourgeois horizon), in so far, i.e., as the capitalist régime is looked upon as the absolutely final form of social production, instead of as a passing historical phase of its evolution, political economy can remain a science only so long as the class struggle is latent or manifests itself only in isolated and sporadic phenomena.
>
> MARX 1867a: 14

Just as the idea of a historical 'lag' does not depend on a timeline of economic development, so the limit of economics, as a science, does not depend on internal coherence. In both cases, the measure is the class struggle. It is the process by which, according to Marx, the guiding principle of the political is constantly redefined (Balibar 2014; Demirovic 2014). The Marxian political is not oriented to decision-making and therefore to political unity, but rather to the deconstruction of the conditions of production and reproduction of society. The class struggle is not simply a conflict, but a 'break' that reproduces itself continuously within the fabric of society: it is not a way of moving forward with history, but the potential repeal of its path as determined by capital. It is not only in Germany that the political economy constantly presents society as an interweaving entity, a fabric, even in moments of rupture. It is precisely this societal tension which appears as anachronism during a time in which class struggle challenges the established relations of power and domination.

It is also for this reason that Germany cannot simply be deemed the place of historical backwardness, of representing a delay in the progressive development which universal history is destined to overcome with time. Rather, Germany is proof that universal history proceeds in a plurality of ways. The specific case of Germany reveals the constitutive incompleteness of universal history itself. Germany, in fact, still occupies an *ancien régime,* which universal history nevertheless claims, in both critique and practice, to be outdated, and yet one which remains impossible to eradicate.

> This struggle against the limited content of the German *status quo* cannot be without interest even for the *modern* nations, for the German *status quo* is the *open completion of the ancien régime,* and the *ancien régime* is the *concealed deficiency of the modern state* [*der versteckte Mangel des modernen Staaten*]
>
> MARX 1844C: 178

The German status quo reveals something about the state in general as a typically modern political structure. It posits that the constitutive link between science and politics does not necessarily fuel constant progress as promised by universal history.

> If therefore the *status quo of German statehood* expresses the *perfection of the ancien régime,* the perfection of the thorn in the flesh of the modern state, the *status quo of German political theory* expresses the *imperfection of the modern state,* the defectiveness of its flesh itself.
>
> MARX 1844C: 181; see also ENGELS 1847

As Marx states even more clearly in *The Jewish Question*, it is the very notion of sovereignty in question. The individual should be the foundation of sovereignty. Yet in order to be so, 'the imaginary member of an illusory sovereignty, is deprived of his real individual life and endowed with an unreal universality' (Marx 1844b: 154). That is, the modern state cannot correspond to its presuppositions given that it is a historical product which already exists in the age of the *ancien régime*. Its laws, despite its universalistic logic, nevertheless inevitably continue to privilege only some. For these reasons, Germany plays the role of the uncanny which reveals to the 'people of modernity' a past that has not yet been overcome. Moreover, precisely because of such a history and subsequent structure of the state, it can in fact, never be overcome. 'The present German regime, an anachronism, a flagrant contradiction of generally recognized axioms, the nothingness of the *ancien régime* exhibited to the world' (Marx 1844c: 178). Beginning from Hegel, Marx defines Germany as the spectacle that merely mimics an ancient, estate-based society. If it no longer makes sense to reenact the behaviors of an era that has now passed, performing 'modern acts' entails running into a double anachronism which affects both the past and the present: 'The pretensions of universal essentiality are uncovered in the self; it shows itself to be entangled in an actual existence, and drops the mask just because it wants to be something genuine' (Hegel 1977: 450; but see also Kouvélakis 2000: 36ff). In other words, all that occurs in Germany, from the customs union to industrial policy, is forced to reconcile itself to a political context which fails to acknowledge it, and to necessarily relie upon a state repeatedly occupied with outdated functions.

Germany clarifies the ever-present past of the state precisely because far from being the Steinian 'state moment' that can govern conflict in society, the state is the fulfillment of the domination that arises in society. The state never presents itself as abstract and impersonal power, but exercises its dominion overall, even if it is constantly to the advantage of some. Germany is the constant refinement of this *ancien régime* which reveals the modern state's structural defect, that is, the necessarily incomplete dialectic of the universal and the particular within it. For this reason, Marx shortly afterwards defines the proletariat as a 'universal estate' and one which leads to the dissolution of society. This is not a semantic oscillation, but an occasional reconfiguration of the term's meaning, given that a few lines earlier Marx had employed 'class' to define the proletariat itself. The reference to the universal estate is intended to break the apparent uniformity of society. An estate embedded in the structure of the bourgeois order is therefore the bearer of its decomposition. Calling it an estate after having spoken of 'universal emancipation' and a 'class burdened by radical chains' entails demonstrating how it disrupts the path of bourgeois civil society. Now in a class-divided society, it presents itself as an estate, with the pretense of representing '*in fact* the dissolution of that world order' (Marx 1844c: 187). It is not yet a question of class struggle, a syntagm that Engels and Marx will begin to use only leading up to 1848, but of a subjective presence which challenges the universalist claims of the state.

The conditions through which the proletariat can reproduce itself is what dominates their own general condition. Simultaneously, and in spite of the distance, the world market connects these conditions. Difference and universality are the characteristics which for Marx distinguish the empirically universal individuals produced by capitalist relations. First, difference means that each of these individuals legitimately claims to change their material condition. Yet they must recognize their dependence on world-historical conditions over which they have no power individually. 'Thus, for instance, if in England a machine is invented which deprives countless workers of bread in India and China and overturns the whole form of existence of these empires, this invention becomes a world-historical fact (Marx and Engels 1845–1846: 27). The 'transformation of history into world history' is by now an established fact for Marx. The lexical tension that he identifies between a historical-world universality, and one linked to the abstraction of law and the state has immediate political ramifications. It is a tension between a possibility of global connection that moves from the differences of single individuals, and one that must necessarily ignore them, literally required to abstract from such differences. This gap in the understanding of the universal becomes for Marx a constant, which, redefining the space and time of the subjects' action, prevents us from thinking about the modification of their material conditions as the result of an act of will or its absence. Instead, we are faced with a systematic domination, unfolded in space as it is articulated according to its specific and composite temporality. The politics of this situation cannot in any case be unilateral, that is, it cannot assume that 'the principle of politics is the *will*.' (Marx 1844e: 199).

For Marx, this is not an occasional acquisition, but one which remains fundamental for his conception of politics. This is evident both in the polemic of 1844 with Arnold Ruge and in the 1875 *Critique of the Gotha Program*. On the question of the Silesian weavers' revolt, Ruge had conceived it as the inability of the Prussian state to represent the perspective of the 'universal'. He consequently asked the administration to take charge of the 'pauperism question' and so to resolve it as an issue of public conscience. To enter into the world, however, the latter would require a social revolution capable of healing the conditions of 'terrible isolation of men from the community [*Gemeinwesen*], but this revolution is impossible without the political part (i.e., without the organising vision from the point of view of the whole)' (Ruge 1975 [1844]: 4).

For Marx, however, (indeed which explains the vehemence of his response) the Silesian weavers turned not against the monarch nor the aristocracy, 'but against the bourgeoisie', demonstrating their ability to more directly grasp who constitutes the enemy: the industrialist ('the invisible enemy'), and the banker ('the hidden enemy'). Their revolt was not sought to bridge the gap from the political institutions, as Ruge claimed; what they detested was not the lack of participation in the sphere of the state, but the need to act against their own condition within society. Thus, it appears that two tensions persist throughout Marx's work. The struggle against what he will call the natural laws of capitalist production requires intense long-term action to modify the conditions of the domination of capital; however, this is not possible without the revolt against political power, knowing, however, that its exclusive action is powerless in the face of those laws. The limit of mere government action is so apparent for Marx that he defines the behavior of the German administration as 'unpolitical', one which does not understand that the needs of an industrial territory, required to be treated as 'as a matter of general concern', and not as 'any local distress due to flood or famine'. The political act is necessary, but at the same time it is always insufficient. It is effectively an 'infantile disorder' of the proletariat. 'Because it thinks in the framework of politics, the proletariat sees the cause of all evils in the *will*, and all means of remedy in *violence* and in the *overthrow* of a *particular* form of state' (Marx 1844e: 204). The point of significance regarding this initial debate on the European question of the German proletariat is summed up, for Marx, in the fact that being included in the state's representative institutions, does not, however, eradicate the isolation between individuals, the isolation fostered by the mechanism of the state. Simultaneously, it would confirm the position of the government as representative of an indifferent universality:

> Therefore, however *partial* the uprising of the *industrial workers* may be, it contains within itself a *universal* soul; however universal a *political* uprising may be, it conceals even in its *most grandiose* form a *narrow-minded* spirit.
>
> MARX 1844e: 205

Over thirty years later many of these arguments would return. First, it would be the criticism of work as articulated in the review to List. 'The bourgeois have very good grounds for ascribing *supernatural creative power* to labour' (Marx 1875a: 81), while work represents the orientating benchmark of individuals within society. From this presupposition, each acquires the right to a certain share of the social product. 'This *equal* right is an unequal right for unequal labour'. In other words, law makes individuals equal who, rather than being different for their own nature, are also materially different in their position within the process of societal production. The law prevents differences from appearing in connection to the relationship of class, because it always brings them back to the individual domain. The law therefore constantly shatters every aspect of individuality in order to allow it to be equated with others. The law 'guarantees' that difference, that is the different share of social product that everyone receives, becomes the measure of equality, precisely because it makes that share the very measure of individuality. 'To avoid all these defects, right would have to be unequal rather than equal', irrespective of whether this evidently contradicts its own assumptions.

Such an impossible equality is central to the issue of transition that Marx here discusses. It is not a question that can be planned and therefore governed by a single and central subject. The transition cannot follow the pattern of the social sciences that design societies, then trying to implement them. This would again be the socialism of German social science which thinks that 'with state loans one can build a new society just as well as a new railway'. However, it is not a question of the mechanism's deficiency as such, but rather the incoherency of the universal subject which it claims to represent. And this requires considering the material composition of the people, which far from being a homogeneous unit is empirically divided into a multitude of social figures, to such an extent that to guarantee its freedom of action, the state can only ignore their differences (Ricciardi 2012). The question of how the order of society could be configured differently cannot be answered 'by a thousandfold combination of the word people with the word state' (Marx 1875a: 95). In any case, given the situation in Germany, a democratic republic cannot be confused with a 'state which is nothing but a police-guarded military despotism, embellished with parliamentary forms, alloyed with a feudal admixture and at the same time already influenced by the bourgeoisie, and bureaucratically carpentered' (Marx 1875a: 96). Nevertheless, even in the democratic republic, which 'vulgar democracy' sees as the 'Millennial Kingdom', that is, as the definitive political form in which the evolution of the modern state culminates, the class struggle is a problem that state mediation cannot solve. Once again, Germany as 'anachronism', is not to be limited to its past but in fact indicates a constitutive deficiency of the modern state and its politics.

CHAPTER 9

In the Anarchic State of Capital

Marx and the Suspended History of Latin America

Michele Cento

1   Introduction[1]

It has become a trope to describe Marx's treatment of Latin America as a *blind spot* – a 'history of a missed encounter' (Boostels 2010: 5). However, in recent decades this idea has been partially revised. Notably, the publication of *Materiales para la Historia de América Latina*, an anthology edited by José Aricó, has done much to challenge this commonly held assumption. Aricó's volume provides a collection of Marx and Engels scattered (yet not so rare) reflections on Latin America. He nevertheless maintains that a Eurocentrist view still problematises Marx's consideration of Latin America. According to Aricó, the revaluation of the autonomous role of the global peripheries in the capitalist world-system – Ireland, Russia, India, China, etc. – begun by Marx in the 1860s did not include Latin America. This has led Aricó to discern a distinctive kind of 'Orientalist' treatment toward Latin America on the part of Marx. Thus, Latin America would have remained outside world history. After all, this was the uncomfortable position to which Hegel had confined it, and Aricó argues that Marx sought to perpetuate that stereotype.

In Marx's work, there are some passages on the peoples of Latin America – i.e., 'degenerate Spaniard' (Marx to Engels 12/2/1854 in MECW 39: 504) – which indeed evoke equally merciless judgments of Hegel's philosophy of history. However, Aricó's argument that Marx is just a 'Hegel redivivus' before Latin American history is questionable. Marx's judgments on Latin American people reflect an 'Orientalist' anthropology broadly shared across Europe, and that certainly was not limited to German idealism (Aricó 2013: 39; Larrain 1991). It is no mystery that Hegelian philosophy of history is openly Eurocentric and orientalist. Hegel's history begins where 'rationality begins to manifest in worldly existence' and shows up when 'society and the state becomes progressively more civilised'. These are considered unfinished processes within

---

1   The author wants to thank Alice Figes for her help in reviewing the English translation.

the American continent. As the 'country of the future', according to Hegel, the American continent remains outside the horizon of his philosophy of history because 'what has taken there up to now is but an echo of the Old World and the expression of an alien life' (Hegel 1981: 134, 137, 171). Therefore, Aricó holds that Marx reiterated the same Hegelian prejudices. He was unable to recognize in the struggles for national liberation the path through which Latin American peoples developed society and a state, beginning to write their history (Aricó 2013: 27–38).

Above all, there is no doubt that the Latin American continent holds a marginal position in Marxian work compared to other non-European areas. One notable example is that Marx does not provide any account of formations of new subjects in Latin America comparable to those observed in the Sepoy revolt in India or the Taiping uprising in China. The emergence of new historical subjects from the world 'peripheries' compels Marx, from the 1850s onwards, to question the linear and Eurocentric conception of history. Following this, Marx was compelled to question the assumption that capitalism's demise would first be put into motion by the proletariat struggles of the most 'advanced' capitalist regimes. (Anderson 2010; Harootunian 2015). There is no passage of Marxian work that seems to assign this task to the Latin American peoples, despite those very same peoples managed to liberate themselves from European domination while the Restoration raged in the Old World. In this sense, we can highlight the insufficient Marxian consideration of the processes of subjectification that take place in Latin America in conjunction with decolonization. However, it does not suffice to say that Marx's account entirely depends on the Hegelian category of people who remained outside history (García Linera 1991).

However, blaming Marx for this or other analytical flaws risks imposing a narrow perspective on his view of Latin America. On the contrary, this essay will focus on how the Marxian perspective emphasizes that Latin America casts a light on the historical truth on the 'arcana' of capitalism, which the political economy claims to conceal and naturalize. Latin America is not a scrap of evolution despite all its 'archaisms'. On the contrary, manifest anachronism reveals the simultaneous coexistence of different temporal layers moving according to different rhythms yet synchronized within the world market. In Latin America, capital abandons any teleology of progress, harmony and *doux commerce* and throws off the mask of modernity. Instead, it exhibits the despotic face with which it came into the world and clearly cannot give up. However, the weight the past exerts on the present, suspending the possibility of a future of emancipation (Ricciardi 2019), is not peculiar to Latin America: it is instead the global truth of capitalism. In this sense, my starting hypothesis is that Latin America does not remain outside history for Marx.

On the contrary, it embodies the 'contemporaneity of the non-contemporaneous' (Koselleck 2004: 160), as it operates in the assemblage of the different temporalities that establish the logical and historical order of the global capitalist space – that is, the world market as a space that combines systemic/universal forms and singular/particular conditions. In other words, the 'contemporaneity of the non-contemporaneous' must be understood as the localized, stubborn, and ostentatious survival of archaic relations of power on which the present world domination of capital is, however, founded. Put differently, there is no capitalist 'modernity' without the Latin American 'archaicity'.

In Latin America, capital as a 'social relation of production' can show its despotic and violent logic without a modicum of shame. In Europe, this corrosive logic is continually disguised behind the glittering modernity of machines, civil codes, and constitutional governments. Marxian texts on Latin America consequently allow us to shed light on the operative logic of the world market, rather than merely revealing the 'multilinear' traces of the history of capitalism (Anderson 2010: 154 ff.). The logic of the world market indeed imposes its systemic order through the synchronization of different temporal layers expressed by the particular parts of the system. This order does not rest so much on the colonial relationship between the centre and 'periphery' but on the logical links that subsume empirical differences and lead them back to the unifying power of capital. Therefore, no peripheral logic of capital is distinguishable from that of the system's core, but a social relationship that branches out and reproduces itself according to the plural phenomenology of valorization processes. In light of the 'logical and historical primacy' of the world market over its local manifestations (Pradella 2015: 119), Latin America enters the history of capital and, as we will see in the following pages, baptises it.

2   In the World Market: The Metallic Link of Despotism

Despite its alleged condition, being 'outside' of world history, Latin America appears from Marx's earliest writings as the midwife of the world market. In the *German Ideology*, the constitution of the world market, and therefore of a space that connects 'world-historical, empirically universal individuals', already appears to be linked to naval exploration: 'Manufacturing and the movement of production, in general, received an enormous impetus through the extension of intercourse which came with the discovery of America'. Thanks to the 'new products imported thence, particularly the masses of gold and silver which came into circulation', from the simple process of 'extension of markets' emerged the systemic form of the 'world market, which had now become possible and was daily becoming more and more a fact' (Marx and Engels 1845–1846: 49, 69).

This argument would be reiterated two years later in the *Manifesto* and developed in the texts of the 1850s, which, starting from the *Grundrisse*, paved the way for the publication of *Capital*. Marx's *magnum opus* deals with the genetic relationship between Latin America and the world market in the last chapters dedicated to the so-called primitive accumulation and colonization. In these twenty years, Latin America enters the work of Marx and, after the publication of *Capital*, fades away. In Marx's account, Latin America as a case study brings to light the *'arcana'* of political economy and allows him to recognize one of the material and logical presuppositions of the world market in the colonial conquest. It is indeed the 'circulation of American silver from the West to East' that has set 'the metallic link between America and Europe, on the one hand, with Asia on the other, since the beginning of the modern epoch' (Marx 1857–1861a: 159). They represent 'a considerable exchange value, in a relatively small volume': gold and silver 'serve as the perpetuum mobile' of capital, providing the constituent elements for the global application of capitalism's despotic logic (Marx 1859a: 385).

This logistical potential is not intrinsic to precious metals but emerges only when they take on the historical form of money. As they are introduced into the circulation process after the discovery of America, these metals acquire a function that transcends their original nature: 'nature does not produce money' – in fact – 'gold and silver are not money in and of themselves'. Indeed, they were not in the pre-Columbian age: 'in Peru and Mexico', Marx argues, 'gold and silver were not used as money, although they can be found as jewellery and a developed system of production existed there' (Marx 1857–1861a: 171). Ceasing to be mere ornaments, Latin American gold and silver begin to acquire a specific 'formal use value': they become the 'general equivalent' of all commodities and adopt the status of 'money' (Marx 1859a: 326, 328). It is when this occurs that the history of capital penetrates Latin America, sweeping away the pre-existing 'natural' connection between individuals which develop 'only to a limited extent and at isolated points', consequently giving birth to an impersonal yet interconnected world market (Marx 1857–1861a: 95).

However, this does not imply that the world market is a mere product of colonialism, at least not in the univocal forms of a predatory power that radiates from the centre to the peripheries. On the contrary, the world market is indeed the space where the different histories of the world are connected, without cancelling the different temporal layers they embody. Here, then, the transmutation of gold and silver into money not only certifies the demise of pre-Columbian civilizations but equally becomes the prerequisite for a global 'foreign power' in the form of 'traffic'. It is this traffic of commodities – and of men reduced to commodities – that generates an increasingly dense web of connections that in the world market 'directly linked up (individuals) to universal history' (Marx and Engels 1845–1846: 49). The equivalence that gold/money is expected to represent is valid not only in the realm of commodities but serves to hold together the asynchronies of history so that different temporalities of development can thus converge within the world 'traffic'. As much as Latin America appears in this sense constrained in history, it is precisely such unforeseen connections that, at the dawn of modernity, make the flow of precious metals toward Europe able to 'change the position of the classes towards one another, dealing a hard blow to feudal landed property' (Marx and Engels 1845–1846: 66).

Gold and silver differ from other commodities because they 'represent independent incarnations, expressions of the social character of wealth' (Marx 1894: 568). They are the manifest form of social power, even if misguided by the artifices of political economy. In other words, they embody the power to command the commodity and the social relationship they express. In the first decades of the 16th century, the landing of Latin American gold and silver first in Seville and then in Antwerp subsequently entailed the transfer of a surplus of social power that ended up in the hands of the great European merchants and manufacturing owners (see Braudel 1992; Braudel 1981), undermining the asphyxiating constraints of the guilds and penalising the more static landed property linked to the feudal organization.

> The great revolutions – Marx argues – which took place in commerce with the geographical discoveries and speeded the development of merchant's capital, constitute one of the principal elements in furthering the transition from the feudal to capitalist mode of production
>
> MARX 1894: 331

since it accelerates the processes, already underway in Europe, of separating free labour from its objective conditions of existence (Marx 1857–1861a: 429–430).

The fall of European feudalism is then prepared in the mines of Latin America, whose precious metals reveal how the unconscious instruments of the Marxian *Weltgeschichte* are multiple and not entirely ascribed to Europe. Latin America is therefore presented as the reserve of that valuable exchange tool through which the history of capital spread worldwide: redrawing the hierarchy of social powers, Latin American gold and silver facilitate the transformation of commercial capital accumulated under the feudal mode of production into industrial capital. In this sense, 'the discovery of the gold and silver lands in America, the extirpation, enslavement and entombments in mines of the aboriginal population ... signalised the rosy dawn of the era of capitalist production' (Marx 1867a: 739): that is, it is a foundational moment of the primitive accumulation. Latin America is thus one of the earliest open-air laboratories of world history.

The mining of Latin American gold and silver holds a peculiar place in the book of the genesis of capitalism. It marks the history of the subcontinent, revealing at the same time how the capitalist world-system is based not on mutual exclusion but the interconnection between different temporalities of development. Notably, as gold in Europe and Asia fuels the spread of modern manufacturing, in Latin America, it determines the affirmation of an extractivist economic model that perpetuates 'semi-barbaric conditions' since 'its production does not require any development of the productive forces. On the contrary, nature here does most of the work'. Simple excavation thus brings to light an inexhaustible source of value, fuelled not only by the exploitation of the indigenous people but also by the very peculiarities of gold and, not least, by its rarity (Marx 1857–1861a: 111–115).

This is the colonial face of original accumulation as it manifests itself in the South of the world. European extractivism, through violence, plundering and the extermination of the Indios, erases the division of labour and the organization of the pre-Columbian production system, which, as we have seen, presents for Marx some traits of modernity. Without any nostalgic attitude, Marx sees in Peru and Mexico forms of communal property and production: 'the labourer has an objective existence independent from his labour'. He can be considered a 'proprietor' not as a free producer, but as much as 'he relates to the others as co-proprietors, as so many incarnations of the common property'. It is precisely this 'existence independent from labour' that must be swept away in order for the cycle of capital accumulation to fully and freely operate (Marx 1857–1861a: 399). The usurpation of territories and slavery are the specific forms of expropriation of producers, i.e., accumulation, that European capital applies to Latin America. Thus, 'treasures captured outside Europe by undisguised looting, enslavement, and murder, floated back to the mother country and were there turned into capital' (Marx 1867a: 741).

This surplus of violence that structures the social relations of production in Latin America responds to the need to dominate a mass of individuals who, having survived the annihilation of pre-Columbian civilizations or forced migration from Africa, are now under the yoke of imperfect absolutism, namely the disorganized and heterogeneous power of the Spanish empire. For Marx, this is the European face of 'oriental despotism': an agglomeration of provinces misgoverned by a state incapable of establishing shared interests

to form a cohesive society, in which cooperation between individuals is stabilized. Instead, viceroys and governors of the provinces exercise an arbitrary
power that is tolerated by the government of the capital 'so long as they take
off its shoulders the duty of doing something and spare it the trouble of regular administration' (Marx 1854b: 396). The Latin American reality then reveals
how 'Oriental despotism' is not as 'exotic' as one might imagine. On the contrary, it expresses a far more intricate web of powers that, ascending from society to the state, reveal themselves wherever the despotism of capital manifests
itself. Namely, the Spanish-style oriental despotism must guarantee in South
America the continuation of slave labour and its formal subsumption, without any need to support advanced socialization processes that base material
subordination on legal equality. As Marx maintains that 'the nature of capital
remains the same in its developed forms as in its undeveloped form' (Marx
1867a: 292), meaning the possibility of an uneven but no less cogent development of capitalism, despotism *sans phrase* is the overall organization of capital's power that ensures the coexistence and interconnection of such forms
within the world market.

Despotism enforces the domination of the past over the present. It thus
identifies

> a particular configuration of power in which forms and figures differing
> in temporality and geographic origin operate to block the processes of
> subjectification, that is, to inhibit the autonomous action of subjects
> standing in opposition to the history and anthropology of capital.
>
> RICCIARDI 2019: 199

As the value extracted from the Latin American continent travels through
the world market, that is the stage of Marx's *Weltgeschichte*, Latin American
peoples are despotically kept at its margin to prevent them from writing their
history. As they are subjected to the history of capital, Latin American people
cannot be outside of it in a Hegelian sense. If they were outside history, they
would be as alien to valorization's logic as caged within immutable anthropology. In Marx's reading, Latin American people appear more likely to be suspended in history than outside of it: their destiny seems to depend entirely on
the eternal return of the identical extraction of value. However, it is not a fixed
destiny. Suspension does not imply a static history but a history whose changes
evoke subject-formation and emancipation processes that, however, struggle
to come out from the despotic envelope that obstructs them.

The progressive overcoming of slavery during the Latin American 19th century confirms this. Nevertheless, capital can renounce slavery but cannot give

up its constitutive anachronism, because for its very logic, 'what capital appro-priates is not the worker, but his labour' (Marx 1857–1861a: 422): it, therefore, depends on a renewal of the productive relations imported from the *conquista-dores* in order to conceal the still despotic nature of the command it exercises over living labour. Thus, Marx observes, in mid-nineteenth-century Mexico, 'slavery is hidden under the form of peonage', that is a condition which 'by means of advances, repayable in labour, which is handed down from genera-tion to generation, not only the individual labourer, but his family, becomes *de facto* the property of other persons and their families'. This is a condition that indeed denies to the peon the status of 'untrammelled owner of his capacity for labour, i.e., of his person', so that he, rather than his workforce, is reduced to a commodity (Marx 1867a: 178). Since peonage reproduces the pattern of 'ordinary usury' – 'advancing of money against future labour' – the result is not the mere reinstatement of slavery as such but, as Marx states in a letter to Ludwig Kugelmann in October 1867, the creation of 'forced labour'. Marx refers to a labourer commanded by the debt contracted with the moneylender and transmitted from generation to generation. The debt ensures the availability of a lasting and ever blackmailable labour force even in a free-labour regime (Marx to Kugelmann 10/11/1867 in MECW 42: 442).

Peonage ended up, however, proving functional to the needs of reproduc-tion of capital within a sparsely populated territory such as Latin America. It indeed subjugated individuals to a double bind of dependence on both the owner and the means of production. In countries with wide availability of uncultivated land, the 'art of colonization' consists precisely in preventing a particular group of individuals from escaping the conditions imposed by the labour market, that is, the condition of constant dispossession over time (Marx 1857–1861a: 508). 'In densely peopled colonies the labourer, although free, is naturally dependent on the capitalist; in thinly peopled ones, the want of this natural dependence must be supplied by artificial restrictions' (Marx 1857–1861b: 212). In other words, peonage serves to avert the possibility that individuals, as far as they are free to move, may reappropriate the means of production, going to reverse the course of the primitive accumulation. This need is all the more felt in a territory such as Latin America, which, although no longer formally subject to a colonial regime, has not yet reached a degree of political organization such as to ensure the certainty and systematic nature of command and obedience relations. This power vacuum in the political realm is thus filled by the social power which the capitalist 'carries ... in his pocket' (Marx 1857–1861a: 94). In addition to peonage, the importation into Peru and Cuba of Chinese 'bonded emigrants', the coolies, who although formally free are the new slaves of the Latin American plantations, demonstrates that the old domination conveyed by slavery is then reintroduced in disguise into free labour (Marx 1857h: 235).

However, in the *Grundrisse*, Marx recognizes that the end of slavery produces the conditions to escape the history of capital at least partially. As the other side of the suspended history of Latin America, Marx presents the case of the Quashees, 'the free blacks of Jamaica' who work in the plantations, exploiting 'their acquired Christianity as a cover for (their) sardonic mood and indolence' in front of the planters. They 'regard loafing itself … as the real luxury article', showing that 'INDULGENCE and IDLENESS' are a constant threat hanging over capital when it introduces free labour. Marx then can only sneer at the indignation of the West Indian planter who, irritated by the freed blacks 'who give a damn about sugar and the fixed capital invested in the PLANTA-TIONS', indulges in nostalgic evocations of the *beaux temps* of slavery. The Quashees, Marx observes, 'have ceased to be slaves, not in order to become wage workers, but SELF-SUSTAINING PEASANTS, working for their own meagre consumption'.

The case of the Quashees, however, doesn't represent an out-of-time version of the idleness which marked the old natural community. Instead, their 'malicious pleasure and sardonic smiles when a planter goes to ruin' expresses their radical refusal of the dominance of 'capital as capital', which in their eyes produces wealth 'either through direct forced labour, slavery, or mediated forced labour, or wage labour' (Marx 1857–1861a: 251). In their reluctance to submit to the yoke of wage labour, Marx reads the emergence of a subject which, if he does not follow the organizational paths of the European industrial proletariat, nevertheless escapes the domination of capital and interrupts the process of valorization. It is that a conclusion all the more relevant if we consider that, in a letter to Engels in 1853, and then only a few years before the *Grundrisse*, Marx seems to share with Henry Carey the idea that the Quashees are 'barbarians', differently from the blacks of the United States that were considered 'capable of being emancipated'. (Marx to Engels 6/14/1853 in MECW 39: 346). Thus, what emerges from the suspended history of Latin America is, on the one hand, the formal subsumption to capital of relations of production deriving from a past that exerts its despotic weight over the present. However, on the other hand, a heterogeneous black proletariat sardonically uses those equally archaic production forms to realize a subversive self-valorization within the capitalist order.

Here then is 'the secret discovered in the new world by the political economy of the old world' (Marx 1867a: 760): capital can renounce to modern factories and civil law to valorise itself as capital, but vitally needs the radical expropriation of living labour, no matter how brutal and archaic this expropriation is. At the same time, living labour in Latin America demonstrates that it can evade the capitalistic order and be able to mock it without, however, being capable of triggering mass organizational processes. Nevertheless, any eventual effort to organize collective forms of resistance is flawed by a lack of societal development that the peculiar capitalist extraction of value in Latin America constantly hinders. As we shall see, this condition is reiterated even and especially at a time when former Latin American colonies attempted at emancipating themselves from European control.

3 Order and Anarchy: The 'Veritable Souloque' and the Old Usual 'Damned Rogues'

Even after the wars of independence, Latin America remained suspended predominately within the history of capital and its accumulation. Independence does not open spaces of liberation since it replicates the post-colonial version of ancient European despotism. It generates a field of tension between subjugation and subjectification, and it is unquestionable that, for Marx, it is the first pole of this relationship that is dominant in Latin America. The result is an insubstantial society, which continues to facilitate the processes of value extraction instead of local production.

Moreover, in Latin American areas, the post-colonial state comes to light as an administrative body lacking a link with the society it claims to represent. Thus, the lack of a consistent social structure projects onto the state. This deficiency had been already fought by what Marx calls the Spanish 'enlightened despotism' of the reformist chief minister of the Spanish monarchy Floridablanca who in 1787 emanates the *Instrucción Reservada*, in order to combine administrative centralization and submission of the different centres of power to shape a cohesive social order in the provinces of the Empire (Marx 1854b: 409). The Juntas that arise after the independence process claims a more vital centralized administrative organization with this exact purpose. However, they barely impose any authority in the magmatic Latin American social space as they confront an endemic social disintegration (Rudan 2009: 220). In this sense, the post-colonial state can be considered an 'outgrowth of society'. It reflects all the contradictions of an unfinished society, although it claims to rise above them (Marx 1880–1882: 329).

The story of Simón Bolívar as narrated in the late 1850s by Marx for *the New American Cyclopaedia* therefore provides an exemplary case. Bolívar was a member of the wealthy Creole aristocracy, los *mantuanos*, who 'were far more oppressive, for the lower classes, than the Spaniards themselves' (Scocozza

1983: 356). It is not surprising, then, that Marx reserves harsh judgments for the Libertador, whose Caesarist ambitions, military incompetence, and cowardice induce Marx to call him 'the Napoleon of the retreat' (Marx 1858e: 226). Because of the authoritarian temptations of a general who willingly gives in to flight in the face of the Spanish enemy, Latin America lies in a condition of constant anarchy.

A condition that Marx blames primarily on the indolent character of the Libertador, who in this respect does not differ from the more general character traits of Latin Americans:

> like most of his countrymen, he was averse to any prolonged exertion, and his dictatorship soon proved a military anarchy, leaving the most important affairs in the hands of favourites, who squandered the finances of the country, and then resorted to odious means to restore them.
>
> MARX 1858e: 221

The insubstantial political structure of the Bolivarian dictatorship is, on the one hand, made apparent by the undue influence granted to the creole elite that surrounds it. On the other hand, the native and the subordinated strata of Latin American 'people' reluctantly joined the armies of the Spanish Crown, whose paternalistic government, from their point of view, was nevertheless preferable to the ruthless domination of the *mantuanos*. Here the deceptive character of independence is revealed, one in which the liberation from colonial rule is merely a precondition for the conquest of political power by the Creole aristocracy.

Latin American independence does not awaken the same emancipatory forces agitating in Ireland against the British landlords but only reproduces the original state of anarchy of the continent. The early decolonization of the continent failed to generate a real bourgeois society in Latin America. On the contrary, the Bolivarian political experiment, in which openly dictatorial attempts are superimposed on a constitutional order of liberal inspiration, establishes an 'arbitrary power' that replicates the forms of the Spanish-style oriental despotism. In other words, the Bolivarian power is not merely authoritarian, but above all unstable and exhibited from the top of a State without any anchorage in a society where there is no original political order.

Once again, Latin America shows that despotism cannot be confined to the Oriental world since the overall logic of power under capitalist production is despotic. In a letter to Engels on February 14, 1858, Marx defines Bolívar as 'a veritable Soulouque' (Marx to Engels 2/14/1858 in MECW 40: 266), and it is well known that, at that time, behind the name of the Haitian dictator was

Napoleon III. The comparison with the French emperor highlights how the anachronistic configuration of the relationship between state and society in Latin America is consistent with the global needs of capital accumulation.

Bolívar is not only the 'Napoleon of the retreat' but also, we might say, the 'Bonaparte of the State'. Like *Napoléon le petit*, Bolívar seized power in a phase marked by unstable social and political conditions. As in France, Louis Bonaparte took advantage of the break-up in alliances between landed elites and industry; in a similar vein, Bolívar exploited the clash between the Spanish political elite and the Creole social elite to strengthen his power position. Both, however, prove incapable of reconstituting a stable organization of power. Therefore, the lucid analysis that Marx provides for the Bonapartist government can be applied to Bolivar. They both represent 'the strength of executive power made independent'.

Nevertheless, to make the executive power independent, they must break the political power of the upper classes. In any case, this is an illusory aspiration: Bonaparte, like Bolívar, bases his political power on the social power of the economic elite and 'by protecting its material power; he generates its political power anew' (Marx 1852a: 194). In both cases, there is a misplaced trust in the autonomy of the state, which is given a task it cannot accomplish: to rise autonomously above society, that is an assumption that Marx had already discarded in the *Contribution to the Critique of Hegel's Philosophy of Law* (Marx 1843). Thus, Bolívar, like Bonaparte, 'produces actual anarchy in the name of order, while at the same time stripping halo from the entire state machine, profanes it and makes it at once loathsome and ridiculous' (Marx 1852a: 197).

Again, under different guises, it is possible to find the Bolivarian 'anarchic state' in Marxian writings on Juarist Mexico, confirming a fundamental character of the Latin American territories political (dis)organization. The seizure of power by Benito Juárez at the end of the 1850s corresponds to the beginning of a rationalising restructuring of government. Juárez promoted a transition to a constitutional republic where the effectiveness of public power, abolition of peonage and substantial autonomy from European powers and the United States made Mexico a case of European-style modernization inspired by liberal principles. The new Mexican political order, combining modernity and autonomy, caused alarm among European powers which consider the Juarez's experiment as a threat to their hegemony. Therefore in 1861, by declaring the Mexican government insolvent because of the unpaid debts contracted with the Europeans, England, France and Spain joined a kind of 'Holy Alliance' of disorder to overthrow Juárez and install the puppet government of his place Maximilian of Habsburg. European capital is concerned with preserving the state of anarchy of Latin America. Indeed, Marx notes that the English press had never considered the Mexican government an 'institutionalized and organized' entity with which one could enter into negotiation. In reality, Lord Palmerston and Louis Bonaparte sought the occupation of Mexican ports and the collection of taxes on commercial transactions in place of legitimate government. As a result, it was easy for Marx to denounce European crypto-colonial policy's incoherence and highlight its machinations, aimed predominantly at undermining the precarious balance of power instituted by Juárez. The 'authoritative interference in behalf of order', as *The Times* dubbed it, for Marx, revealed the full extent of its fallacious nature: even this newspaper, famously described as the public voice of British imperial politics, recognized that 'there is a government in Mexico' (Marx 1861a: 74). Moreover, this was a government led by those same liberal and bourgeois forces that England had supported, while Spain and France allied themselves with the reactionary forces, including the Catholics. Despite diverging political attitudes, European powers nevertheless shared the same struggle against the emergence of an independent and stable government in Central America: falsely claiming to combat anarchy, the new 'Holy Alliance' among England, France and Spain sought to maintain disorder. 'The joint intervention', writes Marx,

> 'with no other avowed end, save the rescue of Mexico from anarchy, will produce just the opposite effect, weaken the constitutional government, strengthen the priestly party by a supply of Spanish and French bayonets, rekindle the embers of the civil war, and, instead of extinguishing it, restore anarchy in its full bloom'.
>
> MARX 1861a: 77

On the other hand, Marx considered the resistance of the Mexicans without real revolutionary expectations: above all, the Mexicans remain for him '*les derniers des hommes*' (Marx to Engels 11/20/1862 in MECW 41: 431). Nevertheless, the French defeats culminating in the deposition of Maximilian and his assassination represent the grotesque final act of the Bonapartist adventure: 'a truly classical epilogue – he wrote to Engels – to the farce of the lower Empire', which anticipated the defeat of Sedan (Marx to Engels 2/13/1863 in MECW 41: 453). Once again, Marx uses Latin America as a backdrop to shed light on the will to power of European capital. Latin America consequently emerges within the Marxian text to highlight the logic of the capitalist world-system, which presents a structurally hierarchical and uneven order: the anarchy prevailing in specific domains is functional to the extractive needs of the capitalist mode of production as a whole. In other words, the reproduction of capital does not require a bourgeois order in Latin America because, for its specific role in the world market, it is not supposed to develop production processes that can compete with the European powers. On the contrary, the incursions of European capital aim to extract value, mainly in the form of precious metals and inject it into circulation to support the production and reproduction of capital elsewhere. Such forced transfer of value is more easily realized in a territory marked by political anarchy and social disintegration.

Therefore, it becomes necessary for Latin America to accept the 'so-called natural destiny' that the capitalist system has reserved to ensure the order of the world market over time. Marx foreshadowed the same destiny in 1848 concerning the West Indies, that is, to supply raw materials to a European capital, the only 'authorized' guardian of the secret of valorization (Marx 1848d: 464). The history of capital then seems to claim its absolute power on Latin American destiny, without ever fully managing to make it 'natural'. The uprising of the formerly enslaved Jamaican Black people, whose earlier sneering indolence anticipates the open rebellion of 1865, reveals the impossibility of neutralising the field of tension between subjugation and subjectification that articulates Marxian history. The revolt was cruelly repressed, but, as Marx writes to Engels, the 'Jamaica BUTCHERIES' shows the inconsistencies and the 'hypocrisy' of the British liberal civilization, as 'True Englishman' is 'as bad as the Russians in every respect'. Thus, despite the famous remarks of Montesquieu on despotism, the 'Jamaica Butcheries' and, more generally, the British colonial rule reveal how despotism can operate even in a constitutional regime since those 'damned rogues' who rebelled against Palmerston's emissaries and European planters would enjoy 'ALL THE LIBERTIES OF AN ANGLO-SAXON CONSTITUTION'. *The Times*, from which Marx draws this last quotation, omits to report that in reality 'they enjoyed the liberty, amongst others, of having their hides taxed to raise money for PLANTERS to import COOLIES and thus depress their own labour market below the minimum'. Marx underlines that the 'Jamaica butcheries' occurred almost simultaneously with the 'Irish affair', i.e., the arrest in 1865 of numerous Fenian leaders and the suspension of habeas corpus. The sacred principles of the English Constitution were sacrificed as higher economic and political interests were at stake (Marx to Engels 11/20/1865 in MECW 42: 199). The despotic power of Downing Street thus appears to serve the more general despotism of capital.

In Marx's work, Latin America performs the narrative function of staging the *arcana imperii* of the capitalist mode of production and the global plots that constitute it. After the publication of the first book of *Capital* Marx's knowledge of the world's 'margins' deepen, yet his interest in Latin America declined. Nevertheless, the fact is that, for Marx, Latin America provides the point of departure to interrogate despotism of capital, but not the movements necessary to bring it down.

CHAPTER 10

The Colonial Lever and the Social Movement in General

Marx and Ireland

Luca Cobbe

It is difficult not to attribute the rise of Marx's interest in the Irish question to his partnership with Engels. As well as his personal links to the country,[1] Ireland was a constant interest in Engels' biography, as can be seen from his 1844 excursus on the Irish population in the Little Ireland neighbourhood of Manchester in *The Condition of the Working Class in England* and his unfinished *History of Ireland* that he began in 1870. Marx's first reference to Ireland and the Irish appears in an 1845 manuscript dedicated to Friedrich List's work, *Das nationale System der politischen Ökonomie* (1841). In this manuscript Ireland represents the extreme measure of poverty, the minimum level beyond which the condition of the agricultural worker cannot go (Marx 1845: 288). These references are rare, and animated by a rhetorical function, but it shows that from the start Ireland was a factor in a discourse referring not only to the theme of colonial rule but also to those of land rent and agricultural labour.

From 1848, he started making more frequent references to the country, concerning the debate that developed after the Polish insurrection of 1846. Even at this juncture, Ireland operates as a term of comparison. Although Marx's interest in the Polish political program is related to its double link with both the democratic and the agrarian question, he did not see the movement for Irish independence as having such a link. The *Repeal Movement* against the Act of Union of 1800, constituted around the figure of the Irish parliamentarian Daniel O'Connell, remains, in his opinion, 'mere political movement' (Marx 1853a: 505) because it proposes a model of national emancipation that does not attack the agrarian question. Even in the 1849 pamphlet *Wage Labour and Capital*, which coincides chronologically with the end of the revolutionary cycle of 1848, the reference to Ireland falls within a discursive context marked by the national question and the relationship between class relations and the revolutionary movements in Ireland, Poland, Italy and Hungary.

---

1 The lifelong partner of Friedrich Engels, Mary Burns, was a working-class Irish woman.

At this point, Marx and Engels noticed the presence of relations of oppression that not only crossed society but also affected relations between states. Their affirmation that 'a nation cannot become free and at the same time continue to oppress other nations' (Marx and Engels 1847: 389) demonstrates that they had begun to detect the presence of a global space made up of relations of domination and differences between states, within the larger issue of the democratic revolution of the state.

The reflection on the world market – which had already found important declinations in *The German Ideology*, at a level of philosophical abstraction appropriate to its polemical references – becomes more concrete in their writings, henceforth. In contrast to the apparent 'proletarian cosmopolitanism' of some passages of the *Manifesto*, at this time Marx begins to reflect on the global scale of the division of labour and the capitalist mode of production, which exceeds the national dimension, not erasing it but rechanneling it within a well-defined hierarchy (Espinoza Pino and Mezzadra 2018). England played a decisive role in this hierarchy, for it represents 'the country that turns whole nations into its proletarians, that takes the whole world within in its immense embrace' (Marx 1849a: 214). Marx's attention to England, however, is not motivated solely by its more advanced degree of industrial development. The dominance that it exerts on the world market not only re-articulates the timing of revolution (Marx 1850a: 117, 134), but also makes clear the limits of thinking the revolutionary process on a national scale, since England remains the rock on which the waves of the revolution are destined to break (Marx 1849a: 214). Thus, if England dictates the timing of the development of capitalism on a global scale, the Chartist movement shows the action of an 'organized perspective of power' (Ricciardi 2019: 121) capable of re-signifying the process of democratic emancipation under the sign of class struggle. The presence of this double level of analysis of objective and subjective power establishes a kind of geography of emancipation in Marx's thought corresponding to a precise hierarchy on the basis of which the various movements of national liberation are subordinate to the socialist revolution in England. Thus, he argues that 'Poland must be liberated not in Poland, but in England' (Marx and Engels 1847: 389), and he could have said the same of Ireland.

Ireland represents the symbol of the domination of the forces of the past – land rent and aristocracy – over the forces of progress, democracy and revolution. Marx at this stage cannot but agree with Ricardo, considering the monopoly of land a remnant of the ancient regime destined to die out along with the aristocracy, 'a relation quite superfluous in, and incoherent with the whole frame-work of modern production' that sets the interests of landowners in opposition 'to the interest of all other classes of modern society' (Marx

1853c: 160–161). He credits Ricardo with revealing an 'unpleasant truth', namely, the fact that 'land rent is nothing but the economic expression of a life-and-death struggle of the industrial bourgeois against the landowners' (Marx 1845: 287, 272).

However, unlike the English classical economist, Marx saw the violent ways in which this process of 'improvement' had taken shape. In Ireland, it gave rise to a veritable 'war of extermination' (Marx 1858b: 137) that relentlessly produced impoverishment and forced emigration. But Marx considered this process to be functional to 'the breaking down of the antiquated system of society'. 'The wheel of improvement' was in fact crushing 'the most stationary class in England', the aristocracy. He sees a 'silent revolution' playing out before his eyes, 'which takes no more notice of the human existences it breaks down than an earthquake regards the houses it subverts'. This was a real 'revolution of capital', a transformation of social relations, in which 'classes and races, too weak to master the new conditions of life, must give way' (Marx 1853b: 530–531).

The civilization brought about by capital is therefore affirmed as a portentous process of the subversion of social conditions rather than as a linear transition. And it can be called a revolution precisely for this reason. However, although Marx read the process of social transformation brought about in Ireland by English capital as a replica of the ejection of small peasants from the English countryside a couple of centuries earlier, he also emphasized differences in the Irish situation, not only in terms of its temporal delay but also in the ways in which the process took shape.

Unlike in England, the capitalist transformation of agricultural production in Ireland did not establish itself by producing the figures of the rentier, the agricultural proletarian, and the capitalist from the past figures of the lord, the serf and the tenant. For Ireland, this 'supposition is quite fictitious'. The system of *rack-renting*,[2] the constant expropriation that 'absentee landlords' exerted against not only the labour but also the capital invested by the tenant, prevented the latter from accumulating the wealth necessary to become a capitalist. Thus, the process of social polarization between the capitalist and the proletariat, which should have progressively rendered the figure of the aristocratic rentier obsolete, remained suspended in a situation where 'on the one side you have there a small class of land monopolists, on the other, a very large class of tenants with very petty fortunes' (Marx 1853c: 158).

In the Marxian imagination, the Irish tenant represented the lowest level of degradation that the agricultural worker subjected to capitalist transformation

---

2   Rent extraction system that relied on a speculative chain of subleases.

could reach (Marx 1850a: 121). The dynamic of impoverishment that acted as a counterbalance to the original process of accumulation seemed to lack that movement of the production of antagonistic social figures that was implicit in the process of proletarianization. What was missing in Ireland was not so much the social condition of poverty but the possibility of a political subjectivity that came into existence in the clash with the capitalist.

In several articles published in the *New York Daily Tribune* between 1853 and 1855, Marx discussed a series of measures discussed in Parliament at the time: the *Landlord and Tenant Bill*; the *Leasing Powers Bill*; and the *Tenant's Improvement Compensation Bill*. He argued that these measures would have improved the condition of the Irish tenant, accomplishing that 'silent revolution' which had previously been suspended by the obstructionism of the landed aristocracy. Under the social pressure of Irish emigration of enormous proportions, Irish members of Parliament had found themselves 'compelled to do what O'Connell had always avoided and refused to do, that is, to explore the real cause of the Irish malady and to make landed property relations and their reform the election slogan' (Marx 1855a: 79). Mass emigration to England, America, and Australia, together with the famine of 1846 and the military occupation with which England had responded to the Irish insurrection of 1848, had helped create the conditions for a veritable 'Anglo-Saxon revolution' in the course of which *'the Irish agricultural system is being replaced by the English system, the system of small tenures by big tenures, and the modern capitalist* is taking the place of the old landowner' (Marx 1855a: 80). These words reveal Marx's impatience with the process of transformation of Irish society that would affect the possibilities for the development of class struggle. They also reveal his 'modernist' conception (Berman 1988: 87–129) of the relationship between revolution and the end of colonial rule that stopped at understanding the development of capitalism as a simultaneous process of democratic movement, the development of productive forces and the anticolonialism of the *free trade movement* (MacDonagh 1962). By calling the revolution 'Anglo-Saxon', Marx wanted to emphasize a process of homologation of society rather than highlighting the political dynamic of military and police conquest and the oppression of an alien territory. The use of this term also shows how Marx inserted the contemporary form of English domination of Ireland into a 'history' of colonial rule that followed a common thread despite changing over time. In other words, Marx identified a kind of continuity between the centuries, demonstrating similarities between his present and 16th and 17th century colonial attempts to impose an English society on Ireland through brutal means such as population transfers, forced conversions to Anglicanism and discriminatory policies against the Catholic religion. In the colonial relationship he identifies a wider 'transmutation' of social relations, a term used a couple of centuries earlier by William Petty (McCormick 2009: 168—208). Although in his day this process mainly concerned the organization of agricultural production and did not include the operations of 'ethnic substitution' used in previous centuries, the logic of the colonial relationship revealed its identity as a process of assimilation and homogenization, which assumed the 'Anglo-Saxon type' as its default outcome. This action, however, no longer coincided with the reintroduction in Ireland of the entire set of English political and social institutions, but in the replication of the conditions that had allowed England to progress, namely in the tripartition of social labour between landlords, tenant capitalists, and landless wage labour (Gray 2002: 142).

On a purely political level, however, Ireland increasingly embodied a space of composition and mediation between the conflicting interests of the English ruling classes, and therefore played a central role in the tensions that crossed the Empire. Marx points out that the reason for the repression that followed the insurrection of 1848 was not so much 'the maintenance of English supremacy in Ireland, but rather the prolongation of the Whig regime in England' (Marx 1855b: 386). The tension generated by the clash between the 'counter-revolution' of the landed aristocracy and the 'silent revolution' of free trade, which was at constant risk of intensifying and producing social movements not aligned with capitalist development, could be suspended by transferring it onto Irish soil. Sacrificed at the altar of compensation between land rent and industrial profit, Ireland thus became the element that allowed the anachronistic English constitution to reconcile Burkean transformation with tradition. It became progressively clear to Marx that the form of political power no longer automatically responded to transformations in social power. Indeed, all proposals for reform relating to Ireland were dead letters due to their obstruction by the landowning aristocracy in the House of Lords, but also thanks to the government's clever use of the system of patronage against Irish MPs. For Marx, the 'landlord rebellion in Great Britain' and their threat to break their feudal promise of loyalty to the Crown represented a 'monstrous anachronism' out of joint with the advancing forces of progress (Marx 1853d: 251).

Faced with the *débâcle* of the 'Irish brigade', the hypocrisy of a nationalism incapable of taking control of the land issue had become evident. Yet something was stirring in those years. However, in January 1859, writing for the *New York Daily Tribune* about the news spread by the English press and government about unrest in Ireland and the proliferation of revolutionary secret sects, Marx seemed to be unaware that the Irish Republican Brotherhood had been founded in Dublin a little less than a year earlier.[3] But it wasn't long until the activities of the secret organization became of extreme interest to him.

Dubbed 'the Fenians' (from Fionn mac Cumhaill, the warrior hero of Irish mythology), these revolutionaries aimed to overthrow English rule and establish a republic. Abandoning the politics of alliance with other social classes of which O'Connell had been the greatest champion and criticizing as middle class the emancipation of Catholics when separated from the cause of national independence, the Fenians represented one of the chief threats to the English government throughout the 1860s (Berresford Ellis 1972: 130–134).

Marx saw in the birth and development of the Fenian movement the effect of a break capable of redefining the entire history of English domination over Ireland. In a letter to Engels on 30th November 1867, he writes:

> What the English do not yet realize, is that since 1846 the economic content and hence the political purpose of English rule in Ireland as well has entered an entirely new phase, and that for that very reason FENIANISM is characterized by socialist (in the negative sense, as directed against the APPROPRIATION of the SOIL) leanings and as a LOWER ORDERS MOVEMENT.

To Marx in the late 1860s it appeared to be 'absurd' to consider English rule in Ireland as unvaried over time (Marx to Engels 11/30/1867 in MECW 42: 486).

The reference to the Fenian 'break' shows that Marx's aim was not simply to develop a clearer understanding of the processes of political domination and their interaction with the dynamics of the constitution and expansion of capital as a social relation. He also wanted to bring to light the capacity of certain movements of insubordination to open cracks in the temporality of the relations of domination, giving rise to particular historical conjunctures in which the reproduction of a social order could be radically challenged and therefore reconstructed on new bases.

The Fenian question was also one of the main issues guiding the internal and external political struggle of the International Working Men's Association. Marx paid close attention to the vicissitudes of the Fenians, to their arrests, escapes and reprisals against British soldiers on both sides of the Atlantic. However, his interest was not accompanied by confidence in their leaders. In a letter to Engels, Marx described the Fenian leader James Stephen's entry in the

---

3   March 17, 1858.

International as 'one of our more dubious acquisitions' (Marx to Engels 12/17/1866 in MECW 42: 338).

In December 1867 Marx was preparing a speech on the Irish Question to be delivered at the *Deutscher Bildungsverein Fuer Arbeiter* in London on the 16th of that month. A few days earlier three Fenian leaders, William Allen, Michael O'Brien and Michael Larkin, had been publicly hanged for killing an English policeman during a jailbreak in Manchester. Marx described the demonstrations that had spread through the main English cities to support the liberation of the prisoners as 'tempestuous' (Marx to Engels 11/7/1867 in MECW 42: 464). What struck him was not so much the Fenian movement itself – as he confessed to Engels, he was often forced to act diplomatically with them, omitting to voice some of his judgments that might have compromised their nascent relations (Marx to Engels 11/28/1867 in MECW 42: 478) – but the fact that 'the business is boiling up in the intelligent section of the WORKING CLASS here' (Marx to Engels 11/7/1867 in MECW 42: 464).

In particular, Marx was interested in delineating the specificity of the current regime of domination with respect to the past and its impact on 'a few points about the character of those who are now called the Irish people' (Marx 1867b: 195). This difference had to do with the fact that oppression 'since 1846, though less barbarian in form, has been in effect destructive, leaving no alternative but Ireland's voluntary emancipation by England or life-and-death struggle' (Marx 1867b: 194).

Beyond identifying the political objective, to which we will return, the notes Marx prepared for his speech portrayed colonialism as a dynamic process (Slater and McDonough 2008). While he was interested in highlighting the specific differences between the colonial regime that began in 1846 and its earlier incarnations, his analysis showed how the colonial relationship evolved through steps that were not always dictated by English decisions, but often by Irish opposition and resistance to their rule. Marx's innovative re-writing of history has often been emphasized, and his response to the Irish question was no exception. For him, going back in history meant not so much reconstructing an evolutionary sequence of stages, but rather engaging in a re-montage (Rancière 1996: 54), that is, establishing another criterion of articulation between historical events, starting from ruptures and those 'non-coincidences' between subjective and structural movements that manifest themselves in the form of anticipations or persistence.

This also explains why Marx saw the American Revolution as 'the first turning-point in Irish history' (Marx 1867b: 198). It was both a break that forced a reconfiguration of power relations between states in the global market and represented the possibility that these relations could be challenged.

Studying the period from the American Revolution to the Union of 1801, Marx changed his earlier opinion on the Irish revolutionary and independence movement that led to the failed insurrection of 1798. Contrary to his 1867 notes, he now attributed this failure to the fact that 'FROM A REVOLUTIONARY STANDPOINT, *the Irish were too far advanced for the* ENGLISH KING AND CHURCH MOB' (Marx to Engels 12/10/1869 in MECW 43: 398). In the experiences of the Volunteers and later of the United Irishmen Marx recognized the development of a point of view on power that was not at all in sync with the development of the productive forces. They deprived the Irish independence movement of its merely political character to give it a social one, while displaying a never-before-seen deliberative capacity and articulating a *pressure from without* on Parliament that would not be seen in England until the Chartist experience (Marx 1869b).

The expression 'from a revolutionary standpoint' clearly shows that Marx does not fix the subjective processes of insubordination to a particular social configuration, or to a specific mode of production or organization of labour. The Fenians, as well as their predecessors the United Irishmen were interesting to Marx because they demonstrated the presence of a class movement that contested certain relations of domination and political subjugation. In different historical periods the Volunteers, the United Irishmen and the Fenians established the 'same' conjuncture, namely the possibility of overthrowing certain regimes of subjugation because they were emancipated from an independentist tradition in which the protagonists had always been the (Irish) aristocracy and middle classes.

Thus, *character* (that of a people) becomes the concept through which Marx investigates the political stratification of class behaviors and not simply the anthropological projection of certain relations of domination and production in the constitution of social customs.

However, emphasizing the presence of a subjective level in history does not mean divesting analysis of its structural dynamics. The Union of 1801 led to the disappearance of all Irish factories. This was the period in which the *rack-rent system* was established. As has already been pointed out, the 'indirect' domination by the *absentee* English landed aristocracy represented a profound historical break with respect to previous phases. But it is with the famine of 1846 that the true contemporary phase of the colonial relationship opened up. Leaving a million people dead and leading to the emigration of two million people within ten years, the famine transformed Irish society from top to bottom. This process soon became a 'conscious and deliberate system' (Marx 1867b: 201) with the abolition of the Corn Laws and the passing of the Encumbered Estates Act of 1853. These measures led to a fall in grain prices and rendered smallholders unable to pay rents but also provided the possibility of selling mortgaged properties, thus allowing the incorporation of small farms into large estates and bringing about the disruption of the modes of subsistence that up until then had ensured the reproduction of this particular society.

Once again, the global extension of the market was decisive in prescribing the development pathways of specific local economies. The development of the wool industry in England and the rise in the price of meat, which took place in parallel with the deprivation of the domestic market to which Ireland was subjected by the Act of Union, were intentionally aimed at 'clearing the estates of Ireland'. While this immediately led to the fact that 'over 1.100.000 people have been replaced by 9.600.000 sheep' (Marx 1867c: 318), in the long run it 'rivet[ed] the labourer to capital' (Marx 1867a: 639) by making a tabula rasa of the previous mode of subsistence in such a way that money, and thus exchange, became the only means of access to subsistence goods and so to the possibility of reproduction (Perelman 2000: 14).

Marx dismisses the idea of colonialism 'in general', showing it to be a kind of replica of the method of political economy, a rational abstraction that highlights the elements common to the various historical phases, and in so doing casts into shadow those differences that characterize its repetition as a relationship of domination (Hall 2003).

It is precisely because each colonial regime had a historical specificity that their differences must be read as products of historical relations that can only be fully understood within those relations. That is, Marx argues that it is not possible to explain colonialism by abstracting it from other social relations of domination, in particular economic relations, although neither should it be explained by reducing it exclusively to economic relations. There is no necessary relation between the development of capitalist relations, the structuring of the colonial relationship and revolutionary acceleration. Ireland's so-called economic backwardness was thus revealed as the effect of particular conjunctures of struggle and repression, of emancipation and domination (Marx 1867b: 199–201), rather than the effect of failed or delayed development. It is thus necessary to understand how the relationship of colonial domination is radically re-organized and re-articulated by the new capitalist mode of production in order to grasp the conjunctural elements in which ruptures, interruptions, and accelerations can occur.

'But Ireland is at present only an agricultural district of England, marked off by a wide channel from the country to which it yields corn, wool, cattle, industrial and military recruits' (Marx 1867a: 694). This is how Marx, in *Capital*, summarizes the status of Ireland in the colonial relationship of his time.

In his battle with classical political economy, Marx realized that for the latter, Ireland was not only a problem of a practical order but represented a testbed on which to legitimize the naturalness of its capitalist laws. Referring to Ireland as the promised land of the 'principle of population' (Marx 1867a: 695) he alluded to classical political economy's obsession with the integration of the Irish exception within the contemporary 'history' of the capitalist mode of production (Boylan and Foley 1992; Lloyd 2010).

The reference to the Malthusian population principle helps Marx to bring to light his hidden epistemic foundation, namely 'the law of capitalist production': the ordered 'correlation between accumulation of capital and rate of wages' that constitutes 'the relation between the unpaid and the paid labour of the same labouring population' (Marx 1867a: 615–616).

It is not the case that the relationship between population and overpopulation is natural, despite what political economy claims. It is created by capitalist accumulation, that is constantly producing its own remnants in the form of a surplus worker population. 'An abstract law of population exists for plants and animals only, and only in so far as man has not interfered with them' (Marx 1867a: 626). To denounce the absence of history in the Malthusian and post-Malthusian narratives of the principle of equilibrium between population and resources is to recognize 'in overpopulation ... a necessity of modern industry' (Marx 1867a: 628), namely that it is capital that constantly produces a part of the population in surplus.

Marx understands that capitalism is a historical social system traversed by interruptions, blockages, discontinuities, ruptures, and contradictions, thus a system that has limits imposed by the historical conditions of its functioning (Hall 2003: 126). For Marx, Ireland shows the historicity of capitalism, namely the fact that its 'material constitution' – the general law of capitalist accumulation – must be constantly safeguarded even with exceptional and violent measures (Marx 1867a: 634).

This is especially evident in the chapters on ground rent, in which he refines his understanding of how capital constantly needs to be synchronized with respect to the other two elements of the 'trinitarian formula', ground rent and wage labour, which unlike capital have a history that predates the current economic formation of society. Indeed, 'the form of landed property with which the incipient capitalist mode of production is confronted does not suit it' (Marx 1894: 611). Only when the process is complete, ground rent 'receives its purely economic form by discarding all its former political and social embellishments and associations' (Marx 1894: 612). However, the process to which Marx refers is purely internal to the logic of capital. Its historical realization therefore comes up against certain temporal discordances that can arise in and between the economic, political and cultural spheres. It is no coincidence that in Ireland this process presented itself with a particularity, namely the fact that 'the manner of expressing landed property in the capitalist mode of production, formally exists without the existence of the capitalist mode of production itself' (Marx 1894: 619). In Ireland, therefore, the violence and political command of the state are fundamental in establishing the social and political conditions for the temporality of capital to coincide with the temporality of rent.

Understanding the temporal register that allows for the coexistence of capitalism and colonial rule is not relevant to placing Ireland's development on a different pathway than England's. Marx recognizes the normality of the Irish historical exception. He thus sees the reconstruction of its historical dimension as the only key to unveiling the normativity of a present that tends to reproduce itself as an ordered combination of different temporalities. From this point of view, ground rent no longer represents the symbol of a vanishing past, but becomes relevant in the present, making it possible to read the relationship between Ireland and England as an articulation between different temporalities within the same social formation and the same mode of production. The mode of production thus represents the structural order through which a particular regime of historicity is articulated, that is, the way in which society deals with its past and experience temporality (Hartog 2015).

Establishing its power through labour commanded by the capitalist and money, capital imposed its temporal register on the Irish worker in terms of a deadly present that envisaged no future improvement. No wonder then, that 'a sombre discontent runs through the ranks of this class, that they long for the return of the past, loathe the present, despair of the future, give themselves up "to the evil influence of agitators," and have only one fixed idea, to emigrate to America' (Marx 1867a: 700), thus projecting into another space the future which was denied to them in their homeland.

Their desire for a return to the past, rather than being the effect of backward thinking and limited intelligence, instead expressed the awareness of the functioning of the law of capitalist development. Indeed, the condition of agricultural workers in Ireland lacked 'the belief of anything better' (Marx 1894: 625), in this sense a situation worse even than that of the slaves in the plantations of the southern United States, who at least could hope to become free. Irish ground rent thus acquires its present status in the relationship of capital as an anachronism, as the contemporaneity of a past in the present that seems to belong to it only as its final destination. And it is precisely as an anachronism that it affects the behaviour of Ireland's rural proletariat.

The temporal dynamic present in Marx's reflection on Ireland shows that, contrary to the rhetoric of classical political economy, the Irish could not be considered as an 'outside' that were waiting – more or less recalcitrantly – to be conquered by capital. For the Irish difference arose in the encounter with capital and colonial rule. Thus, for Marx, it was not a question of emphasizing the 'naturally' irreducible character of the Irish, but rather of putting their insubordinate character in communication with that of the English working class. If the capitalist mode of production revealed itself as a process of articulation between different modes of exploitation and reproduction, then posing the problem of revolution coincides with the question of how to produce a connection capable of interrupting this historical articulation.

As Marx wrote to Engels in 1869:

> For a long time I believed it would be possible to overthrow the Irish regime by ENGLISH WORKING CLASS ASCENDANCY. I always took this viewpoint in the New-York Tribune. Deeper study has now convinced me of the opposite. The English WORKING CLASS will never accomplish anything BEFORE IT HAS GOT RID OF IRELAND. The lever must be applied in Ireland. This is why the Irish QUESTION is so important for the social movement in general.
>
> MARX to ENGELS 12/10/1869 in MECW 43: 398

This is a radical change in perspective from earlier Marxian judgments on colonialism (Mohri 1970: 34): Ireland represented a principal battleground for the social movement in general and should no longer be considered simply as a national issue subordinate to the more important class struggle in 'the metropolis of capital'.

However, even at this stage Marx's political subject remains the English working class. It is therefore vital to understand what it was that intervened in Marx's understanding of the relationship between the English working class and the Irish question.

A few years earlier, on 2nd November 1867, Marx had emphasized in a letter to Engels that the goal of his reconstruction of the history of English rule in Ireland was 'to incite the English workers to demonstrate in favour of FENIANISM', adding: 'I once believed the separation of Ireland from England to be impossible. I now regard it as inevitable' (Marx to Engels 11/2/1876 in MECW 42: 460). Still in the 1870s, England represented in Marx's eyes 'the metropolis of capital'. This centrality seems, however, to have been complicated by the continuous processes of the re-definition of the shapes of the capital relationship and of class behavior set in motion by the global dynamics of capitalism at the time.

What is first redefined is the system of levers for triggering revolutionary processes. His new understanding of the relevance of 'aristocratic' anachronism in the political governance of the capital relation leads Marx to reposition the Irish question with respect to the Irish workers' movement.

> If England is the BULWARK of landlordism and European capitalism ... Ireland is the BULWARK of English landlordism. If it fell in Ireland, it would fall in England. In Ireland this is a hundred times easier because *the economic struggle there is concentrated exclusively on landed property*, because this struggle is at the same time *national*, and because the people there are more revolutionary and more exasperated than in England.
>
> MARX 1870a: 119

Ireland thus becomes the *bulwark* of the *bulwark*, the lever through which other levers can be activated, accelerating the global revolutionary process (Rodden 2008: 610).

Something clearly continues to shift in Marx's understanding of revolution. The changes in his understanding of the leverage associated with Ireland are important to analyse, since they point to a wider continuous shift in his understanding of the revolution. The term 'lever' is used to describe the external pressure put on the immanent dialectic between the productive forces and the relations of production. It means highlighting how the processes of articulation between the different modes of the extraction of surplus value act as different fulcrums from which it would be possible to apply levers. Although he argued that England remained 'the only country where the class struggle and the organization of the working class by the *TRADES UNIONS* have acquired a certain degree of maturity and universality', the shift in Marx's attention towards Ireland and the Fenian movement revealed that he had changed his opinion on the English working-class movement. The English, despite possessing 'all the *material* necessary for the social revolution', lacked '*the spirit of generalization* and *revolutionary ardour*' (Marx 1870a: 118). It is not clear exactly what Marx meant by the spirit of generalization; however, it is evident that he believed their political relevance could no longer be derived simply from their being at a more advanced position along the line of progress. The global movements set in motion by capitalism had complicated the political work of the workers' movement by redefining its fundamental social relation and consequently the possibilities of its attack on capital.

In the second half of the 19th century, the Irish represented about a third of the industrial working class employed in England. What Marx wanted to highlight was not so much the worsening of working-class conditions produced by this transformation of the composition of living labour, but how this changed composition affected workers' behaviour.

> In *all the big industrial centres in England* there is profound antagonism between the Irish proletarian and the English proletarian. The average English worker hates the Irish worker as a competitor who lowers wages and the *STANDARD OF LIFE*. He feels national and religious antipathies for him. He regards him somewhat like the *POOR WHITES* of the Southern States of North America regarded black slaves.

The synchronization between different temporalities carried out by capital took the form of a process of division and at the same time the imposition of a dynamic of competition within the labour market. This prevented 'the revolutionary fire of the Celtic worker' from merging 'with the solid but slow nature of the Anglo-Saxon worker' (Marx 1870a: 120).

National antagonism was clearly one of the reasons for the division that ran through the working class in England. With respect to the Fenian explosion at Clerkenwell, in which numerous English people lost their lives and which Marx judged to be 'a great folly', his concern was that 'the London masses, who have shown much sympathy for Ireland, will be enraged by it and driven into the arms of the government party' (Marx to Engels 12/14/1867 in MECW 42: 501; Newsinger 1982). The relevance assigned by Marx to the Irish question within the International, the diplomatic position to which he was forced in relation to the Fenians, and the obstinacy with which he tried to encourage the English trades unions to adopt a position favourable to the Repeal of the Union of 1801 testified to how central it was for him to keep the English and Irish working classes united.

But Marx also emphasized the role that the Irish colony, and the other dependencies of the Empire, played in what has been called a kind of 'domestication' of the English proletariat (Lim 1992: 173). In a letter to Meyer and Vogt in 1870, Marx stated that, with respect to the Irish, the English worker 'feels himself to be a member of the *ruling nation* and, therefore, makes himself a tool of his aristocrats and capitalists *against Ireland*, thus strengthening their domination *over himself*' (Marx to Meyer and Vogt, 4/9/1870, in MECW 43: 474). Beyond this clash of nationalisms, Marx recognized how Irish rent 'returned to the metropolis' and thus affected the social relationship between capital and labour, producing segmentations in the working class according to different nationalities, wages and skills (Gray 1990). No longer destined to represent solely the portion of total value that remunerates the landowning class, ground rent slotted into the relationship between capital and labour by, on the one hand, establishing those hierarchies necessary for its governance, and on the other, by defusing the political potential of the struggle over wages through the progressive institutionalization of Trade Unions and government concertation (Stedman Jones 1984: 126). Ground rent, indissolubly linked in that phase to the colonial dimension of English capital, thus represented a compensating factor that made it possible to neutralize those social movements activated by the growth of capitalism.

Marx is evidently aware of the difficulty of establishing working class politics within a context constantly redefined by global dynamics. He did not believe the capital relation arranged the different forms of subjugation and exploitation into a progressive scale (Ricciardi 2019: 187). Since capital operates as a synchronizer, and therefore valorizer, of these different forms of exploitation and subjugation, its disruption had to be realized through a connection between the different temporalities expressed in the processes of insubordination. Thus, the disruption of the complex regime of historicity – the temporal articulations of different forms of subjugation – that characterized the British imperial space could not be thought of in a nationalist way. Dealing with the political separation between Ireland and England, Marx stated that this would immediately lead to a social revolution in Ireland, 'though in outmoded forms' (Marx 1870a: 120). If what was considered backward or archaic became the element that could allow the future – as revolution – to invade the present, then this meant taking a distance from a logic of the time of revolution imagined in progressive terms. Political disruptions introduce associations of prior pasts into the contemporary context that jar with the presumed stability of normative social time (Harootunian 2015: 23). Furthermore, thinking about the combination in the present of these different temporal registers of revolution means recognizing that the global dimension appears in society in the form of processes of decomposition that impose the need for 'generalization'. In the face of these difficulties, Marx identified the General Council of the International as the instrument that could 'thus accelerate the truly revolutionary movement in this country, and consequently *everywhere*' (Marx 1870a: 119). In the same way as the state functioned as a placeholder of capital to produce the historical conditions of its domination (Harootunian 2015: 66), the General Council of the International thus provisionally seemed to represent that lever necessary for workers' uprising on a global scale, a political lever that was external to the pure economic dynamics proper to the relationship between the forces and relations of production.

CHAPTER 11

The French Revolutions and the Meaning of Politics

Marx and France

Federico Tomasello

This chapter investigates the way in which the interpretation of the political, social, and intellectual history of revolutionary and post-revolutionary France shaped Marx's thought in the decade 1842–1852. Throughout this first phase of his theory's development, Marx focused on the French context to address a specific topic: the status of politics in the modern age. I therefore propose the expression 'the French question' to designate the way in which, in the decade under investigation, Marx tackled the issue of politics, developed a critique of it as an abstract sphere separate from concrete, material life, and ultimately advanced a different interpretation of the essence of politics, centred on the notion of class struggle. In order to trace this development, I will set out by analysing the first 'critique of politics' that this author formulated in 1843–1844 by interpreting the significance and destiny of the French Revolution (§ 1). I will then employ the expression 'Parisian moment' to describe Marx's encounter with the social and working-class context of Paris and the development of his critical engagement with French socialism, which revolved around the understanding of class political action and revolutionary initiative (§ 2). After that, I will consider Marx's reception and development of the concept of class as formulated by bourgeois liberal historians in France, and the way in which this notion was used to interpret the 1848 revolution in France and the subsequent coup by Louis Bonaparte (§ 3). What will emerge from this discussion is primarily the role played by making reference to the French Revolution as a means to interpret all the major events that Marx found himself facing in the decade under investigation. Therefore, I will end by addressing the development of Marx's interpretations of the great Revolution of 1789 in order to show how they reflect certain tensions and antinomies that are typical of this thinker's way of envisaging the very notion of politics (§ 4).

1   Kreuznach's France and the Critique of Politics

'Kant's philosophy must be rightly regarded as the German theory of the French revolution', Marx wrote in the *Rheinische Zeitung für Politik* in August 1842 (Marx 1842b: 206). This passage already reflects the influence of the motif of the '*European Triarchy*', which constitutes a crucial lens for understanding how Marxian theory incorporated and developed a reference to France as the defining aspect of a broader vision. In other words, the overall Marxian framework appears to be shaped by a reading of *Die Europäische Triarchie* (1841), in which Moses Hess – co-editor-in-chief of the *Rheinische Zeitung* and later a contributor to the German French Annals – aimed to re-establish Hegelian philosophy from a revolutionary European perspective. He pointed to Britain as the country in which economic development had made social contradictions most evident, and hence the revolution most imminent, after Germany had paved the way for spiritual liberation through the Reformation and philosophy, and France for political and social liberation through the great Revolution. Marx fully draws upon this perspective by adopting the idea of a sort of *division of tasks* in the process of emancipation between the British, German, and French peoples, envisaging the French as the exponents of *true politics*. On the basis of this theoretical framework, Marx turns the revolutionary and post-revolutionary history of France into a fundamental point of reference that informs his analysis throughout the decade 1842–1852, particularly as regards its quintessentially political contents.

We can detect this perspective in the manuscript which Marx drafted in Kreuznach in the summer of 1843 to formulate a critique of the Hegelian philosophy of public law:

> Since in modern times the idea of the state could not appear except in the abstraction of the *merely* political state or the *abstraction of civil society from itself*, from its actual condition, it is a merit of the French to have defined, produced this abstract actuality, and in so doing to have produced the *political* principle itself.
>
> MARX 1843: 13

We must therefore set out from this idea of France as the cradle – or 'midwife', to use the famous Marxian metaphor – of modern politics. By 'producing' the abstract state, the 'modern French' have isolated the '*political* principle', and Marx's analysis in 1843 appears to be marked by a constant tendency to define the content of this principle by investigating the French Revolution's political significance (Abensour 1997). While criticizing its outcomes, this manuscript envisages the abstraction of the political state as a historical necessity that France has had the 'merit' of affirming, and which must now be pushed beyond its formal limits. This approach coincides with the development of a *radical-democratic* perspective whereby Marx sets both the Hegelian conception of the constitutional state and the egoistic individualism of modern civil society, founded on private property, in contrast with democracy as 'a relation that is not *merely representative but actually exists*' between the social and the political sphere. By envisaging legislative power simply as the *'formation'* of society, this democratic political principle aims to make political existence the 'true, general, essential mode of being' of civil society, thereby abolishing the split between the political and the social sphere engendered by the rise of the modern state (Marx 1843: 121).

'The French have recently interpreted this as meaning that in true democracy the political state is annihilated', writes Marx (1843: 30), introducing the problem of the state's extinction that was to acquire considerable prominence in future Marxist debate. However, what is being presented here is not merely the perspective of abolishing the state, but rather the idea of 'reducing' it: in a 'true democracy', 'the state as particular is *merely* particular' (*ibid.*). It is not so much a matter of abolishing the state as of minimizing it as an organizational principle: the state ceases to be separate from and superior to the other spheres of social existence and cooperates with them within a more substantial and original political principle: the democratic one (Abensour 1997). This principle is destined to superimpose itself upon that of the state, and its essence must be envisaged in the light of how the French 'in modern times' have revolutionized the very nature of politics by re-inventing the functions and significance of the legislative assembly.

This radical-democratic 'moment', however, soon vanished from the Marxian horizon, as is already clear from *The Jewish Question* (1844), which reflects a more crucial influence from Feuerbach and his philosophy of man centred on *Gemeinwesen*, the communal essence of the human species. This perspective shifts Marx's gaze from democracy to the question of *emancipation*, a shift which goes together with an increasingly detailed critical analysis of the French Revolution's significance. The latter is now taken to exemplify a process of *'merely political'* emancipation: a process that only involves the separate, abstract, and merely formal sphere of the state without affecting the real and substantial one of civil society. Marx thus reinterprets the events of 1789 as an emancipatory process that only concerns the *citoyen's* 'ethereal' bureaucratic life in the context of the 'imaginary community' of the state rather than his real existence in the concrete sphere of civil society, which has been legitimized and established as the domain of modern propertarian individualism. This

thesis is developed through a critical investigation of the principles underlying the *Déclaration des droits de l'homme et du citoyen* produced by the great
Revolution. Marx's analysis reveals the revolutionary figure of the *citoyen* as an
'imaginary member of an illusionary sovereignty', the holder of a purely formal right and of a kind of equality that only exists within the abstract sphere
of the law and the state (Marx 1844b: 154). Beyond this abstraction, the real
homme that emerges from an analysis of his 'natural' and 'imprescriptible'
rights to *liberté*, *propriété*, *égalité*, and *sûreté*, as proclaimed by the revolutionary *Declarations*, is the *bourgeois*, the property-owning individual who acts
egoistically in civil society.

The watershed of 1789 thus produced the citizen as an equal holder of sovereignty within the abstract horizon of the political community of the state,
while *at the same time* freeing the real, egoistic, and bourgeois man, legitimat-
ing his individualistic activity within material bourgeois society. This outcome
embodies the essential hallmark of modern politics, legally enshrined by the
bourgeois revolutions. The result of this process is that the citizen's political
life ultimately proves to be a 'mere *means*' to ensure the rights of the private
bourgeois property-owner in civil society (Marx 1844b: 164). No attempt to
push the Jacobin revolution to its ultimate consequences, to the point of trans-
lating it into a 'true' substantial democracy, can therefore have a real impact
on the problem of social individualism, since it presupposes it. Any emancipation process designed to transform the political sphere – including the
most radical democratic process – is necessarily encompassed and confined
within this bourgeois revolutionary logic, which has redefined the political
sphere by separating it from that of society and thus basing it on the assumption of propertarian individualism that governs the latter. This development
of Marx's investigation of the French Revolution's significance brings about an
intensification of his criticism of modern politics. It is a kind of criticism that
identifies the hallmark of the revolutionary transition in the opening up of
civil society to the individualism of private property through the institution of
the state, which rests on and safeguards it. By legally establishing the modern
abstraction of the political state, the turning point of 1789 'naturalized' modern
civil society – the domain of egoism and private property –, turning it into the
assumption on which the political sphere rests.

This analysis developed in 1843 – and expounded in *Kritik* and *Judenfrage* –
is usually regarded as the first *Marxian critique of politics* (Tosel, Luporini and
Balibar 1979; Bongiovanni 1981). As we have seen, it largely stems from a reflection on the significance of the French revolution. The most evident outcomes
of this work are the affirmation of the ontological primacy of civil society,
an understanding of the latter – and, with it, of the French Revolution – as

bourgeois, and hence the development of a somewhat *heteronomous* conception of politics (Rubel 1971). The scenario is actually far more complex. In these and the followings years, Marx never ceased to explore the significance of politics in the modern age, which he rather sought to redefine – or *translate* – *within* civil society by means of the theoretical device of class struggle (Tomasello 2012, 2018a). However, for the purposes of the present enquiry, we can take the arguments examined so far as a useful starting point to understand France – and French revolutionary history – as the general epistemic perspective through which Marx interpreted politics and its significance in the modern age. He did so by developing an original framework for the critique of politics which denounced its separate, abstract, and merely formal character vis-à-vis the real substance of social existence.

This intellectual framework is effectively exemplified by the 1844 essay on the Silesian weaver's uprising. Marx defines this as the first major action taken by the German proletariat, in the light of the categories he has developed in his previous critical analysis of politics. He does so once again through a reference to French history: he draws a comparison with the great Lyonnais weavers' uprisings of 1831 and 1834, when the workers' struggle had become one with that waged by the republican movements (Rude 2007; Tomasello 2018b). 'It has to be admitted that the German proletariat is the *theoretician* of the European proletariat, just as the English proletariat is its *economist*, and the French proletariat its *politician*', writes Marx (1844e: 202). Here, he reframes the motif of the European Triarchy from a proletarian perspective and presents France's political intensity as the primary reason for the defeat of the Lyonnais weavers: insofar as 'their political understanding concealed from them the roots of social distress, thus it falsified their insight into their real aim, thus their *political understanding deceived* their *social instincts*' (Marx 1844e: 204). The main cause of the failure of these workers' struggle is thus found in the French tendency to think 'in the framework of politics' (Marx 1844e: 204), to understand all problems within the limits of politics. By contrast, the Germans' lack of familiarity with the language and logic of modern politics – their political *backwardness* – enabled the Silesian weavers not to limit themselves to the illusory search for solutions in the 'narrow' and separate sphere of politics, governance, and the state. The 'industrial revolt' of the German workers immediately sought to act upon the social root of the problem through the destruction of machinery, account books, and property deeds, thereby reflecting a lucid and profound understanding of the social – more than simply political – roots of their problems.

This article that Marx published in *Vorwärts!* clearly illustrates the outcomes of the *first critique of politics* he had developed in 1843. This critique identifies France as the 'country of politics' – and hence a crucial point of reference to investigate the forms and significance of politics in modern times so as to denounce its limitations, and particularly its abstract, heteronomous, and separate nature. Nevertheless, we will now see how Marx's critical dialogue with French socialism is entirely centred on politics, and how a recurrent reference to French history lends a distinctly political depth to his whole intellectual development that leads up to the texts on the 1848 uprisings in France – which define his *second critique of politics*.

2   The Parisian Moment and the Engagement with French Socialism

If we could use dates to present the turning points in an author's thought, as we do with historical developments, one of these dates for Marx would be 11 October 1843. This is the day when he settled in Paris for the first time: the 'new capital of the new world', as he wrote to Ruge before leaving; when he announced that 'the world has long dreamed of something of which it only has only to become conscious in order to possess it in reality' (Marx 1844f: 142, 144). In the summer of 1844, this 'something' which the world had long dreamed of was to take the name of communism.

If we wished to speak of a *Parisian moment* in Marxian thought, this would first of all designate the effort to define the subject of emancipation, which coincides with the reception of the categories of proletariat, workers, and class at the centre of the Marxian lexicon. This is a 'theoretical encounter, but also a personal and lived encounter' with such concepts (Balibar 1997), which Marx made through his close engagement with the political and intellectual climate of France as much as with the social movements he became involved with in the capital (Cornu 1962; Ducange and Burlaud 2018). In Paris he approached secret societies, the League of the Just, and especially workers' and craftsmen's circles. These experiences influenced him and contributed to focusing his attention on the issues of labour and production, as is evident from the *Economic and Philosophic Manuscripts of 1844*. These are informed by Marx's eye-opening encounter with that 'practical process' in which

> the most splendid results are to be observed whenever French socialist workers are seen together ... the brotherhood of man is no mere phrase with them, but a fact of life, and the nobility of man shines upon us from their work-hardened bodies.
>
> MARX 1844a: 313

In Paris, Marx chiefly devoted himself to the project of founding a journal – the *Deutsch–Französische Jahrbücher* – which he had been working on
ever since the suppression of the *Rheinische Zeitung für Politik* by the authorities: the *German Annals* founded by Ruge became the *German-French Annals*,
not least to stress the 'need for a Franco-German scientific alliance' (Marx to
Feuerbach 3/10/1843 in MECW 3: 349). Thus, before leaving Germany, Marx
stressed the need of not raising a dogmatic barrier against the communism of
Cabet or Dézamy or the 'socialist doctrines' of Fourier or Proudhon, but rather
of establishing a dialogue with them as 'a special expression of the humanistic
principle' (Marx 1844f: 143). All attempts to invite collaboration with French
socialists failed, however, chiefly owing to the distrust shown towards the
Annals' anti-religious stance by the authors invited to submit contributions.
Among them were the Catholic Lamennais, the founder of *l'Avenir* in 1830; and
Lamartine, who in 1831 had founded the *Revue Européenne*, which presented
Christian morality as the basis for the re-establishment of a *politique rationelle*
committed to the pursuit of liberty and equality. Another author was Pierre
Leroux, the founder in 1824 of the liberal newspaper *Le Globe*, which he had
brought into the sphere of Saint-Simonian socialism before distancing himself
from this political movement in the name of an ideal of 'religious democracy'
(Abensour 2013). Similar distrust underlies Considérant's refusal to contribute
to the *Annals*. As the leading exponent of the Fourierist current of *Démocratie
pacifique*, Considérant interpreted *phalansteries* as avenues for reconciliation – *harmonie* – and for a 'broad and pacified politics' hostile to all forms
of antagonism. Likewise, Cabet envisaged his community of *Icarians* as the
apostles of a new civil religion founded on Christ's gospel of social redemption
(Collina 1990).

These disagreements on religious matters reflect issues typical of post-
revolutionary France, which was generally marked by a mistrust of the previous century's philosophy, blamed for the excesses of the Revolution and its
Terror. Even secular thinker Louis Blanc accused the editors of the *Annals* of
being atheists indebted to the materialism of the 18th century, which in France
was regarded as a thing of the past. The post-revolutionary French climate was
indeed marked by a general tendency to rethink social bonds in terms other
than the Roussovian 'social contract' between 'wills'. In this context, new plans
for social emancipation were also formulated as claims to re-establish civil
morality on a religious basis (Riot-Sarcey 1998). The first socialist movements,
which sprang up in the 1830s, interpreted their own mission in terms of the
reconciliation of a society marred by the traumas of the political and industrial revolutions – to the point of presenting themselves in certain cases as the
genuine modern interpreters of *true Christianity* that had been betrayed by the

Church. Marx's critical dialogue with French socialism is primarily marked by these kinds of issues. Consequently, the struggle against the mystical-religious overtones of socialist groups and against their influence on French workers' and German craftsmen's movements was to become a significant aspect of his engagement in the second half of the 1840s. This is attested by various passages of the communist *Manifesto* of 1848, which regards the first social-ist movements' 'fanatical and superstitious belief' in a new 'social gospel' as the cause of their degeneration into 'reactionary sects' and inane experiments to re-establish 'duodecimo editions of the New Jerusalem' (Marx and Engels 1848: 516).

Among the French intellectuals who in 1843 turned down the invitation to contribute to the *Annals* was Proudhon too, whose *Qu'est-ce que la propriété* (1840) was an influential text for Marx, who praised it in *The Holy Family* (1845). The two thinkers often met in Paris and, after emigrating to Brussels, Marx asked Proudhon to join the Communist Correspondence Committee – but the latter once again turned down the invitation. Their correspondence illustrates this growing disagreement, which culminated in the publication of *Misère de la philosophie* (1847), a work written directly in French, not least to give resonance to a polemic with an intellectual who was particularly in vogue. Marx criticized the murky and ill-defined character of Proudhon's economic doctrine, which he set in contrast with the more rigorous nature of the categories used in Ricardian political economy. Hence, he denounced the inconsistency of the measures Proudhon had suggested to promote more equitable exchanges – labour vouchers, labour-time certificates, and so on. In Marx's view, these solutions deny 'the struggles and dangers necessarily result-ing therefrom'. They simply – and misguidedly – seek to turn the proletariat into the bourgeoisie. Thus, the *Manifesto* lists Proudhon among those expo-nents of 'bourgeois socialism' who 'desire the existing state of society minus its revolutionary and disintegrating elements'. They seek to 'depreciate every revolutionary movement in the eyes of the working class' by coming up with 'administrative reforms', failing to see that a change in 'bourgeois relations of production ... can be effected only by a revolution' (Marx and Engels 1848: 513–514). The same ideas crop up again in the texts on the 1848 uprisings in France, where Marx praises the Blanquists – who were closer to the traditional republi-can perspective than the socialist one, but still tenaciously engaged in political struggle. By contrast, he criticizes 'doctrinaire' socialists for their incapacity to act on the political terrain of conflict and their efforts to pursue inane mea-sures designed to alleviate the suffering of the proletariat, instead of waging its struggle (Marx 1850a; Marx 1852a).

The polemic against Proudhon and French 'doctrinaire' socialism therefore chiefly centres on a perceived lack of politics. The *Manifesto* attributes the same limitation to the various currents in communist and socialist literature: an incapacity to deal with the *political question*, to grasp the crucial relevance of political-revolutionary struggle and of class conflict. The same idea also lies at the core of Marx's verdict on 'utopian' socialism and the 'systems of Saint-Simon, Fourier, and Owen', notwithstanding the fact that they had advanced a radical critique of capitalist society and offered a crucial contribution to the early developments of the workers' movement. This ambivalent verdict on utopian socialism (Abensour 2016) reflects Marx's theoretical indebtedness to these thinkers, and especially to Saint-Simonian doctrine, from which he would appear to have derived a series of formulations and categories of fundamental importance for his thought's later development. First of all, the Saint-Simonians were the first to have reframed the bourgeois historian's theme of the clash of races into a *proto-socialist* perspective (cf. *infra* § 3) by extending it to include the issues of private property, exploitation, and changes in modes of production. We then have the conception of society as an organic whole whose laws of historical development must be studied scientifically in view of the dissolution of the state into a new, human form of association founded on its real *basis*, namely industry. Hence, even Marx's few references to the future communist society are clearly indebted to the Saint-Simonian notion of the 'workers' association' (Dardot and Laval 2012: 43–62, 238–241). The lexicon which Marx began to develop in his Parisian period is therefore deeply influenced by Saint-Simonian categories. However, it constantly transcends them insofar as it reveals their political inadequacy for a theory of emancipation, class conflict, and revolution. It was precisely this political depth that the Saint-Simonians and other utopian socialists lacked: Marx apparently sought to draw upon their critical side, while at the same time denouncing their political inadequacy.

The *Manifesto* traces this inadequacy back to an objective historical limit, namely the fact that such theories were developed in what was still an immature stage of capitalism, which prevented the first socialist theorists from clearly grasping the reality of class conflict. This historical limit amounts to an incapacity to see the possibility of – and need for – autonomous political initiative on the part of the proletariat. Thus, instead on focusing on the conditions for the latter's emancipation through its 'establishment as a class', the utopian socialists, to create them, 'search after a new social science, after new social laws': they replace political initiative with 'their personal inventive action ... an organization of society specially contrived by these inventors' (Marx and

Engels 1948: 515). The *Manifesto*'s argument about the various currents of French socialism therefore also raises the issue of Marx's engagement with the budding social sciences in France – which, after all, found a most authoritative pioneer in Saint-Simon. What emerges is a radical criticism of any perspective based on the mere sociological description of society, a perspective which simply enunciates its laws without including the dimension of power relations and that of the political action that transforms them. 'So long as they seek science and merely make systems ... they see in poverty nothing but poverty, without seeing in it the revolutionary, subversive side' (Marx 1847a: 178). The 'utopians' – like the 'doctrinaire' socialists – are such because they fail to see the need for political struggle; hence, they understand the proletariat's existence exclusively in terms of suffering, without grasping its revolutionary nature, which is the transformative historical significance of its condition. Marx tirelessly rails against the structural inadequacy of a merely scientific-sociological approach to the structure of society, stressing the need to establish the political dimension of class struggle and conflict at the centre of a new materialistic theory of the history of human societies and of a scientific theory of the historical laws governing their development. It is precisely this theoretical effort that brings out the crucial relevance of Marx's engagement with the liberal bourgeois historians of early nineteenth-century France, from whom he derives his conception of class struggle as the driving force of history.

3   The Rationale of Class Struggle and 1848 in France

During his stay in Paris from October 1843 to February 1845 – when a decree issued by Guizot forced him to leave France – Marx continued his study of the French Revolution, planned a text on the Convention, and traced the outline of a text about the state drawing upon half a century of French history. In this period, he also delved into the writings of 'bourgeois' historians such as Mignet, Thiers, and especially Thierry and Guizot (Mazauric 2009). From them Marx would appear to have derived not just the idea of class as a political concept and a conception of history as the effect of class struggle, but also the definition of the nature of this struggle, i.e. the whole idea of class conflict as the driving force of history.

The Marxian theory of class struggle may be regarded as a sort of 'strategic redefinition' of the historical theory of the war between races – which envisaged the national history of France in terms of an enduring conflict between the native Gauls and the Franks who had entered the country with the barbarian invasions. Certain well-known formulas used in the *Manifesto* are directly and patently indebted to the development and reinterpretation of this theory by the liberal bourgeois historians of the early 19th century (Dardot and Laval 2012). As regards the contents of this historiography, I shall refer the reader to Isabella Consolati's contribution to the present volume. What I wish to stress here is that, from the historiography in question, Marx derives an idea of the 'class' as a formation whose structure emerges from an analysis of the history of human societies. This idea is established at the centre of a teleological conception which assigns the modern proletariat the same kind of universalistic value that post-revolutionary liberal historians had assigned to the European bourgeoisie. From their historiographical theories, Marx draws the notion of a fundamental connection between the ontology of social classes and their mutual struggles throughout history: each class is born and transformed through its conflict with other classes; and it is this conflictual dimension that determines its existence, structure, and development (Dal Pane 1939; De Mauro 1958). What emerges here is a notion of class as a primarily historical-political factor, firmly set within the struggles that have marked the course of human societies, and indissolubly linked to the existence of conflicts. This is evident in certain texts on the 1848 events in France, where Marx aims to describe class struggle as the original political substance that must be constantly rediscovered behind the distorting and illusionary language of parties and the state. This struggle is the 'thing' which materialistic enquiry brings to light behind 'a nebulous existence, an existence in phrases, in words' (Marx 1850a: 69), behind 'this superficial appearance, which veils the *class struggle*' (Marx 1852a: 127).

It is through this framework that Marx interprets the whole history of the 1848 revolution in France, as he constantly finds himself having to reinterpret the idea of social class and having to put it to the test on the political terrain. The months between the February revolution and the workers' insurrection of June 1848 apparently seem to confirm the scheme of polarization into two classes outlined in the *Manifesto*. Yet, the class-based interpretation of the subsequent events leading up to the Bonapartist coup of December 1851 proves to be more complex. Here social classes hardly emerge at all as an established social structure. Rather, they essentially appear to depend on the dynamics of conflict that constantly redefine them. Thus, the bourgeoisie – the historical force most clearly brought into focus in the previous works – becomes caught up in a regressive spiral that makes it impossible to speak of this class in the singular, given the opposition between financial, land-based, and industrial capital, as well as the recurrent conflicts with the petite bourgeoisie. In other words, the binary scheme of the *Manifesto*, based on the idea of class polarization, seems to crumble before the dynamics of events, and the bourgeois class only acquires a unitary appearance in those moments when it finds itself facing the rising opposition of the proletariat and thus catalysing different interests, demands, and discourses against a common enemy. Then there is the condition of the *peasants* – the 'mass of the French people' – who through their votes determined the ultimate outcome of the 1848 events, but who in themselves 'do not form a class', owing to their isolation from one another. Rather, they represent the 'simple addition of homologous multitudes' which could only acquire the status of a class by representing its own interests in opposition to the bourgeoisie through a political alliance with the 'urban pro-letariat' (Marx 1852a: 187). But the latter too finds itself marked by the 'rift' of the *Lumpenproletariat*, a category which Marx resorts to in order to account for the two major events in these revolutionary developments: the workers' uprising of June 1848 and the Bonapartist coup of December 1851 (Draper 1972; Raymond 1988). As a result, a peculiar perspective emerges whereby classes prove unusable as descriptive social categories, since they only become fully intelligible within the dynamics of conflict.

In Marx's interpretation of the 1848 events in France, the very ontology of social classes therefore appears to depend not so much on the structure of French society as on the dynamics of conflict that unfold within it. In other words, it seems as though it is the intensity of the conflict and the eruption of struggles that lends intelligible and evident form to the structure of social classes. The latter emerge, first of all, from the opposition to other groups' initiative, from a polarization that engenders antagonistic subjectivities. For this reason, the 'revolution made progress, forged ahead, not by its immediate tragi-comic achievements but on the contrary by the creation of a powerful, united counter-revolution, by the creation of an opponent in combat' (Marx 1850a: 47). It is this dynamic of antagonism – the intensifying of conflict, of political enmity – that determines the conditions for a revolutionary break, for it alone can make it clear who the actors involved are, engendering the nec-essary class polarization. This perspective, then, is based not on the sociology of classes but on the nature of their conflict, which establishes a generative relationship between struggles and the definition of class subjectivity. It is the enemy's gesture that makes one class 'rise up' before the others, which is why

> proletarian revolutions ... deride ... the inadequacies, weaknesses and paltrinesses of their first attempts, seem to throw down their adversary only in order that he may draw new strength from the earth and rise again more gigantic, before them ... until a situation has been created which makes all turning back impossible.
>
> MARX 1852a: 106–107

Hence, the *Eighteenth Brumaire of Louis Napoleon* presents a polemological dia-lectic of the struggles through which Parisian 'workers' politically constitute them-selves as a class – or as the 'revolutionary proletariat' – by leading their counterpart to display an increasingly clear and staunch reaction. This finds its most intense expression in the Bonapartist coup and its hypertrophic growth of 'state machinery' and of 'executive power, with its enormous bureaucratic and military organization' (Marx 1852a: 185). It is at this level, in relation to the issue of the state, that the idea of a generative relationship between political conflict and class subjectivity becomes most evident. In order to interpret Louis Bonaparte's coup, Marx here seems to apply to the centralization of state power the Manifesto's notion that the process of capital's concentration generates the antagonist destined to destroy it. Through this framework, he describes the process by which the Parisian workers constitute themselves as a class through a struggle which, in turn, triggers a reaction from their counterpart that calls for increasing the strength of the machinery of state repression, thereby triggering a growingly intense spiral of conflict. Only this antagonistic dynamic can account for the genesis and affirmation of the Second Empire: to face the proletarian revolution, the bourgeoisie was 'compelled by its class position ... to render irresistible ... the executive power hostile to it' (Marx 1852a: 139). In turn, Marx argues, it is precisely the vast increase of this power that, by way of antagonism, determines the resumption of the workers' class struggle, which now 'sets it up against itself as the sole target, in order to concentrate all its forces of destruction against it' (Marx 1852a: 185). The growing consolidation of state *Gewalt* – the violence organized as the 'state machine' that the Bonapartist coup of 1851 developed to the most intense degree – stems from the workers' struggles. These have constituted the Parisian workers as a revolutionary class, and in doing so have led to the 'arising' of a counter-revolutionary antagonist that has progressively come to coincide with the hypertrophic growth of the state's executive power – thereby setting the ground for the coup.

In view of the dense reflection on political and state power and on representative institutions that emerges from this line of reasoning, the texts on the 1848 events in France are generally regarded as a *second Marxian critique of politics* after the one established in 1843 by interpreting the great Revolution's significance. Let us therefore consider some aspects of this topic by returning to Marx's interpretations of the watershed of 1789. Ultimately, my aim will be to show how they reflect certain antinomies and characteristics that distinguish this author's conception of politics.

4   The Interpretations of the French Revolution and 'Permanent' Politics

The 1848 events brought Marx face-to-face with the immanence of a revolutionary process already underway, thereby enabling him to test the concept of revolution that he had been working on since the *Parisian moment* of 1844

(Cornu 1948; Frosini 2009). In that year, a reflection on the nature of critique led Marx to identify *Praxis* as its most developed form, and to present *revolution* as the only practice '*à la hauteur des principes*' (Marx 1844c: 182). This transition occurred in the first text he wrote in Paris, an *Introduction* to the critique of Hegel's philosophy of law, in the last pages of which we witness the *irruption* into the Marxian lexicon of the term *proletariat*. Through the latter, Marx now 'discovered' – or 'invented' – the subjectivity called to embody this revolutionary praxis in history by virtue of its negativity, of its 'own chains', of its condition of 'universal suffering'. This 'sphere … cannot emancipate itself without emancipating all other spheres of society': this 'dissolution of society as a particular estate is the proletariat' (Marx 1844c: 186). This notion is still enunciated without referring to the categories of wage labour, capital, exploitation, and so on. It is a purely political figure symbolizing exclusion that Marx would appear to have developed through his encounter with the Parisian context at the time of the social question's emergence. More precisely, Marx would appear to have been inspired by the place that the term proletarian had acquired in French public debate, starting from the famous and inaugural self-defence uttered by Blanqui in 1832. When the judge asked him what his profession was, Blanqui answered 'proletarian', stating: 'this is the condition of thirty million Frenchmen who live off their own labour and are deprived of political rights' (SAP 1832: 2–3). Twelve years later, this category entered Marx's lexicon according to the same purely political logic of exclusion: 'a class of civil society which is not a class of civil society, an estate which is the dissolution of all estates' (Marx 1844c: 186; cf. Rancière 1992).

Marx sees this revolutionary vocation in the very existence of the modern proletariat because, with his eyes fixed on 1789, he envisages the revolution as the 'moment' in which 'a particular class' of civil society ceases to be a part, to become the whole: 'a moment in which its demands and rights are truly the rights and demands of society itself' (Marx 1844c: 184). The 1844 *Einleitung* thus recalls Sieyès's adage to enunciate the need for 'that revolutionary audacity which flings at the adversary the defiant words: *I am nothing and I should be everything*' (Marx 1844c: 185). In brief, to quote Lichtheim (1964: 55–56), the '*critical theory* of 1844 … is intended as the theory of a political revolution patterned on that of 1789–1794, but with this difference: instead of *the people* we now … encounter *the proletariat*'. Marx's theory of revolution would indeed appear to be modelled after his interpretation of 1789 France, which indicates the general, but also *changing*, epistemic perspective from which he envisages the revolutionary politics of the proletariat. Changes in this interpretation shape the Marxian concept of politics and reflect its instability and polysemy: it fluctuates between the idea of a revolution of bourgeois civil society (which characterizes the 1843 texts and was to become the *Marxist* interpretation) and that of a revolution of politics and the state that never ceases to manifest itself in new ways and to engender fresh consequences (Furet 1986; Bongiovanni 1989a, 1989b).

This interpretive and theoretical development primarily appears to be reflected in the extension of the timespan that Marx considers in relation to the effects produced by the watershed of 1789. In *The Jewish Question*, the latter is regarded as the 'moment' in which 'the political state as such is born' violently out of civil society, whereas the stage of the *Terror* is seen to embody an attempt by 'political life' to establish itself as 'real' life, to crush its prerequisite – civil society – by appropriating it, to make itself dominant with respect to the other spheres of civil life by 'declaring the revolution to be *permanent*' (Marx 1844b: 156). Hence, the idea of the 'permanence' of revolution enables Marx to gradually project the persistence of the principle of the autonomy of politics – or of the primacy of the political – into the subsequent decades of French history, down to the constitution of the Bonapartist Second Empire in 1851. In *The Holy Family*, this interpretative framework is extended to Napoleon's First Empire and to the Restoration, which is seen as another attempt made by the political realm to impose itself on the social system of the bourgeois domain. 'Napoleon represented the last battle of *revolutionary terror* against the *bourgeois society*'. This 'battle', resting on a conception of the state as an '*end in itself*', was waged 'by *substituting permanent war* for *permanent revolution*' until the revolution of July 1830 established, once and for all, the government and the state as 'the *official* expression' of the exclusive power of the bourgeoisie: 'the *political* recognition of its own *special* interests'; the final affirmation of the control of bourgeois civil society over political institutions (Marx and Engels 1845: 123–124).

But the 1848 revolution once again radically challenged this development, which is why the *Eighteenth Brumaire* newly addresses the issue of the political sphere's tendency to acquire an autonomous and dominant position with respect to civil society, tracing it from the French Revolution to the Bonapartist coup of 1851. As a consequence of the latter event, 'against civil society, the state machine has consolidated its position so thoroughly' that 'the state seem[s] to have made itself completely independent' (Marx 1852a: 186). Yet this vast increase in executive power is only possible through the centralization produced by the 'first French Revolution'. Adopting a perspective reminiscent of de Tocqueville's *The Old Regime and the Revolution*, Marx acknowledges a point of continuity between absolute monarchy and the French Revolution in the process of administrative 'centralization', which continued throughout the post-revolutionary years:

Napoleon perfected this state machinery. The Legitimist monarchy and
the July monarchy added nothing but ... new material for state administration. ... Finally, in its struggle against the revolution, the parliamentary
republic [established in 1848] found itself compelled to strengthen ... the
resources and centralization of governmental power. All revolutions perfected this machine ... The parties that contended in turn for domination
regarded the possession of this huge state edifice as the principal spoils
of the victor.

    MARX 1852a: 185–186

We can see how the rise of the Second Empire is included within a trajectory
that begins with 1789 and finds continuity through the reproduction and diffusion of that political and state principle established by the 'modern French'
(cf. § 1 above). The long-term developments that began with the watershed
moment of the French Revolution are envisaged in terms of a revolution affecting the sphere of politics and the state at least as much as that of bourgeois and
civil society. More accurately, Marx's interpretation constantly appears to be
marked by an irresolvable fluctuation between these two poles, which shapes
the very Marxian concept of revolution. By striving to establish an increasingly
tight connection between the existence and growth of the industrial proletariat and a revolutionary tension that is seen to lie at the heart of modern
society, the Marxian theory of revolution envisages capitalist development as
a dynamic that ushers in its own end by engendering the antagonist destined
to destroy it. However, this paradigm does not really clarify what the actual
role of political action is – of the specific initiative of the revolutionary class,
whose necessity Marx nonetheless affirms – within a transition that essentially
appears to fall within the historical dialectic between the relations of production and productive forces.

    The tension shaping Marx's interpretations of the French Revolution
reflects this antinomy: the fluctuation – affecting Marx's theory as a whole –
between the strategic logic of class struggle and the scientific one of capital
(Dardot and Laval 2012). It is a constant and fundamental struggle between the
subjective perspective of revolutionary class initiative and the objective one
that envisages the development of relations of production as a law of historical
evolution, and hence also of political and social transformation. This unsolv-
able fluctuation between the *autonomy* and the *heteronomy* of politics may be
regarded as a central aspect of the way in which French historical events stim-
ulated Marx's thought in the decade under consideration, lending it enduring
political depth.

In this respect, Marx's move to London – or, more precisely, the publication of his last text on the 1848 French revolution in 1852 – and his increasing focus on the British rather than French context, marked a substantial turn. What seems to emerge is an actual eclipsing, or at any rate de-emphasizing, of the *political question* in the subsequent two decades of Marx's work. However, it was once again the events occurring in France that forced Marx to abruptly return to this field of analysis when a new insurrection of Parisian workers in March 1871 raised the question of the 'government of the working class', of the use that the revolutionary proletariat must make of political power and of the state machine once it has vanquished its class enemy. The Paris Commune thus confirmed the French singularity and its political essence, which Marx had brought into focus in the early 1840s (cf. § 1), and forced this author to re-examine the key points raised in his texts on the 1848 revolution (cf. § 3). What new form of power the Commune was called to establish, by seizing the state in order to destroy it, was to remain an enigma; but the events of 1871 unambiguously pointed to the unavoidability of that distinctly political problem which, in relation to Marxian thought, we might then describe as the *French question* (Tomasello 2018a).

CHAPTER 12

The Nation within Capital's Political Relations

Marx and Italy

Michele Filippini

1   The Italian Question

In his early work Karl Marx confronts the problem of human emancipation and the resolution of the real antinomy between civil society and the state, a problem which had been raised by G.W.F. Hegel in the German context characterized simultaneously by political backwardness and an advanced theoretical consciousness. Already in 1844, in *Contribution to the Critique of Hegel's Philosophy of Law: Introduction*, Marx writes: 'If therefore the *status quo of German statehood* expresses the *perfection of the ancien régime* … the *status quo of German political theory* expresses the *imperfection of the modern state*, the defectiveness of its flesh itself' (Marx 1844c: 181). Right from the start, then, Marx's theory confronts a spurious, historical object, one whose internal contradictions call not for linear unfolding but instead for a unique combination of critical tensions and steps, in which the very backwardness of conditions may preface a total upheaval beyond the limits of a 'revolution which leaves the pillars of the house standing' (Marx 1844c: 184). Radical analysis and the radical subject charged with carrying out the transition from the weapon of criticism to criticism by weapons are here consubstantial. His study of England and the critique of political economy will come later, during a longer and less tightly packed phase of upheavals, after 1848 partially demolishes the foundations of a discourse capable of holding together Hegelian logic and radical democratism, the national question and the proletariat (cf. Finelli 2015).

The history of Marx's relations with Italy recalls this same trajectory, given the backward character of its political forms (with unity not yet achieved, ruled as it was by different kingdoms) and its particular backwardness from the point of view of capitalist development, but above all considering the seemingly inevitable role played by the 'national question' in every attempt at social emancipation. Additionally, from the point of view of theoretical consciousness, if 'Germany's *revolutionary* past … is the *Reformation*' (Marx 1844c: 182), so too could Italy make reference to the Renaissance – not by chance Croce calls Marx 'a Machiavelli of the labour movement' (Croce 2016: 46) – just as Mazzini and the Carbonari tried to do during the struggles of the Risorgimento. But Marx, contrary to Mazzini, did not remain satisfied for long with the formulation of the problem of human emancipation in these terms. 1848 marked the beginning of a rethinking of the imminence of revolution as much as the bond between the national and the social.

Following the trajectory of Marx's remarks on Italy – from the revolts of 1848 to the first rumblings of the Italian workers' movement in the 1870s – one can reconstruct what is effectively the history of the disappearance of the centrality of the national issue in Marx's thought. This disappearance is consistent with the peculiar form of politics that Marx develops in the following years (Ricciardi 2019), which seeks to think its object not in terms of unity – of social recomposition and of national independence – but in terms of scission – of class struggle and of conflict between sides.

The story of the emergence and the submergence of the 'Italian question' in Marx's writings may be read as a litmus test for the formation of a theory of revolution that progressively emancipates itself from notions that are national and martial in character, instead becoming embedded in contexts that are social, diffuse, and conflictual. Emancipation can no longer emerge through a 'foreign' war, through a bloodbath which serves as a founding myth for the national spirit. For Marx this kind of war ceases to be the catalytic event for all aspirations, it no longer serves the salvific function of promising to resolve every contradiction. Instead, a longer timeframe is opened, one marked by the cycles of capital accumulation and the organizational efforts of the workers' movement, in which the 'foreign' war between nations transforms into a domestic war, a civil war, between classes. This approach will culminate in Marx's essay on the Commune, *The Civil War in France*.

The conflictual relationship between Marx and Mazzini can also be read through this lens. The passage from the war of national liberation to social revolution involves a series of reversals which the Italian republican could not accept refusing sectarian political action and necessitating a mass politics, replacing 'patriots' with 'the class with the most radical chains' as the subject of emancipation, and identifying the class division as a fundamental caesura in society in place of the recompositional myth of national independence.

The historiography (not only Marxist) concerning Marx's scarce interest in Italian events can thus be reconsidered in light of these considerations. In fact, Italy becomes an increasingly peripheral scenario if one looks at it, as Mazzini had, from the point of view of its nationalism: weak, elitist, cross-class, conspiratorial (Mazzini 2009). Its political history undoubtedly reveals a subaltern nation whose fate was determined by European powers pursuing their own interests during the Risorgimento. If, on the other hand, one's gaze shifts to consider Italy from the point of view of capital, class conflict, and the working class in formation, then the peninsula ceases to be peripheral.

It also must be acknowledged that Marx's and Engels's evaluations of the Italian situation are woven together according to a geographical division of tasks that the two pursue over their entire history of collaboration. Engels will write more widely on Italy in part due to his interest in military history and strategy, which will play such a strong part in the Italian events of the Risorgimento. Here, however, we will focus our attention on Marx alone, hoping to reconstruct an orientation that, as noted above, turns out to be consistent with the more general development of Marx's thought.

2   The Manifesto and 1848

The *Manifesto of the Communist Party*, published in London in February of 1848, contains numerous passages in which the international horizon and interests of the working-class clash with the need for its own national political organization:

> Though not in substance, yet in form, the struggle of the proletariat with the bourgeoisie is at first a national struggle. The proletariat of each country must, of course, first of all settle matters with its own bourgeoisie.
>
> MARX and ENGELS 1848: 495

Even if, as individuals, 'the working men have no country', when they present themselves as a class, when they organize themselves as a political force that seeks to overthrow the bourgeoisie, then for Marx their action must take, at least initially and instrumentally, a national form: 'the proletariat must first of all acquire political supremacy, must rise to be the leading class of the nation, must constitute itself *the* nation' (Marx and Engels 1848: 502–503). This difference in form and in content signals a political contingency in which 'the *Manifesto* seeks ... to reconcile the indication of a necessary national phase of revolution with the internationalist position of the communists' (Ricciardi 2019: 122).

It is this centrality of the national form of political action before 1848 that makes Italy – a country in which capitalist development and the relative presence of a working class pertain only to Lombardy, to Piedmont (to a lesser extent), and to Venice (in terms of trade) – an interesting terrain within the framework of international European politics. For Marx 1848 represents a turning point, as much for the nascent working class's organizational experiences of political struggle as for the international relations of force created at the intersection of the principle of 'freedom of peoples' and the objective function that each country plays in the European arena vis-à-vis the Restoration. Already in June of 1848, in a letter to the democratic Florentine newspaper *Alba*, Marx, who had just taken over the *Neue Rheinische Zeitung*, reassures the Italians that 'we shall defend the cause of Italian independence, we shall fight to the death Austrian despotism in Italy as in Germany and Poland' (Marx 1848a: 11). The magazine at that time has a different position with respect to the national aspirations of the Slavic peoples, considered 'people without history', in the sense of being unable to create an autonomous state through economic, political, and demographic development. Engels's evaluation of these peoples is indeed disdainful, in part due to the role that they play in the reaction to 1848:

> [T]he Slavs of Austria had no right to national existence because they sided with the counter-revolution in 1848; and they necessarily sided with the counter-revolution because they had already proven themselves incapable of national existence in the past and only the reaction left them any hope of preserving their 'imaginary Slav nationality'.
>
> ROSDOLSKY 1986: 110

On the other hand, 1848 puts Italy in a position which is in no way peripheral. In fact, it represents one of the possible terrains on which the European revolution may be ignited. In addition to this, Marx and Engels take the opportunity to insert the Italian question into public debate in Germany. On July 3, 1848, with an article titled 'Germany's Foreign Policy' in *Neue Rheinische Zeitung*, the latter takes a position in favor of the Italian national revolution, tying it to the interests of revolution in Germany:

> Now that the Germans are throwing off their own yoke, their whole foreign policy must change too. Otherwise, the fetters with which we have chained other nations will shackle our own freedom, which is as yet hardly more than a presentiment. Germany will liberate herself to the extent to which she sets free neighbouring nations .... Is Austria's war against Italy's independence or Prussia's war against the restoration of Poland popular, or on the contrary do they not destroy the last illusions about such 'patriotic' crusades? ... Meanwhile, everything possible must be done to prepare the way for the democratic system on this side and the

other side of the Alps. The *Italians* have issued a number of declarations
which make their friendly attitude towards Germany perfectly clear.

ENGELS 1848: 166–167

Giving support to revolutionary national movements, above all to Italy's, thus
allows Marx and Engels to play with German public opinion, to argue that revolution in Germany has as its necessary condition the victory of democratic
revolutions in other European countries. They extend support most of all to
the Poles and to the Italians, both for their anti-Habsburg function and as a
polemical weapon against nationalist plans of *Grossdeutschen*. Marx writes on
July 12 in 'Germany Foreign Policy and the Last Events in Prague':

> Despite the patriotic shouting and beating of the drums of almost the
> entire German press, the *Neue Rheinische Zeitung* from the very first
> moment has sided with the Poles in Posen, the Italians in Italy, and the
> Czechs in Bohemia.
>
> MARX 1848b: 212

Marx thus follows developments in Italy and believes in the possibility of the
revolution starting in an economically peripheral theater. It is perhaps not
by chance that in January 1848 a revolt first broke out in Palermo, extending
itself quickly to all of Sicily and Southern Italy, until arriving in Naples in May,
where it would be violently repressed. These episodes initiated the European
uprisings, and in *The Class Struggles in France: 1848–1850* Marx will recall their
importance for developments in France in 1848: 'the bloody uprising of the
people in Palermo worked like an electric shock on the paralysed (French)
masses of the people and awoke their great revolutionary memories and passions' (Marx 1850a: 51–52).

After the defeat of the uprisings, and of the Italian national movement more
generally with the Five Days of Milan, Marx takes up his pen again to denounce
France and the hypocrisy of its Second Republic, which, after vague statements
about emancipation and the 'brotherhood of peoples', follows with the most
classic *realpolitik* in all the European arena, acting like a cynical national
power. The bourgeois Republic, Marx writes on October 22, 1848, in 'English-
French Mediation in Italy', does '*Rien pour la gloire!*':

> They calmly allowed the shocking scenes in Naples, the shocking scenes
> in Messina and the shocking scenes in the Milan region to take place
> before their very eyes .... The officers of the French fleet let themselves be
> treated to a banquet by the Neapolitan officers and cheered the health of

the *King of Naples, the idiotic tiger* Ferdinand, on the still smoking ruins
of Messina.

MARX 1848c: 481

And so, the defeat of 1848 in Italy and in Europe brings Marx, in the 1850s,
to a critical reconsideration of the relationship between national revolution
and social revolution. This reconsideration will fuel the continuous polemic
between him and Engels, on the one hand, and Mazzini, on the other, and it
will also address the causes of the revolutionary defeat in 1848.

With his concurrent relocation to London, Marx's plan now places relations
of capital squarely at the centre of his analysis, as these have proven to be the
true obstacle to revolution: 'The February republic finally brought the rule of
the bourgeoisie clearly into view, since it struck off the crown behind which
capital kept itself concealed' (Marx 1850a: 54–55). Consequently, this also
changes the political strategy adequate to the phase of the bourgeois regime's
consolidation: both Germany and Italy pass into the background after 1848.
Their weight in international politics indeed was tied to the possible international victory of the revolution. The marginalization of the national question and the reorientation of analysis (and of political-organizational efforts)
toward countries where the working class seems stronger and more developed
come out of this 'season of movement' that Marx experiences in the first part
of his life.

3   The Critique of Mazzini

This radical change of scenario can be gathered immediately from Marx's
references to the Italian events of the early 1850s. While in 1848 every movement, disturbance, and insurrection had been viewed as a possible spark of
the Italian and European revolution, after settling the Italian national question
within the power struggle between European powers, any insurrectional surge,
while arousing Marx's sympathies, is interpreted through the lens of a realism
that condemns it inexorably to failure.

This orientation is outlined both in Marx's correspondence and in a series
of articles that he writes for the *New York Daily Tribune*. On May 6, 1852, Marx
writes to Engels regarding Mazzini:

Unless these gentlemen suffer defeat and receive a drubbing twice a
year, they feel ill at ease. That world history continues to unfold without their help, without their intervention, and without, indeed, official

intervention, is something they refuse to admit. If things go wrong, as
they are sure to do, Mr Mazzini will have a renewed opportunity for self-
assertion in outraged letters to a Graham *quelconque*. Nor will his diges-
tion suffer in consequence.

MARX to ENGELS 5/6/1852 in MECW 39: 101

Not even one year passes before the two drubbings arrive, right on sched-
ule: on February 6, 1853, in Milan, several hundred workers and peasants attack
Austrian guard posts before being pushed back and violently repressed once
again. Five days later Marx reports the first fragments of news in the *New York
Daily Tribune*: the revolt broke out and was immediately suffocated, but the
situation in the other Italian cities remained one of great turmoil; 'as regards
the chances of the present insurrection at Milan, there can be little hope of
success, unless some of the Austrian regiments pass over to the revolutionary
camp' (Marx 1853e: 509). Ten days later, the flimsiness of any insurrectionary
attempt of an overt, conspiratorial type is clear. Marx writes:

> The Milan insurrection is significant as a symptom of the approaching
> revolutionary crisis on the whole European continent .... But as the finale
> of Mazzini's eternal conspiracy, of his bombastic proclamations and his
> arrogant *capucinades* against the French people, it is a very poor result.
> Let us hope that henceforth there will be an end of *révolutions improvisée*,
> as the French call them.
>
> MARX 1853f: 514

On March 22 and April 4, Marx writes two articles in the *New York Daily Tribune*
on the Italian situation, both entitled 'Kossuth and Mazzini' (Lajos Kossuth
was the head of the Hungarian democratic-republican national movement),
in which Marx polemicizes over the failure of the Milanese uprisings within
which Mazzini and Kossuth were active. In the second article Marx reports
excerpts from a letter by Aurelio Saffi, in which the Mazzinian organizer of the
uprisings writes: 'the upper classes were sunk in listless indifference or despair
..., the people of Milan, abandoned without direction to their own instincts,
preserved their faith in the destiny of their country'. Marx comments:

> Now, it is a great progress of the Mazzini party to have at last convinced
> themselves that, even in the case of national insurrections against for-
> eign despotism, there exists such a thing as class distinctions, and that
> it is not the upper classes which must be looked to for a revolutionary
> movement in modern times. Perhaps they will go a step further and come

to the understanding that they have to seriously occupy themselves with the material condition of the Italian country population, if they expect to find an echo to their *'Dio e popolo'*.

MARX 1853g: 536

In the footnotes to this article Marx announces his intention 'to dwell on the material circumstances in which by far the greater portion of the rural inhabitants of that country are placed, and which have made them till now, if not reactionary, at least indifferent to the national struggle of Italy' (Marx 1853g: 536). He will do this occasionally and many years later, for example in the article 'Sicily and the Sicilians' from May 17, 1860 (Marx 1860a: 370–372), written after the Gancia revolt on April 4th, in which he retraces the history of the Sicilians from the Greek period to the present, their economic conditions and their uncountable rebellions. Marx is now interested in the peninsula's economic conditions and their political consequences. The Italian peasants are in fact almost extraneous to the circuit of the European capitalist economy and precisely for this reason they perform the particular function of holding back the possibility of building a mass mobilization. What also reappears in Marx's observations is the importance of passing from conspiratorial politics to mass politics, from the patriotic thrust to the economic determination of relations of force. This is true not only for the economically depressed zones and their reactionary role, as in Southern Italy, but also for that part of the Italian territory, which is for the most part developed, which under Austrian domination is essential for the political stability of the Empire. In 'The Austrian Bankruptcy' Marx carefully analyses the balance sheets of the Empire in its final years, observing how its financial sustainability depends strictly on the obedience of its Hungarian and Lombard territories, which furnish the tax revenue necessary for sustaining the Empire's growing military expenses, enlarged due to rebellions in these same territories:

> We arrive then at the irrefragable conclusion that on the possession of Hungary and Lombardy depends not only the political but the economical existence of the Austrian Empire, and that with their loss the long-delayed bankruptcy of that state becomes inevitable.
>
> MARX 1854a: 49

Marx insists on this again in 1858 in his polemic with Mazzini, annotating in the article 'Mazzini and Napoleon' a letter in which the former reproaches the latter for the failed promises of economic prosperity and widening freedom in France and in Europe.

M. Mazzini, too, does not now disdain to dwell on social realities, the interests of the different classes, the exports and imports, the prices of necessaries, house-rent, and other such vulgar things ... It is only to be hoped that he will not stop at this point, but, unbiased by a false pride, will proceed to reform his whole political catechism by the light of economical science.

MARX 1854C: 486

From the middle of the 1850s, Marx's interest in national revolutions that can trigger international revolution has definitively faded. The equation is reversed, and his attention shifts to international conditions that can create the possibility of a national revolution.

4   Savoy, Italy, and Napoleon III

Given the failure of the uprisings of 1848 and 1853 and the new role played by the France of the Second Empire, the European political terrain forces Marx to rethink the forms of victorious revolution within unfavourable geopolitical conditions, evaluating the most favourable constitutional contexts and the objective relations of force between the States of the European arena. In this context we can also situate a series of articles on the Kingdom of Sardinia and on the Savoys, including 'La Sardegna' from November 27, 1855:

In the storm of the war of 1848 a constitution was drawn up, liberal at its base, which opened a new political era in Piedmont. Shortly afterward the Piedmontese armies were overwhelmed by the Austrians; the reaction however did not take hold of the government, and the constitutional regime became the patrimony of the nation.

MARX 1855C: 128

The survival of the Statuto Albertino thus made the Kingdom of Sardinia an exception with respect to the reaction raging at its borders, and Marx praises its 'progressive' political role without much hesitation: 'many things ardently desired by the friends of freedom remain to be done, but we applaud the good that has been accomplished, even if it is limited, in the face of conflicts so fraught with danger' (Marx 1855c: 129). The article concludes, somewhat presciently, with hopes that the Kingdom will play a leading role in the future independence of Italy: 'Sardinia is the nucleus of the future Italy. It is the bulwark against which Austrian bayonets will be broken and which will at least partially curb the control of clerics over the people' (Marx 1855c: 130).

This unprejudiced analysis of the character of the Kingdom of Sardinia with respect to European reaction certainly does not prevent, several months later, a disenchanted Marx from detecting the intrinsic weakness of the house of Savoy, given the small size of its territory and army. The Piedmontese political class deludes itself if it thinks that its constitutionalist experiment can 'become a conquering power. Such an idea could but originate with the great men of a little state' (Marx 1856a: 4), he writes on May 31, 1856, in 'Sardinia'. It is a state incapable of carrying forward an independent foreign policy because it is squeezed between two incomparably more solid states: France and Austria. Of the Savoy monarchy, Marx writes:

> It can but play the part of an Italian liberator in an epoch of revolution suspended in Europe, and of counter-revolution ruling supreme in France. Under such conditions it may imagine to take upon itself the leadership of Italy, as the only Italian state with progressive tendencies, with native rulers, and with a national army .... In case of serious friction between these neighbouring empires, it must become the satellite of one and the battlefield of both.
>
> MARX 1856a: 4

For Marx the Savoy monarchy is 'an Italian Belgium', whose fate is tied to France's destiny. A great monarchy on the other side of the Alps could only consent to a small, neighbouring monarchy; an Empire would at most tolerate a constitutional monarchy; in the event of the return of the republic to France, however, the future of the Piedmontese monarch would be doomed: 'The hopes of the house of Savoy thus are bound up with the *status quo* in Europe' (Marx 1856a: 4).

Marx's predictions are confirmed by the Second War of Independence, which in 1859 brings Italy back to the center of the international scene as the Savoys acquire Lombardy. But the prominent role played in the war by the French army is so clear that the Savoys will need to submit to the humiliation of receiving Lombardy 'as a gift' from the French, which in turn they had received from Austria with the peace of Zurich. Marx writes on May 18 in 'Fair Professions':

> It was only the sudden development of a peculiar interest on the part of Napoleon in Italian affairs that gave the Italian question any pressing

importance in the eyes of the other European Powers. Though Austria has been the first to commence hostilities, the fact still remains that but for encouragement given by Napoleon to Sardinia, in which neither Prussia nor England concurred, and the steps taken by her in consequence, there is no reason whatever to suppose that hostilities would have commenced.

MARX 1859b: 307–308

Before the war, on February 4, 1859, Marx had written to Lassalle:

The war would, of course, have serious, and without doubt ultimately revolutionary consequences. But initially it will maintain Bonapartism in France, set back the internal movement within England and Russia, revive the pettiest nationalist passions in Germany, etc., and hence, in my view, its initial effect will everywhere be counter-revolutionary.

MARX to LASSALLE 2/4/1859 in MECW 40: 382

Napoleon III is the real protagonist of the following events, and the alleged local leaders of the wars of liberation are no more than instruments of his foreign policy. On June 25, 1859, in an article in *Das Volk* titled 'Spree and Mincio', Marx reiterates the political centrality of Louis Bonaparte:

Voltaire, we know, kept four monkeys in Ferney, to which he had given the names of his four literary opponents, Fréron, Beaumelle, Nonnotte and Franc de Pompignan. Not a day passed without the writer's feeding them personally, kicking them liberally, pulling their ears, sticking pins in their noses, stepping on their tails, dressing them in clerical hoods and mistreating them in every possible way. The old man of Ferney needed these monkeys of criticism to draw off his bile, satisfy his hatred, and calm his fear of the weapons of polemics, just as much as Louis Bonaparte needs the monkeys of the revolution in Italy. And Kossuth, Klapka, Vogt and Garibaldi too are fed, given golden collars, kept under lock and key, cajoled or kicked, depending on whether hatred of the revolution or fear of it predominates in the mood of their master. The poor monkeys of the revolution are thus to be its hostages; they are to assure the man of December 2 an armistice on the part of the revolutionary party, so that he may, undisturbed, destroy the arsenals of Orsini-type bombs and fall on the enemy, whom he dreaded so long in the Tuileries, in his own camp, and strangle him.

MARX 1859c: 380

His judgment of the war in Italy is therefore opposite to that of 1848, and Marx's subsequent articles in the *New York Daily Tribune* will be no more than war reports. Piedmont, in this case under the wing of France, does nothing but strip portions of territory away from the Austrian empire and hand them over to the French sphere of influence, which maintains its position as the fundamental political guarantor of the Savoys. Beyond having widened its sphere of influence in Europe, 'the Italian war', Marx writes to Lassalle, 'has temporarily strengthened Bonaparte's position in France' (Marx to Lassalle 11/22/1859 in MECW 40: 537). If ten years earlier the war of national liberation in Italy could provide the spark for European revolution, when indeed it had not received help from anyone, in the Europe of 1859 it had the sole function of reinforcing domestically and internationally the most advanced political regime in Europe in terms of relations between bourgeoisie and proletariat, which Marx saw as the main obstacle to a revolutionary upswing. The critique of the Bonapartist regime is in fact in this period at the center of the 'Italian articles' by Marx as well as by Engels. Marx will remember ten years later:

> In 1848–1849 in the *Nuova Gazzetta Renana* I fought the Italian cause against the majority of Parliament and the German press. Later, in 1853 and during other periods, in the *New York Tribune* I took up the defense of a man with whom I had found myself in permanent opposition of principles: Mazzini. In a word, I always held the parties of Italy to be revolutionary against Austria, but the war of 1859 had been quite another thing: I denounced it as something that would prolong the existence of the Bonapartist Empire for another decade, subject Germany to the Prussian chain, and make Italy what it is today.
>
> MARX 1872: 39

At the end of the war, in 'What Has Italy Gained?' from July 27, 1859, Marx's account is peremptory: the fate of Italy has been decided 'at a short interview between the Emperors of France and Austria ... without the formality of even seeming to consult the parties who were the subjects of it' (Marx 1859d: 407). Not only did the Piedmontese elite play no substantive role in the negotiations, but the Italian masses were themselves treated as mere instruments of a war fought between foreign armies. What is really missing from the peace negotiations – Marx continues in the article 'The Treaty of Villafranca' from August 4, 1859 – is in fact the Italian movement. 'The Congress of Vienna itself, if its transactions be compared with the Villafranca job, may well be suspected of revolutionary principles and popular sympathies' (Marx 1859e: 417).

Marx is still closely following the developments of the Italian situation at the end of 1859, with French pressure for the restoration of the Princes in the duchies of central Italy, and with the resistance of the populations who supported the provisional governments after their expulsion. He does not pass up the opportunity to unmask the hypocrisy of Napoleon III and his instrumental use of rhetoric concerning the freedom of nations. He writes in 'The Current Position of Italy', on September 16, 1859:

> After having incited the populations of the duchies to oust their rulers and to side with France and Sardinia in the war against Austria, after having come to the point of inviting his cousin, Prince Napoleon, to assume command of their forces, with the peace of Villafranca, the French emperor abandoned them in a cowardly manner, accepting their old rulers as having been restored. But the populations of the duchies were decisively opposed to this agreement.
>
>   MARX 1859f: 345–346

Further confirming the fact that Marx's interest in Italian affairs is, in this phase, linked only to events on the European scene, especially in France, we find no significant articles on the unification of Italy after the Second War of Independence. In his analysis of unification movements in Italy Marx appears to reaffirm the connection between political emancipation and subordination to capital: national revolutions can no longer trigger social revolution because their outcome can only be successful if they submit to the European balance of power or to the direct blackmail of capital.

5   Conclusion

One brief and final phase of Marx's interest in Italy will come after 1871, when both he and Engels, through articles sent to Italian newspapers, or by speaking about Italian affairs in German or English newspapers, intervene in the debate by contributing to the formation of the Italian workers' movement. There are around thirty interventions, written by Marx and above all by Engels between 1871 and 1879, which criticize the various tendencies of the Italian movement in the context of the battle for communist hegemony within the First International. This intervention into the Italian debate has been reconstructed by Gianni Bosio, a key figure of the 'heterodox' Left who composed the first anthology of Marx's and Engels's writings on Italy (Bosio 1955) taking explicitly critical aim at the Italian Communist Party's (PCI) historicist and orthodox reconstruction, which, in the 1950s, viewed Italy solely through the lens of capitalist backwardness:

> How to reconcile, on the one hand, Marx's and Engels's interest in the Italian workers' movement and the actions they carried out, through direct intervention in Italian affairs, to try to form a class current during the years from 1871 to 1879, with, on the other, the thesis according to which the delayed development of modern capitalism in Italy would have guaranteed a delay in the formation of a class current in the Italian workers' movement? It is only a question that we pose, but it could lead us to rethink the simplistic thesis of the 'natural' delay of the formation of a class current in Italy .... Marx's and Engels's actions vis-à-vis Italy in the years from 1871 to 1879 is based on an historically mature evaluation of the Italian situation framed by the development of international capitalism.
>
> BOSIO 1955: 13–14

These interventions are in reality rather episodic and of merely relative importance, and they appear to take the form of normal communications between two established leaders of the international communist movement and small groups of Italian communists.

On the other hand, a more fruitful suggestion on this subject, even if hitherto disregarded, is one which Antonio Gramsci consigns to a note of the *Prison Notebooks*, pointing out the need for a collection of writings on Italy that comprises, in part: '1. writings with specific reference to Italy; [also] 2. writings on 'specific' arguments of historical and political criticism which, although not referring to Italy have a relevance to Italian problems' (Gramsci 1971: 416). The examples that Gramsci cites are 'the article on the Spanish Constitution of 1812 [which] has a relevance to Italy because of the political function that this constitution had in Italian political movements up to 1848' and 'the critique in *The Poverty of Philosophy* against the falsification of Hegelian dialectics made by Proudhon ... [since] this falsification finds its reflection in corresponding Italian intellectual movements (Gioberti, the Hegelianism of the Moderates, concept of passive revolution, dialectic revolution/restoration)'.

Regarding the Spanish constitution of 1812, Gramsci refers to the sixth of eight articles that Marx sent to the *New York Daily Tribune* between August and November 1854 under the title 'Revolutionary Spain' (Marx 1854b). This is a precise examination of the Spanish constitutional framework developed by the Cortes of Spain which resisted the occupation of Napoleon, who governed broad swaths of it through his brother Joseph. The document, which outlined a liberal constitutional monarchy, beyond being one of the first constitutions of the 19th century, was promulgated during a uniquely important conjuncture with respect to the national theme: that of the French occupation and the consequent abdication of the sovereign Ferdinando VII in favour of Joseph Bonaparte. The Cortes that had promulgated the constitution in Cadiz in 1812 thus included representatives who were quite liberal with respect to the Spanish elite of the time, which had a century of absolute Bourbon rule. For this reason, in the first half of the 19th century this constitution served as a model for different European constitutions, serving also as a point of reference for the Italian Carbonari during the Italian revolts of 1820–1821. This particular fact interested first Marx and then Gramsci, who shared curiosity in what could be defined as a relative autonomy of the constitutional plan with respect to economic development, a topic of some interest for the reconstruction of political and constitutional development of economically 'peripheral' countries such as Spain and Italy.

Gramsci's second insight concerns his critique of the theoretical current in Italy which interpreted the Hegelian dialectic as a continual overcoming of contradictions which presented themselves as already potentially resolved, where the predictability of moments and subjects permits one to treat the clash always as a function of its overcoming. This is the well-known Gramscian criticism of Gioberti, but above all of Croce ('Croce's position is similar to Proudhon's that was criticized in *The Poverty of Philosophy*; domesticated Hegelianism') (Gramsci 2007: 372), and to their conservative domestication of 'antitheses' which necessarily bring about a 'passive revolution' (Gramsci 1995: 373–376). In this case, as well, Marx's investigation on different grounds – his critique of Proudhon – becomes interesting in the Italian context, in terms of the investigation of the forms of philosophical critique appropriate to the particular 'national' declension of this 'domesticated Hegelianism'.

Ultimately, the reconstruction of Marx's journey from the prospective and partial point of view of his interest in Italy – from the centrality of national movements to its subaltern role in the international relations of force, up to the development of a class current in its nascent workers' movement – appears to show once again how Marx immediately presents himself equipped with a global thought, one that grasps the specificity of historical regions and events only within a comprehensive perspective of all relevant movements. In a thought oriented in this way, indeed mimicking a characteristic of capital, even a peripheral terrain such as Italy can offer a politically useful view of the overall movement.

CHAPTER 13

From the Commune to Communism?

Marx and Russia

Luca Basso

The theme of *Marx and Russia* is a complex and controversial one, not least in the light of 20th century events (Dörig 1960; Shanin 1983). From this standpoint, it is important to consider if, and how, the question of the communist revolution in Russia fits into the Marxian perspective. The following interpretation of the Marx-Russia relationship disagrees with two opposing interpretations which I find to be problematic, for different reasons. The first, typical of a 'traditional' Marxism, consists in underestimating the function of Russia, considering the country to be substantially irrelevant where Marx is concerned, not yet capitalistically developed and therefore unable to spawn a communist revolution without a capitalist model of production first being fully deployed. There are two key aspects to this view of things, namely the devaluation of Russia and the presence of a somewhat mechanical schema as concerning the passage from capitalism to communism. On this assumption, the communist revolution could have been brought about only in capitalistically advanced countries such as Britain or other Western European states. This approach has been followed in recent years by others, post-Marxist, predicating an interaction of the Marxian system with *Postcolonial Studies* (Spivak 1999; Chakrabarty 2000), on the basis of a critical stance taken with regard to every 'grand narrative' of the west, steeped in colonialism. In this scenario, the question of Russia takes on a special importance, since that country had not yet experienced the 'birth pangs' of the capitalist mode of production, and consequently one sees a high value being placed on the Russian commune. The interpretation given in this essay differs from both the approaches indicated. The first is marked by an excessive rigidity in the passage from capitalism to communism, and risks explaining the entire political horizon on the basis of a single model, drawn from the more advanced capitalist experiences, and in any event almost only as related to Europe. One cannot ignore the fact that Marx, from the 1850s onwards, expressed a growing interest in countries beyond Western Europe, like Russia, and non-European countries such as China and India. But, if the first approach is unsatisfactory, then the second is problematic in the extreme, as it paints the picture of a Marx who is 'archaic', anti-modern. From this point of view, any analysis of Russia must be conducted eschewing simplistic models that do not take in the ambivalences, and even the ambiguities, of Marx's thinking.

To explore the question posed here, one needs to bear in mind the relationship between the various levels of the discourse, between the theory and the politics: on the one hand, the spheres in question are closely linked, so that the theory cannot be discussed in isolation from the history and the politics; on the other hand, Marx does not bring about a full 'compaction' of the levels. The politics is not deduced from the theory, as it eludes a generalizing interpretation, and the theory cannot be 'pressed' onto the politics, as it has a character of abstraction. Marx's thematization of Russia is affected by this approach and sits unstably between an overall exposition of community-based structures and a specific plan of political intervention (Basso 2015: 85–99). Two preliminary observations must be added here, however. The first consideration is chronological in nature: the writings of Marx examined in this essay are from the 1850s to the early 1880s, and therefore I do not explore those of the 1840s. The reason for this exclusion is that, in Marx's early works, the references to Russia were not particularly significant, and took the general view of Russia as a 'backward' country. The second consideration relates to the fact that I will use various historical and political texts and various letters, with this methodological warning: Marx's analysis of Russia does not find any organization in the critique of political economy, since he never comes to affect a genuine connection between the writings in question and *Capital*.

A significant stage is datable to the 1850s, when Marx studies pre-capitalist situations; these are eloquently described at length in a pertinent section of the *Grundrisse* (Hobsbawm 1965; Terray 1969; Sofri 1969; Hindess and Hirst 1977; Janoska 1994): the first pre-capitalist form is identified as a natural community dedicated to pastoral farming, founded on the family and on the union of families, on the tribe, on the basis of a direct relationship with the land. One of the historical-geographical examples offered along these lines in the *Grundrisse* is that of the Slav community, in which there is no ownership, but only individual possession, given that the true 'owner' is the commune (*Gemeinde*). And so, from those years forward, Marx also conducts research on Slavs, and in particular on Russians. This exploration is intensified during the composition of *Capital*. Also highly significant, from a later period, are the ethnological and anthropological notebooks (1881–1882). Marx takes notes in particular from Lewis Henry Morgan, *Ancient Society* (1877), and from Henry Sumner Maine, *Lectures on the Early History of Institutions* (1875), but also from other authors such as Kovalevsky, Tylor, Lubbock, Phear. From this standpoint, the present essay discusses a theme also covered in the *Ethnological Notebooks*, namely that of the Russian commune, and whether or not it prefigures communism.

Following the death of Marx, certain writings of Engels, especially *The Origin of the Family, Private Property and the State* (1884), would give the sense of executing a legacy left by Marx. The main reason why Marx explores the Russian situation somewhat cursorily in the 1840s – and thereafter changes his stance – is to be found not only in terms of an intellectual reappraisal, but rather in a more thorough understanding of the social and political changes taking place in Russia.

Mention may be made here of certain systems that operated for several centuries, in a Russia founded on serfdom (Poggio 2017: IX–LI). The *Artel* was an associative form occurring spontaneously and connected with various trading, fishing and farming enterprises: one of its constitutive elements is the solidarity of its members toward the community. The *Obshchina* was a community of peasants, life tenants of the land they work and occupy, organized as a cooperative. The *Mir* was the assembly, the decision-making body of the community in question. As Gitermann points out, certain significant changes take place within the Russian scenario during the 1840s and 50s: in particular, the widespread adoption of a practice whereby the lord of the estate would release the peasants on his lands entirely or in part from their feudal obligations and allow them, on payment of a personal tribute in cash, known as *obrok*, to engage in any other profitable activity. Undoubtedly, even those peasants who paid *obrok* continued, under the law, to live in a condition of serfdom, although in reality they were no longer serfs in the full meaning of the word (Gitermann 1945).

The emergence of the *obrok* system caused the institution of serfdom gradually to crumble. Tsar Alexander II made certain important and significant reforms during the years 1861–1863. It was in 1861 that serfs, bound to the land hitherto, were recognized as free men with civil rights enabling them, like other Russian subjects, to enter into contracts and marry of their own volition without first asking permission of their lord. Serfs were accorded the chance to redeem small parcels of the land they worked from their lords, with the aid of loans granted to them by the state. The village assemblies, or *mir*, would stand guarantor for the debt incurred by the peasants. But the repayments were too heavy, foreshadowing the peasant revolts that occurred from 1861 to 1863. From this standpoint, Russia had undergone considerable changes from the 1840s to the early 1860s, tending at least in part toward a growth of capitalism, which generated hugely serious contradictions in social terms.

Marx explores this change in Russia during the 1860s and shows up the constitutive ambivalence therein. On the one hand, there is a move, albeit incomplete, beyond the patriarchal models of the past (Gitermann 1945, uses the expression 'greenhouse of capitalism'): 'The movement for the emancipation of the serfs in Russia strikes me as important' (Marx to Engels 4/29/1858 in MECW 40: 310); 'In my view, the most momentous thing happening in the world today is the slave movement – on the one hand, in America, started by the death of Brown, and in Russia, on the other' (Marx to Engels 1/11/1860 in MECW 41: 4). On the other hand, Marx also notes the devastating consequences of the change within this specific scenario (for example, the total domination of the usurer). If the conditions of the peasants freed from serfdom are extremely difficult, this does not mean – *sic et simpliciter* – that there has been a bourgeois evolution in the strict sense. This partial erosion in Russia of an unacceptable social system, based on a patriarchal structure, does not however herald an effective reconfiguration of social relations.

Just as it emerges that there is distance between the economic and social forms of Russia and those of Western Europe, so the political forms of Russia and those of Western Europe are far apart. If the state, though not reducible mechanically to the interests of capitalists, nonetheless presents the configuration of a structure suited to the production and reproduction of capital, the Russian Empire, interpreted in Marx's early writings as the stronghold of reaction (on the basis of an analysis covering the period 1789–1848), possesses characteristics that are profoundly different from those of the state. The case of Russia is singular due to its geopolitical position: in one sense, it cannot be considered an extra-European country, whilst in another, it covers an enormous expanse of Europe and Asia, so it is not a part of Europe purely and simply. According to the most classic Marxist reading, the Russian Empire is the political form suited to oriental despotism. Over time, Marx persists in his harsh criticism levelled against the autocracy of Tsarist Russia, but then tending to consider the Russian Empire not so much as the stronghold of reaction but more as the weakest link in the world market, albeit a country experiencing a certain internal dynamism, as witnessed by the reforms of the 1860s.

Within this new situation, presenting a mesh of economic, social and political factors, it now becomes necessary to explore the extremely complex and controversial theme of whether or not it may be possible, in Russia, to transition from a system as yet not truly capitalistic, to communism. The analysis of this question plays out on a hybrid level, concerning not only the historical and theoretical picture of the Russian world, but also the accessibility or otherwise of a revolutionary outbreak, and thus taking on a political character *sans phrase*. Marx sees and explores the rural commune as an emblem of the Russian situation. But the theme of natural communal ownership cannot be confined to the example of Russia, as Engels also makes plain:

> The *communal property* of the Russian peasants was discovered in 1845 by the Prussian Government Councillor Haxthausen and trumpeted to the world as something absolutely wonderful ... In reality, communal property of the land is an institution found among all Indo-Germanic peoples

at a low level of development, from India to Ireland ... In Western Europe, including Poland and Little Russia, at a certain stage in social development, this communal ownership) became a fetter, a brake on agricultural production, and was increasingly eliminated. In Great Russia ... on the other hand, it persists until today ... The Russian peasant lives and has his being only in his *obshchina* ... This is so much the case that, in Russian, the same word *mir* means, on the one hand, 'world' and, on the other, 'peasant community' ... Very great differences in degree of prosperity are possible and actually exist among the members of the community. The predominance of this form in Russia proves the existence in the Russian people of a strong impulse to associate ... which (however) serves the workers less than it does capital ... Under such conditions and under the pressure of taxes and usurers, communal ownership of the land is no longer a blessing; it becomes a fetter.

ENGELS 1875: 45–47

Similarly, Marx does not paint an irenical and idyllic picture of the Russian scenario: 'The whole business, down to the smallest detail, is absolutely identical with the primaeval Germanic communal system. Add to this, in the Russian case ...: a) the non-democratic, but patriarchal character of the commune leadership and b) the collective responsibility for taxes to the state, etc'. (Marx to Engels 11/7/1868 in MECW 43: 154).

In subsequent writings too, Marx remarks on the fact that the egalitarian nature of the Russian commune has been eroded, through the private accumulation of movable property such as livestock, money, and in some cases even servants. This property, which is removed from the control of the community, becomes of more and more account within the agricultural economy. From this standpoint, the position of Marx cannot be set alongside that of the Russian populists. It should be borne in mind, however, that there were very significant differences between these as well, and they cannot therefore be bracketed together readily and without difficulty (Venturi 1972; Walicki 1969; Tvardovskaja 1969). At all events, Marx is distinctly critical toward any idealization of the Russian commune, any mystical glorification of the 'Slavic mission'. Besides the anarchist Bakunin and the panslavist Herzen, mention must be made of other Russian authors studied by Marx and Engels, like Tkachyov, Chernyshevsky (Natalizi 2006), Bervi-Flerovsky and Mikhailovsky. Add to this the fact that it would be questionable to see all Russian populists as holding an anti-modernist position. Marx, while never engaging in an acritical exaltation of Russia, did nonetheless develop an increasingly solid interest over time in the rural commune.

The central question is one of whether the Russian commune might originate communism. More generally, one has to look at Marx's historical schema
and in particular the idea that communism would become possible only when
the capitalist mode of production had been fully rolled out. From this standpoint the Russian scenario is quite complex, as on the one hand it presents an
economic structure nothing like that of other European countries, whilst on
the other, it has been the scene of great changes during the 1860s. With the
passage of time, not least on the back of further anthropological and ethnological researches, Marx did not come to question, but rather rehearsed and
problematized his previous historical view. Looking to understand the uneven
course of history, its non-linear nature, Marx had developed ideas long before
the anthropological notes of later years: in this regard, for example, several
aspects of interest emerge from the Marx-Engels letters of the period 1868–
1870. Marx is also well aware that the collective distribution of land had been
customary among Germanic peoples up until the 19th century. And here, Marx
takes up various points from the work of legal historian Ludwig von Maurer
(*Geschichte der Dörfer Verfassung in Deutschland,* 1865–1866), especially the
idea that it was Asian forms of ownership which were the first to appear in
Europe. The question of communal land property is a complex one and cannot be explained simply by labelling it as something from long ago, a hang-
over from mediaeval times. Marx would come to the conviction, not least after
studying the work of Lewis H. Morgan, that features of the rural community
are found also among the native American Indians. Thus, it happens that capitalist production is fully developed in only one part of the world, but not universally: events similar in nature but taking place in different historical and
geographical environments have produced dissimilar outcomes (Anderson
2010). In this sense, the question of Russia and the Russian commune fits into
an overall picture abounding with points of reference. There are three particularly significant aspects: the ethnological and anthropological interpretation
of the forms of commune; the nature of the historical and political Russian
backdrop, and a specific political intervention.

In a letter to the journal *Otechestvenniye Zapiski,* Marx makes the following
observations:

> The chapter on primitive accumulation does not pretend to do more
> than trace the road by which in Western Europe the capitalist economic
> order emerged from the entrails of the feudal economic order ... Now, in
> what way was my critic [Zhukovsky] able to apply this historical sketch
> to Russia? Only this: if Russia is tending to become a capitalist nation, on

the model of the countries of Western Europe ... it will not succeed without having first transformed a large proportion of its peasants into proletarians ... It is absolutely necessary for him [my critic] to metamorphose
my historical sketch of the genesis of capitalism in Western Europe into a
historico-philosophical theory of general development, imposed by fate
on all peoples, whatever the historical circumstances in which they are
placed ... By studying each of these evolutions on its own, and then comparing them, one will easily discover the key to the phenomenon, but it
will never be arrived at by employing the all-purpose formula of a general
historico-philosophical theory whose supreme virtue consists in being
supra-historical.

> MARX to *Otechestvenniye Zapiski* 11/1877 in MECW 24: 199–201

Marx engages in a reassessment of his analysis on primitive accumulation
in the first book of *Capital* (Luxemburg 1913; Harvey 2003): the question of
the progression from feudalism to capitalism needed to be expressed in less
mechanical terms (Patterson 2009: 130). Marx always looked in his thinking for
a mutual interaction, albeit on the basis of an essential instability, between a
broad appreciation of the course of history, and attention to the specific situation in which a political action took place (Assoun 1978; Garo 2012). With the
passage of time, the importance of geographic specificity, not related *ipso facto*
to a generalizing schema, becomes more and more apparent. This does not
mean a refusal to express an overall conception of history, in relation to which,
however, the singularity of historical and geographical factors can appear,
case by case, on the basis of differentiated geometries, to be both 'within' and
'against'. This approach, which comes across as a destructuring of philosophy
as it had been understood up until that point, rejects the *'passe partout* of a
philosophy of history'. Consequently, Marx's thinking cannot be taken either
as a philosophy of history (indeed it is not always possible to define uniquely
what this concept effectively conveys) or as an anti-philosophy of history, given
that it entirely posits the need for a strong interaction between history and
theory, but without ever imagining that the former could be subordinated to
the latter. In effect, this way of setting out the question would be undermined
precisely by that spirit of 'critical criticism' for which Marx had been sharply
reproaching 'Bruno Bauer and company' since the 1840s. Emerging here are,
on the one hand, a historical-theoretical narrative tending to see Russia in an
ever broader scenario, and on the other, a question that is *sans phrase* political, concerning the possibility or otherwise of a revolutionary way forward.
The two elements are connected but cannot be made to coincide (Maffi 2008:

31–32). Marx explores and criticizes the disciplines of his time – historical, economic and social – seeking to destructure them, but not staying on a purely theoretical plane. It could be said that, rather than a critical theory (as would be delineated in the 20th century), this is more a critique of theory, a questioning of the manner in which the relationship between theory and practice has been formulated thus far, and laying the ground instead for a continuous, yet unstable interchange between conceptual analysis and social and political transformation. Compared to the schema of the *Theses on Feuerbach*, however, the later Marx does not recognize any kind of linearity between an expansive philosophical outlook and the revolution, since this is a rocky road, full of surprises, in which philosophy no longer has a sort of primacy.

In this context there is a need to examine the correspondence between Marx and the Russian revolutionary Vera Zasulič (Geierhos 1977), which affords various points of interest, but also of potential misunderstanding. The circumstance of the letter from Marx to Vera Zasulič is worthy of note: Marx, in poor health at the time, was seeking to bring the first Russian Marxist group into being as smoothly as he could manage. He wrote a number of pages in four drafts, much longer than the letter ultimately sent, and full of corrections; the actual letter does contain all of the argumentation laid out in the draft. 'Its constitutive form allows this alternative: either the element of private property which it implies will gain the upper hand over the collective element, or the latter will gain the upper hand over the former. Both these solutions are *a priori* possible ...' (Marx to Zasulič 8/3/1881, First draft, in MECW 24: 352).

Again, there is the question concerning the ambiguity of the Russian commune in this period, its oscillation between communitarian aspects and new privatization dynamics. Always bearing in mind, first, that the communitarian dimension must not be idealized, and second, that in Russia it is not configurable in democratic terms, which of the two forces in play would dominate? Marx writes to Zasulič that the schema of *Capital* neither admits nor excludes the possibility of a transition from Russian commune to communism:

> ... the analysis provided in Capital does not adduce reasons either for or against the viability of the rural commune, but the special study I have made of it, and the material for which I drew from original sources, has convinced me that this commune is the fulcrum of social regeneration in Russia, but in order that it may function as such, it would first be necessary to eliminate the deleterious influences which are assailing it from all sides, and then ensure for it the normal conditions of spontaneous development.
>
> MARX to ZASULIČ 8/3/1881 in MECW 24: 371

Tracking this development – entirely hypothetical, in effect – Marx draws attention to the possibility that the Russian commune could function as a propulsive force in establishing collective production on a national scale:

> ... it is first of all evident that one of its [of the Russian commune] fundamental characteristics, communal ownership of the land, forms the natural basis of collective production and appropriation ... It is precisely this point which demonstrates the 6great superiority of the Russian 'rural commune' over archaic communes of the same type. Alone in Europe it has kept going on a vast, nationwide scale.
>
> MARX to ZASULIČ 8/3/1881, First draft, in MECW 24: 355–356

> What is threatening the life of the Russian commune is neither historical inevitability nor a theory; it is oppression by the state and exploitation by capitalist intruders, who have been made powerful at the expense of the peasants by the very same state.
>
> MARX to ZASULIČ 8/3/1881, Second draft, in MECW 24: 362–363

> As far as this is concerned, it is no longer a matter of solving a problem; it is simply a matter of beating an enemy. To save the Russian commune, a Russian revolution is needed ... If revolution comes at the opportune moment ..., the latter [the rural commune] will soon develop as an element of regeneration in Russian society and an element of superiority over the countries enslaved by the capitalist system.
>
> MARX to ZASULIČ 8/3/1881, First draft, in MECW 24: 359–360

The question cannot not be fully resolved on the theoretical level of a historical dialectic, since it is radically political in character. Notwithstanding there are certain ambiguities in the drafts of the letter to Zasulič, one has to remember that this was a case of making a political gamble on Russia. On the one hand, Russia could no longer be considered the stronghold of reaction, whilst on the other, this is a country in which there had not yet been a true reorganization on capitalist lines as in western countries. This state of ambivalence would have highly significant consequences as touching both the revolutionary subject, given that the majority of the population was made up of peasant farmers, and the way that struggles were carried on, since the political and trade union organizations existing in Western European countries had not yet been developed.

From a careful examination both of his letters to various Russian revolutionaries and theorists, and of other writings from the 1870s and 1880s, it will be seen that Marx took up a fairly prudent position, providing no undeniably affirmative response to the idea that the Russian commune might transition to communism. Indeed, he states two non-negotiable conditions for this. The first is that the retention and transformation of the Russian commune as a basis for the establishment of communism would be conceivable only if the revolutionary insurgence were to take place swiftly and incisively. But a revolution in Russia could not, on its own, create a communist society. Accordingly, the second condition is that the Russian revolution must be completed by a working-class revolution in the West. Without this, in effect, the passage from Russian commune to communism would be almost unachievable: it did not suffice, seemingly, to rely on the potentially expansive aspects of Russian associative structures. On this point, it is evident that the outlook of Marx and the thinking of Russian populists do not readily match up, even considering the different positions adopted by the latter, as emerges clearly in Marx's *Preface* to the second Russian edition of the *Manifesto of the Communist Party*.

> The first Russian edition of the *Manifesto of the Communist Party*, translated by Bakunin, was published early in the sixties ... Russia and the United States of all places are missing here [in the *Manifesto*]. It was the time when Russia constituted the last great reserve of all European reaction ... But in Russia we find ... more than half the land owned in common by the peasants. Now the question is: can the Russian *obshchina*, a form of primeval common ownership of land, even if greatly undermined, pass directly to the higher form of communist common ownership? Or must it, conversely, first pass through the same process of dissolution as constitutes the historical development of the West? The only answer possible today is this: If the Russian Revolution becomes the signal for a proletarian revolution in the West, so that the two complement each other, the present Russian common ownership of land may serve as the starting point for communist development.
>
> MARX 1882: 425–426; cf. BONGIOVANNI 1989b: 171–189; HECKER 2014

In the first place, the *Manifesto of the Communist Party* was not faulted, but was nonetheless amended, beginning with a specific analysis of the historical and political events that occurred over more than thirty years from 1848 onwards (Balibar 1974). Pertinently, Marx remarks in the above noted *Preface* that Russia and the United States, two countries so crucial to global affairs and so different one from another, are not even mentioned in the *Manifesto*. This was not so much an abstract theoretical reappraisal, as an attentive examination of the changes that had taken place in recent decades, not least in relation to the Russian situation (Lenin 1908). In addition, there is a reference to the notion of whether or not a transition from Russian commune to communism could occur. Hence the dilemma: might the *obshchina* be a 'touch-paper' to ignite communism, or would the 'birth pangs' of the capitalist mode of production inevitably be experienced as part of a long historical journey still to come? If the first hypothesis were to prove true, hence without requiring a full roll-out of capitalism, it would be conditional not only on a Russian revolution taking place swiftly, but also on the existence of an external factor, namely a communist revolution in the West.

In Marx's late output, on the 'objective' level, the social and political perspective is redefined on the basis of a wider geographical scope than considered before: materially and metaphorically, the world had grown beyond what had been delineated previously and could no longer be confined to the boundaries of Western Europe alone (with reference in particular to Germany, France and Britain), as seemed mostly to be the case from Marx's train of thought up until 1848. In addition to the Russian analysis, the studies of China and India are especially significant. In some ways, the reference to Russia seems to be even more important than those made to the Asian countries in question, at least in view of the frequency with which the topic reappears in the later writings, and of the very marked attempt, albeit with the ambivalences highlighted, to invest it with a political significance *sans phrase*. And in *Capital*, especially in the notes, one finds numerous 'traces' of other non-European countries, such as Latin American countries. As mentioned at the beginning of the essay, taking up this position does not mean that Marx can be seen straightforwardly as a kind of herald of post-colonial studies, and it is doubtless impossible to understand his most important work, *Capital*, without constantly bearing in mind the reference to the British scenario.

Increasingly in Marx there is at work an awareness that the capitalist mode of production has not been developed everywhere and has not unfolded uniformly. Thus, one has a coexistence of capitalist systems that are developed, and systems that are not capitalist or not fully developed. Moreover, as Marx emphasizes in a letter of 1858 to Engels (Marx to Engels 10/8/1858 in MECW 40: 346–347) and as recurs continually in his writings, the pull toward the world market is inscribed in the very concept of capital. Beyond the trust in an immediate revolutionary breakthrough, linked not least to the political investment (ultimately a failure) in the great panic of 1857, the propitious aspect of the letter in question lies in the realization that our continent is no more than 'a little corner of the world'. It follows that the gamble of a social revolution cannot but reach out totally into those expanding spaces that are no longer reducible to the confines of Western Europe. Russia, endowed with a position at once decisive (not least by reason of its enormous size, and a notable influence on

European history) and eccentric (given the difference of its economic, social and political structures from those of Western Europe), is included by Marx in an analysis of the world market, no longer relegated to the role of being a wreckage of the past. The theme of the relationship between different contexts also has a subjective connotation, correlated to its objective counterpart but without being mechanically deducible therefrom. Where Russia is concerned, the response of Marx is ambivalent, if not tentative, neither excluding nor even univocally predicting a revolutionary explosion. The *Gemeinwesen*, typical of non-capitalist or not entirely capitalist organizations (like the *obshchina*), is neither rejected nor idealized. In effect, on the one hand, it is important to avoid putting forward a simplified and linear representation of the historical process, in keeping with the 'grammar' of Western modernity. On the other, there is the need to focus attention on the complex and at times even contradictory nature of the common dimension.

Marx differentiates between pre-capitalist communities, in which the free growth of individuals appears to be impossible, the community typical of the state, with its demarcation of territorial limits, physical and metaphorical, and the communist association. It seems that the terminological choices he makes are not always guided by rigour, but it is significant that the word *Gemeinschaft*, which in *The German Ideology* referred not only to the capitalist system but, on the basis of a 'transvaluation', to communist society as well, is practically never used again thereafter to characterize communism. Symptomatically, to avoid any organicist misconstruction, the rejection of this term occurs coincidentally with the use of others like *Verein, Vereinigung, Assoziation*, to indicate the possible (not inevitable) emancipated scenario of the future. In this context, an important role would be played – not without ambiguities and not without alternations (as witness its use, in the *Grundrisse*, to denote both pre-capitalist forms, and money), and with a long history in Marx's writings – by the concept of *Gemeinwesen*, which, compared to *Gemeinschaft*, carries a greater sense of dynamism (Sereni 2010: 143). As observed by Engels, 'we would ... suggest that *Gemeinwesen* be universally substituted for *state*; it is a good old German word that can very well do service for the French *Commune*' (Engels to Bebel 3/18–28/1875 in MECW 24: 71; for a contemporary redefinition of this question, see: Hardt and Negri 2009; Dardot and Laval 2014). The Russian commune can be translated into German using the term *Gemeinde*, which also indicates the administrative and institutional structure, but *Gemeinwesen* captures its expansive, unpredictable potentialities, which cannot be reduced to a blueprint defined once and for all. This examination of the common dimension should make no one forget that Marx's entire output (even the late writings) is devoid of any communitarian bias, and consequently, communism is never delineated with an anti-individualistic and organicistic approach; rather, the tendency is to create a dynamic give-and-take between individual and common property, in radical opposition to private property (Basso 2012). Moreover, one cannot ignore the fact that the rural commune in Russia during the 1870s and 1880s, the period of Marx's particular interest, was undergoing processes of accumulation: the Russian structure in that situation does not qualify *sic et simpliciter* as non-capitalist. The theme of the *Gemeinwesen*, again, as related to Russia, must be interpreted allowing for its ambivalence, and therefore accepted politically as a challenge, a gamble, requiring a continual readiness to acknowledge shifts and adjustments in one's understanding of the question.

CHAPTER 14

'A Sea of Revolution'

Marx, India and China

Giorgio Grappi

The bourgeoisie, by the rapid improvement of all instruments of production, by the immensely facilitated means of communication, draws all, even the most barbarian, nations into civilization. The cheap prices of commodities are the heavy artillery with which it batters down all Chinese walls, with which it forces the barbarians' intensely obstinate hatred of foreigners to capitulate. It compels all nations ... to introduce what it calls civilization into their midst, i.e., to become bourgeois themselves. In one word, it creates a world after its own image.

MARX and ENGELS 1848: 488

• • •

Thus, events strikingly analogous, but occurring in different historical milieux, led to quite disparate results. By studying each of these evolutions on its own, and then comparing them, one will easily discover the key to the phenomenon, but it will never be arrived at by employing the all-purpose formula of a general historico-philosophical theory whose supreme virtue consists in being supra-historical.

MARX 1877: 201

• •
•

In this chapter I will discuss Marx's extensive engagement with India, and to a lesser extent with China, analysing the articles he wrote between 1853 and 1861 as part of his prolific journalistic activity at the *New York Daily Tribune*. Although not systematic in nature, they are the only body of texts devoted to the subject – elsewhere Marx touches on it only in isolated passages – and are among the few texts Marx wrote in English. Newspaper articles have a unique character within Marxian production, bringing together a reportage style, with analysis and political polemic. In a letter to Engels, Marx made it clear that he was engaged in a 'clandestine campaign' against the hypocrisy of the American protectionists, who found ample space in the *Tribune*. He writes that his campaign also includes his 'first article on India, in which England's destruction of native industries is described as *revolutionary*', something that 'they will find very shocking', given that 'the whole administration of India by the British was detestable and still remains so today' (Marx to Engels 6/14/1853 in MECW 39: 346; Perelman 2008; Espinoza Pino and Mezzadra 2018).

In the Communist Manifesto, Marx and Engels had pointed out the ability of the bourgeoisie to 'create a world after its own image' by using the low cost of its goods as 'the heavy artillery with which it batters down all Chinese walls' to drag every nation into bourgeois 'civilization'. When, five years after the publication of the Manifesto, he starts writing about India, the tone is similar. In the course of these writings, however, his point of view changes and is enriched by open questions. Beginning from an analysis of the range of capital's action that was in fact limited to Europe, and within a historical process that seemed to him unstoppable, Marx comes to grasp elements of a difference that become an integral part of the very nature of capital, *complicating* its linear movement.

I am not interested in philologically reconstructing his position through texts in which there is no shortage of contradictions, which are largely drawn up on the basis of government reports and official documents, and where Marx often uses categories that reflect the common sense of a European gaze that was opening towards Asia (Krader 1975). Nor do I want to suggest that newspaper articles can be equated with systematic political theories. The aim of this chapter is instead to identify, where possible, the passages that relate to this *complication*. The scope is to highlight not so much the coherence of Marx's discourse on India and China, but the elements that allow us to grasp its problematic, open and evolving aspects, which contribute to making Marx's thought mobile, its value depending more on a 'strategic' character in constant confrontation with concrete conditions and revolutionary political practice, than on a scientific systematic approach (Mezzadra and Samaddar 2020; Consolati 2019).

1 Destruction and Regeneration

In his first articles on India, published in 1853, Marx argued that England had a double mission in India, 'one destructive, the other regenerating' (Marx 1853i: 217). Even if the intervention of the British led to 'the annihilation of old

Asiatic society' (Marx 1853i: 217), that Marx describes as a 'strange combination of Ireland and of Italy' (Marx 1853j: 125), it also produced some necessary conditions for its regeneration. These include the political unity of the territory and the formation of a new class of natives, 'imbued with European science' (Marx 1853i: 218). The mission was not yet complete due to the persistent 'dissolution of society into stereotype and disconnected atoms', but Marx was confident that the railways and new means of communication would definitively break the 'self-sufficient *inertia of the villages*' (Marx 1853i: 219–220). However, India would not be able to enjoy the fruits of regeneration

> till in Great Britain itself the now ruling classes shall have been supplanted by the industrial proletariat, or till the Hindoos themselves shall have grown strong enough to throw off the English yoke altogether
> MARX 1853i: 221

a possibility in which Marx displays a certain confidence. If this is the general outline of Marx's views on India, he tries to go deeper in his other articles, to define both the character of Indian society and that of the British government of India.

He employs the model of the *hydraulic* society prevalent at the time to argue for the centrality of the 'department' of public works and irrigation in Asian governments, calling the other two departments that made up Asian governments, those of finance and war, 'the plunder of the interior' and 'the plunder of the exterior', highlighting the parasitic nature of 'Asiatic despotism' (Marx 1853j: 127; Gunawardana 1976: 25–27). The fact that the British, despite having inherited the finance and war departments, had 'neglected entirely [the department] of public works' (Marx 1853j: 127), was the main reason why once cultivated and prosperous regions had become deserted. Moreover, while the government was failing in its duties, 'British steam and science' had flooded what was 'the very mother country of cotton with cotton' and British artefacts, destroying the old village system characterized by 'the union between agriculture and manufacturing industry' (Marx 1853j: 125–133). But Marx also observed that 'these idyllic village-communities, inoffensive though they may appear, had always been the solid foundation of Oriental despotism' (Marx 1853j: 132) and, in a polemic against a nascent Orientalist romanticism, declared from the outset that he did not share 'the opinion of those who believe in a golden age of Hindostan' (Marx 1853j: 126). If capital exploited labour power by subjecting it to the laws of labour and accumulation, traditional village societies did nothing more than subject human power to superstitions that consolidated a hierarchical structure. This presumed nature was thus actually 'contaminated' by distinctions, slavery and rigid social relations that constituted, in Marxian analysis, the true foundations of the 'Oriental despotism' (Habib 2006).

In *Capital* we read that the social structure centred on the village community functions 'in accordance with an approved and authoritative plan' (Marx 1867a: 362), in which 'each individual has no more torn himself off from the navel-string of his tribe or community, than each bee has freed itself from connection with the hive' (Marx 1867a: 339). It is for this reason that, however 'vile' England's interests were and however unjust and barbaric its conduct, Marx wonders whether 'mankind' could 'fulfil its destiny without a fundamental revolution in the social state of Asia' (Marx 1853j: 132). He argues that if the answer to this question is no, then 'whatever may have been the crimes of England she was the unconscious tool of history in bringing about that revolution' (Marx 1853j: 132). Therefore, despite the 'bitterness' produced by the spectacle of the 'crumbling of an ancient world' (Marx 1853j: 132), Marx sees English penetration in Asia as an element in the direction of historical progress, capable of overwhelming traditional societies that prevent the full expression of human faculties.

Arguing with those who were scandalized by the destruction of the 'native *States*', Marx further argues that they were largely puppets of the British, and that 'they virtually ceased to exist from the moment they became subsidiary to or protected by the Company' (Marx 1853k: 198). The argument about their eventual annexation was therefore misplaced and the real issue was not 'the native States, but the native *Princes* and Courts', which were 'the strongholds of the present abominable English system and the greatest obstacles to Indian progress' (Marx 1853k: 198). With these observations, Marx pointed out another kind of obstacle to Indian regeneration beyond the archaic and isolated system based on the village community: the de facto parasitic class of Indian nobles and notables, fully integrated into and nurtured by the English system. Yet this does not mean Marx excludes the possibility that the energy for radical change may emerge from India itself. Indeed, as well as considering the possibility that Indians might become strong enough to break British rule on their own, he disagrees with those who, like Sir Thomas Munro and Lord Elphinstone, argued that it was necessary to maintain a native aristocracy to prevent India's decline. Marx notes that, apart from an aristocratic class in the service of the English, 'the natives, under direct English rule, are systematically excluded from all superior offices, military and civil', while he agrees with George Campbell, author of a detailed account on government and institutions in India, that in order to meet new needs it is necessary to form 'a fresh class' and that 'from the acuteness and aptness to learn of the inferior classes, this can be done in India as it can be done in no other country' (Marx 1853k: 199).

2   The Value of Dominion

In 1853 Marx noted that '[t]he English oligarchy have a presentiment of the
approaching end of their days of glory' and therefore sought to establish the
conditions to maintain 'for themselves and their associates the privilege of
plundering India for the space of 20 years' (Marx 1853l: 104). He sarcastically
commented that, in the on-going debates in England on the reform of the
Indian government, the classic question 'who shall be the governing power?'
was being replaced for the first time since Aristotle by the 'irregular' question: 'who among us is the actual governing power over that foreign people of
150 million of souls?' (Marx 1853m: 178). While everyone agreed they wanted
to make India a source of wealth, there was no agreement on how to do it. It
was therefore a question of trying to reconstruct how the relation of England
with India changed from that of a simple trading company into such a political
conundrum.

The British government, Marx writes, 'has been fighting, under the Company's
name, for two centuries', managing to subjugate India to English *suzeraineté*
'under various forms', while all parties, including those who now criticize the
Empire, agreed in silence because they 'had to get it', before subjecting it 'to
their sharp philanthropy' (Marx 1853n: 152). Here we can see that the 'Indian
question' has acquired a more general political relevance to England itself
and the 1853 Charter renewal debate than it had in previous debates. During
this period, the nature of trade relations between England and India had
changed: if during the 18th century Indian wealth had been acquired mainly
'by the direct exploitation of that country, and by the colossal fortunes there
extorted and transmitted to England', by 1813 trade had very quickly tripled and
India was 'inundated with English twists and cotton stuff' (Marx 1853n: 154).
Thus, as domestic production was destroyed 'at the same rate which the cotton manufactures became of vital interest for the whole social frame of Great
Britain, East India became of vital interest for the British cotton manufacture'
(Marx 1853n: 154). This caused the end of the convergence of different British
interests and 'India became the battle-field in the contest of the industrial
interest on the one side, and of the moneyocracy and oligarchy on the other'
(Marx 1853n: 155).

This explains the increasing interventionism of the English government
in the affairs of the Company, to the point of constituting a real '*double
Government*' (Marx 1853m: 178). The result was a joint stock company that governed an immense empire, formed not by nobles, as in Venice, but by a 'permanent and irresponsible *bureaucracy*', the weird '*creatures of the desk and the
favour* residing in Leadenhall-st' (Marx 1853m: 183). At its head was a Court

of Directors made up of Company shareholders and elected by 'elderly ladies and valetudinarian gentlemen, possessing Indian stock, having no other interest in India except to be paid their dividends out of Indian revenue' (Marx 1853m: 182). This *'succursal* to the English moneyocracy' was in fact a large patronage structure, which managed a huge set of administrative and military posts on a personal basis by excluding Indians from the most important positions (Marx 1853m: 182). A few years later, Marx noted that in the last hundred years the British Parliament had legislated several times to financially support the Company and save it from bankruptcy. It was therefore clear that to understand 'what is the real value of their dominion to the British nation and people' it was necessary to look not at the government, but at English society and 'to the profits and benefits which accrue to individual British subjects' (Marx 1857a: 349).

According to Marx, the shareholders who received annual dividends and the directors and officials who received a salary were at the top of a large clientele made up of thousands of civil and military officers and other subjects 'employed in trade or private speculation'. Their private gain 'goes to increase the sum of the national wealth', but this had to be balanced against the fact that the expense of maintaining the Company's power, 'paid out of the pockets of the people of England', has constantly increased. It was therefore doubtful whether 'on the whole' their dominion did not cost the English people more than they could get out of it (Marx 1857a: 352). However, the Company survived thanks to its 'political revenue' and the large interests around its operations, which drove Parliament to act to pay its creditors and to meet its growing expenses. Through recapitalization, its debt was in fact transformed 'by a Parliamentary sleight of hand' (Marx 1858c: 444) into a debt belonging to the whole English people.

At the same time, 'a disproportionately large part' of the fiscal interest of the Anglo-Indian government depended upon the profits derived from the opium trade with China and on its 'contraband character', due to the ban on opium consumption imposed by China (Marx 1858d: 18, 20). Marx argued that this marked the East India Company's transition from a mercantile configuration to a form of government: the Company losing its commercial privilege with China, trade was transferred to private enterprises, but cultivation and smuggling were in fact organized and managed by the Company itself and constituted 'integral parts of its own financial system' (Marx 1858d: 16). Thus, while the 'semi-barbarian' took the side of morality by prohibiting the consumption of opium, the 'civilized' turned to its production and smuggling, thus showing the hypocrisy of free trade imposed by the force of the cannon and based on the monopoly of the strongest, since 'while openly preaching free trade in poison, it secretly defends the monopoly of its manufacture' (Marx 1858d: 16, 20).

3   'Something Is Brewing'

In May 1857, an episode that seemed to be a simple mutiny of 'native' troops, the Sepoys, quickly spread into a real 'revolt' with unprecedented characteristics: not only were English officers killed for the first time, but 'Mussulmans and Hindoos, renouncing their mutual antipathies, [had] combined against their common masters' (Marx 1857b: 298). The Sepoys had been underestimated by 'the English people', who had been convinced that 'the Sepoy army constituted their whole strength in India', and now 'all at once they feel quite satisfied that that very army constitute[d] their sole danger' (Marx 1857c: 315–316). But things were different. The rebels took control of Delhi and events showed how 'a general union against the British rule, of all the different tribes, was rapidly progressing'. Marx added, 'by and by there will ooze out other facts able to convince even John Bull himself that what he considers a military mutiny is in truth a national revolt' (Marx 1857c: 315–316). Overall, the events that Marx referred to as 'the Indian insurrection' would lead him to look at the subcontinent from a slightly different perspective than that which he had taken in his earlier interventions (Marx 1857d: 327–330). Whereas in 1853 Marx considered the unification of India to be an element of progress introduced by the British, he now observed that the conditions of British supremacy had changed following the conquest: the Company was 'no longer conquering, it had become *the* conqueror' and 'found itself placed at the head, and the whole of India at its feet'. The troops serving the Company in India, Marx added, 'from soldiers ... were converted into policemen'. This means that some two hundred million 'natives' were now being 'curbed' by the Sepoys, an army of men of their own rank, who in turn were 'being kept in check' by an English army of only forty thousand men (Marx 1857b: 297).

The mutiny showed that this equilibrium after the conquest of India was short-lived and was the culmination of an 'insurrection' against the colonial rulers whose significance went beyond India: it was in fact part of 'a general disaffection exhibited against English supremacy on the part of the great Asiatic nations', which was 'intimately connected' with the Persian and Chinese wars (Marx 1857b: 298). What emerges from these chronicles is a Marx at times fascinated by military strategies, and also torn between his interest in the evolution of the international exchequer and his recognition that something new was happening. In the first respect, which was that which most interested his editors, Marx relied mainly on Engels and on 'a little [of] dialectic', admitting that he had no great expertise on the subject (Marx to Engels 8/15/1857 in MECW 40: 152). However, analysing the course of the war allowed Marx to note its profound political effects on Indian society and the Empire, so much so that

> no greater mistake could be committed than to suppose that the fall of Delhi, though it may throw consternation among the ranks of the Sepoys, should suffice either to quench the rebellion, to stop its progress, or to restore the British rule.
>
> MARX 1857e: 306

The size of the revolt, the 'prologue of a most terrible tragedy' (Marx 1857b: 300), was not yet completely clear, but it had already produced some important consequences. Marx wrote that, no longer able to rely on native troops, the British 'command only the spot of ground held by their own troops, and the next neighborhood domineered by that spot', adding that 'any idea of collecting the regular taxes throughout the Bengal presidency must be abandoned' (Marx 1857e: 307).

Exposed to 'the incessant sorties of the rebels' and the 'ravages of the cholera', in some provinces 'the British forces were gradually drifting into the position of small posts planted on insulated rocks amid a sea of revolution' (Marx 1857f: 344, 348). Peasants, princes, *zamindar* and *taluqdar*, joined the Sepoy for different reasons. The growth of a general 'disaffection' towards English rule as a whole was also seen in the financial 'panic' widespread among 'the native capitalists' in the Bombay money market, the 'very large sums ... withdrawn from the banks', and in the fact that 'Government securities proved almost unsalable' and that 'hoarding to a great extend commenced, not only in Bombay but in its environs also' (Marx 1857e: 308). Marx saw in the lack of financial confidence of the 'Indian capitalists' the measure of the Indian people's mistrust and the depth of the political crisis enveloping the Empire. The issue of public debt securities in Calcutta 'turned out a complete failure' and the Indians, Marx wrote sarcastically,

> appear not to understand the beauty of a plan which would not only restore English supremacy at the expense of Indian capital, but at the same time, in a circuitous way, open the native hoards to British commerce.
>
> MARX 1858c: 445

This 'financial muddle', Marx pointed out in a letter to Engels, 'must be seen as the real result of the Indian Mutiny' and 'John Bull has cheated himself, or rather has been cheated by his capitalists' because 'India's payments are merely nominal, whereas those of John Bull are real' (Marx to Engels 4/9/ 1859: 412–413). On the whole, Marx had previously observed with some satisfaction in another letter to his friend, 'in the view of the drain of men and bullion which she will cost the English, India is now our best ally' (Marx to Engels 1/16/1858 in MECW 40: 249). I would not go so far as to argue, as Anderson does, that Marx regarded the uprising itself as a direct ally of the revolutionary movement in the West but would say that his articles and letters confirm that he was increasingly intrigued by the form taken by the insurrection in India (Anderson 2010: 37–41). The whole structure of the British control of India seemed to be crumbling before his eyes. The Indian revolt started not among the *ryots,* who were 'tortured, dishonored and stripped naked by the British', but by the Sepoys that where 'clad, fed, petted, fatted and pampered by them'. This confirmed the historic rule of 'retribution', whose instruments were forged 'not by the offended, but by the offender himself', which had already been seen in the French Revolution, when 'the first blow dealt to the French monarchy proceeded from the nobility, not from the peasants' (Marx 1857g: 353). However, Marx argued, it would be 'a curious *quid pro quo* to expect an Indian revolt to assume the features of a European revolution', because the basis and forms of political power were different. He wrote that while the Indian princes, 'like true Asiatics, are watching their opportunity, and the people in the whole Presidency of Bengal ... are enjoying a blessed anarchy', in fact, 'there is nobody there against whom they could rise' (Marx 1857d: 329).

Military supremacy would mean the British would regain control of rebel strongholds in the following years, but what Engels described as 'the second conquest' of India was a harbinger of future crises and, he writes, 'has not increased England's hold upon the mind of the Indian people' (Engels 1858: 610). In a letter to Danielson over twenty years later, Marx confirmed this judgement by stating: 'In *India* serious complications, if not a general outbreak, is in store for the British government'. The reason lay in the continuous 'bleeding process' by which the English took annually from India, 'in the form of rent, dividends for railways useless to the Hindoos, pensions for military and civil servicemen, for Afghanistan and other wars, etc. etc'., an amount of money that was '*more than the total sum of income of the 60 million of agricultural and industrial labourers of India!*' (Marx to Danielson 2/19/1881: 63). Against all this, he writes, 'there is an actual conspiracy going on wherein Hindus and Mussulmans cooperate'. But, he argues, even if the British government 'is aware that something is *brewing*, this shallow people (I mean the governmental men)' prefer to follow the *parliamentary wisdom* 'to delude others and by deluding them to delude yourself'. But the prospect of disaster does not seem to upset Marx, who concludes the letter by exclaiming: '*Tant mieux!*' (Marx to Danielson 2/19/1881: 64).

4   Slowdowns and Differences

The temporary end of the conflict allowed Marx, prompted by his publisher, to return to India's financial difficulties: the Company had been running annual deficits for at least twenty years, aggravated by the outbreak of the revolt. It was not only the military expenditure that was weighing on the country, but also the increase in liabilities and the loss of tax revenue due to the suspension of tax collection. This was why Marx believed that the 'financial panic' at the time was 'a matter of secondary importance, if compared with the general crisis of the Indian Exchequer' (Marx 1859g: 282). The resumption of trade between India and England was distorted by the 'the artificial demand raised by the Government during the Indian rebellion', from the stimulus 'given to commercial activity by the subsiding of the revolutionary disturbances' and by 'the contraction of most of the other markets of the world, consequent upon the general crisis of 1857–1858' (Marx 1860b: 407). Moreover, whereas the American civil war drove up cotton prices and led to India becoming the first market for British exports, 'England pays now, in fact, the penalty for her protracted misrule of that vast Indian empire'. In particular, he wrote that the poor conditions of production, the lack of means of communication and transport and the plight of the farmers were 'difficulties' which 'the English have themselves to thank for' (Marx 1861b: 19). In this context, the Russian advance in Asia would 'be the end of John Bull's world market, a demise that [would] be hastened by the United States's protective tariff policy' (Marx to Engels 3/6/1862: 349).

But there were also other conditions that contributed to the difficulty of English trade penetration in Asia. Speaking of China, Marx argued that the obstacles encountered by English trade derived in particular from 'the economic structure of the Chinese society'. He emphasized this point, against the arguments of the British mercantile world that instead attributed these difficulties to 'the artificial obstacles foreign commerce was supposed to encounter on the part of the Chinese authorities', a 'great pretext' for any interference (Marx 1859h: 536–537). On the basis of the information he found in the *Blue Book* compiled by Lord Elgin, Marx showed how 'the most advanced factory system of the world' was unable to beat the prices of a system of production that revolved around 'the combination of minute agriculture with domestic industry' (Marx 1859h: 536, 538). He wrote that it was this very combination 'of husbandry with manufacturing industry', which 'for a long time, withstood, and still checks, the export of British wares to East India' (Marx 1859h: 538). This showed that although the system of rural communities and common land ownership in India had been corroded and destroyed by the British, who had been able to 'forcibly' convert part of India's self-sufficient communities 'into mere farms', the situation was far from settled and the work of destruction was proceeding unevenly, all the more so because 'in China the English have not yet wielded this power, nor are they likely ever to do so' (Marx 1859h: 539). We find similar arguments in the third book of *Capital*, where Marx noted that 'the work of dissolution' of the local economy operated by English commerce in India 'proceeds very gradually' and 'still more slowly in China, where it is not reinforced by direct political power' (Marx 1894: 332).

Added to this is the fact that colonial rule was distorted by the application of 'purely English prejudices or sentiments' to 'a state of society and a condition of things to which they have in fact little real pertinency' (Marx 1858f: 548). It was in fact the clash between government and parliament, between the centralization of powers and the defence of the conservative order based on the landed gentry, that explained why property, on the one hand defined as 'the great desideratum of Asiatic society', was above all 'a great *bone of contention* among English writers on India' (Marx 1853i: 218; Marx to Engels 6/14/ 1853 in MECW 39: 348). Lord Canning's proclamation of the Company's acquisition of all land titles held by Indians in the state of Oudh highlighted the difficulty surrounding the issue, particularly with regard to the position of the *zamindar* and the *taluqdar* within the economic and political system of India, and whether they should be considered 'as landed proprietors or as mere tax-gatherers' (Marx 1858f: 546).

Marx observed that it was well-known that in India, as in much of Asia, the ultimate owner of the land was the government. If, however, the government in Asia was considered as an embodiment of the sovereign in a feudal type of system, collecting taxes on land would be within its prerogative to meet its expenses, but land ownership in India would be largely private 'as in any other country whatever' (Marx 1858f: 546). Thus, if property existed, it remained to be seen who was 'the real proprietor', whether it was the *zamindar* and the *taluqdar* or the 'village corporations', who then had the power to assign it to individuals for cultivation (Marx 1858f: 547). There had been many discussions on this, and 'very serious practical mistakes' had been made (Marx 1858f: 546). The British made the *zamindar* and the *taluqdars'* proprietorship 'the foundation of the famous landed settlement of Bengal' in 1793, but, if the village corporations were the real proprietors then they would be merely government officials, 'middlemen' that were 'nothing but officers of the Government' whose role was 'to look after, to collect, and to pay over to the prince the assessment due from the village' (Marx 1858f: 547). The exclusive property rights they claimed as a result of the *permanent settlement* were thus 'to a certain extent [a] legal' source of 'usurpations' and undue political power, both in relation to common village property and to the Asian system of government (Marx 1858f: 547).

The discussion on forms of property in India occupied a lot of space in the Marxist debate on the 'Asiatic mode of production' (Gunawardana 1976; Krader 1975; Sofri 1969). In addition to the well-known passages in the *Grundrisse*, Marx addresses this topic in several articles, showing that he is aware of the scarcity of European knowledge and the complexity of property in Asia, arriving at more articulate descriptions than the simple definition of the *zamindari*, the *ryotwari* and the village as 'only so many forms of fiscal *exploitation* in the hands of the Company' (Marx 1853o: 121; see also Marx 1853i). Marx defines the *zamindar* and the *ryotwar* 'agrarian revolutions, effected by British ukases', with peculiar characters: the one is in fact

> a caricature of English landlordism, the other of French peasant-proprietorship; but pernicious, both combining the most contradictory character – both made not for the people, who cultivate the soil, nor for the holder, who owns it, but for the Government that taxes it.
>
> MARX 1853p: 214

The *zamindar* was, however, a 'curious sort' of English landowner, while the *ryotwar* was a 'curious sort' of French farmer, with no permanent title to the land and with taxation that changed every year in proportion to the harvest (Marx 1853p: 214). Even as he argued that the role of England was to regenerate India, then, Marx struggled to find terms of comparison capable of comprehensively encapsulating the features of the colonial system in India, using parallels that were always partial, and which, as such, never seemed to satisfy him completely. Thus,

> in Bengal, we have a combination of English landlordism, of the Irish middlemen system, of the Austrian system, transforming the landlord into the tax-gatherer, and of the Asiatic system making the state the real landlord. In Madras and Bombay we have a French peasant proprietor who is at the same time a serf, and a *métayer* of the state.
>
> MARX 1853p: 215

Against the backdrop of these differences, Marx noted the impossibility of considering the tax question in India, which was linked to the discussion of property, from a purely quantitative point of view, bringing out some elements of the colonial *difference*. In fact, not only had it at that point been documented 'beyond doubt' that the taxation imposed on India 'crushes the mass of the Indian people to the dust', but it was also known 'that its exaction necessitates a resort to such infamies as torture' (Marx 1858g: 578). These observations thus shed light on the colonial pretence of erasing the material conditions of domination while 'torture formed an organic institution of [English] financial policy' in India (Marx 1857g: 353) and nothing was given back to the population in return. Marx points out that 'in estimating the burden of taxation, its nominal amount must not fall heavier into the balance than the method of raising it and the manner of employing it' (Marx 1858g: 579). English hypocrisy produced bitter arguments in the metropolis and led to the establishment of numerous commissions of enquiry. And yet the British shielded themselves behind the Indian officials, claiming that the European employees of the government 'had always however unsuccessfully, done their best to prevent' the use of torture (Marx 1858h: 338). These considerations were contested by the natives, and Marx himself demonstrated their inconsistency: torture was in fact systematic not because of local distortions, but because the extortion applied to India proceeded either through the theft of public money, or by imposing new taxes and 'there [was] no legal means of punishment whatever for the employment of force in collecting the public revenue' (Marx 1858h: 337).

Torture was therefore not to be considered an accident, but a real 'institution', and other elements showed how the colonial government operated through making distortions a rule and creating an imbalance in international politics. If the seizure of Oudh showed how the British government violently appropriated independent territories 'in open infraction even of the acknowledged treaties', the events that led the British to bomb Canton following the Arrow liner incident led Marx to denounce

> the novel doctrine in the law of nations that a state may commit hostilities on a large scale against a Province of another state, without either declaring war or establishing a state of war against that other state.
> MARX 1858i: 538, 533

The issue of opium, which was at the heart of the new war with China, revealed another example of the duplicity of a government that, while 'in its imperial capacity it affects to be a thorough stranger to the contraband opium trade, and even to enter into treaties proscribing it', in India directly supervised its production until, in the final step of this 'matter of fact complicity', it passed into the hands of smugglers (Marx 1858d: 19–20).

5   Conclusions

One of the accusations levelled at Marx, particularly on the basis of his writings on India, is that he shared the Eurocentric values that dominated the mid-nineteenth century (Said 1978: 153–155). Although it should be noted that prejudices about the Asian social system and its politics are not extended to the common people in Marx's writings, these accusations contain useful elements for critically re-reading Marx's focus on non-European contexts. However, it is useful also to ask how Marx's focus on India and China, rather than simply reflecting defined positions, affects his general thought.

As Marx wrote to Engels in 1858, '[s]ince the world is round', the realization of the world market 'seem[s] to [be] completed' and no longer simply the content of a tendency. Europe had become 'a little corner of the earth', where revolutionary perspectives had to contend with what was happening where 'the movement of bourgeois society [was] still in the ascendant' (Marx to Engels 10/8/1858: 347). The writings considered in this chapter demonstrate that this ascendant movement was strewn with elements that complicated its trajectory. In fact, Marx's gaze on India filled his discourse with references to strange combinations of government, atypical market operations, and hybrid ownership structures, for which the only reference models were purely idealistic or the result of complex assemblages that took only certain characteristics from known experiences. Thus, for Marx, India was an economic, industrial and budgetary problem intertwined with social transformations and political and economic interests in the metropolis, but from which emerged the symptoms of a political difference that ran through the creation of the world of capital.

The contradictions that developed in the metropolis were dumped onto the colonial dimension, where they found no solution. What was happening in India, far from being peripheral, concerned England itself, whose constitutional order was being transformed by the new imperial dynamic through the centralization of power in the hands of the government (Marx 1853n; Ricciardi 2019: 136–142). At the same time, the form of government in the colonies made structural what was considered to be archaic or against the law in England: property was overturned, torture was an institution, and the opium trade became the example of an interweaving of the informal dimension of production and the apparatus of government, calling into question England's idea of itself as a civilized country. The financial crises that seemed to structurally accompany the management of colonies and the instability of trade did not simply mean putting a brake on the expansion of the world market as a whole but represented a sign of decline of the *English* world market and a complication in the paths of political legitimation and the trajectories of capitalist development in the face of unexpected social and political conditions. Beyond the ever-present Marxian judgement on the barbarity of domination, India's process of modernization and industrialization seemed to get lost under British presence in the country, which merely imposed its own accumulative rapacity while meeting resistance from the natives. And it is precisely in the way Marx analyses the revolt started by the Sepoys in 1857 that we see anticipations of points that he would later address with the Russian revolutionaries, when he made it clear that the 'historical inevitability' described in *Capital* was '*expressely* limited to the *countries of Western Europe*' and opened up the idea of a possibility of a revolution without undergoing 'all the fatal vicissitudes of the capitalist system' (Marx to Zasulič 3/8/1881: 71; Marx 1877: 199). Marx made clear that the Indian uprising could not be compared to a 'European' revolution but saw in its unfolding a prelude to greater upheavals and recognized the concreteness of the possibility, only briefly touched upon in his early writings, of the people of India becoming the authors of their own destiny. The Indian revolt thus seemed to interrupt the historical trajectory of the bourgeoisie in creating 'a world after its own image' as imagined in the *Manifesto*.

Oscillating between the material determinations of the world market and the global projection of the English market, Marx's observations in various articles thus contained elements for an articulated understanding of capitalist development: on the one hand, mutual dependence could be seen as already a fact in the mid-nineteenth century; on the other hand, the recognition of the growing importance of the difference in social and political conditions complicates the idea of the purely economic character of accumulation and of productive forces (Mezzadra 2014). Debt, revolts, distrust and wars were not only necessary moments within a progressive path, but factors that changed its course and results, showing how the realization of the world market was different from the realization of a world with European characteristics. In his articles on India, Marx picked up on several elements of this path, which allows us to separate him from the long-standing consideration among various 'Marxisms' of the struggle in the colonies as a second-order struggle, subsequent to the triumph of socialism in the metropolis (Sofri 1969: 86–88). Instead, Marx sought to expand his knowledge far beyond what was reported in his articles, as shown by the notes he left on Indian history and in the *Ethnological Notebooks*. There is certainly no point in forcing Marx's thought to make him say something that he doesn't in fact say to make his thought more attractive. But once freed from the double constraint of criticizing Marx as Eurocentric or making him a champion of anti-colonialism, we can see that there are already flashes of a Marx beyond Marx in his relationship with India and China, and that is what makes it so significant.

CHAPTER 15

Between Slavery and Free Labour

Marx, the American Civil War and Emancipation as a Global Issue

Matteo Battistini

> In my view, the most momentous thing happening in the world today is the slave movement on the one hand, in America, started by the death of Brown, and in Russia, on the other ... I have just seen in the *Tribune* that there's been another slave revolt in Missouri, which was put down, needless to say. But the signal has now been given. Should the affair grow serious by and by, what will become of Manchester?
>
> MARX to ENGELS 1/11/1860 in MECW 41: 4–5

∴

1 Outside Historiography, within Global History[1]

Marx's letter to Engels ten months before Lincoln's election shows how the authors of *The Communist Manifesto* (1848) supported the Union against the Confederacy. Marx looked at the heart of British industry and its working class while establishing the social and political centrality of slavery and the insurrection against it at that time. In this way, Marx distanced himself from what he defined as the 'vulgar-democratic phraseology' (Marx to Engels 12/2/1864 in MECW 42: 49) of Atlantic liberalism: the Manchester School of free trade and laissez-faire and Henry Carey's American School of Political Economy. According to Marx, Atlantic liberalism raised the abolitionist flag of free labour against slavery only under pressure from the 'slave movement' and the workers' struggle. In his view, the working-class struggles unexpectedly followed the path of the world market after the revolutionary uprising of 1848. In this sense,

---

1 A long version of this essay is published in *International Labor and Working-Class History*. See Battistini 2021.

slave and free labour was the global point of view through which Marx read the 'irrepressible conflict' (Marx to Philips 5/6/1861 in MECW 41: 277).[2]

Unsurprisingly, then, while Marx is quoted in most of the 20th century historiographical works on the Civil War, his writings are considered irrelevant or not particularly significant for its historical understanding. If consensus historiography of the fifties has obscured the meaning of the war, of slavery and the fight against slavery in order to represent a nation united in the cold war against Communism, then the new historiographies following the ideological and narrative fractures of the 1960s and 1970s (Rodgers 2003) have given slavery and abolitionism an unprecedented visibility. Yet, they have highlighted above all the undisputed affirmation of capitalism and its economic, legal, and cultural institutions, or else they have analysed a multiplicity of conflicts and tensions of race, gender and religion between social groups and lower classes with such different interests as to impede any overall vision. Thus, although new interpretations of the Civil War are emerging in the last decade that deconstruct the myth of the free North by re-establishing the centrality of slavery in American and transnational history (Beckert and Rockman 2016: 6–13), the fight against the 'peculiar institution' seems to diminish and the abolitionist movement to be further downsized. Furthermore, the role of wage labour, which Marx considered 'the true political power of the North', appears to be weakened (Marx 1865a: 19–21). In this sense, the history of the Civil War risks slipping back into the national narrative of the liberal triumph of free labour.

We can therefore understand why in the historiography of the Civil War Marx appears as someone who has to be cited, but who is irrelevant or not particularly significant for the historical understanding of the Civil War. Marx has in fact been accused of having given in to liberalism in order to support the Union (Genovese 1971: 315–353. Cf. Doyle 2015: 150–155; Carwardine and Sexton: 2011: 85–89). Moreover, although his work on the United States has contributed to the development of new historiographies, his influence is not considered direct, but instead as coming via W.E.B. Du Bois' pioneering study *Black Reconstruction* (2007 [1935]). Marx's writings on Civil War and slavery, on the American state and capitalism, have not been explicitly used or deeply discussed by the new historiographies on the Civil War.

In fact, the fragmented and dispersed body of his work on the United States has not yet been assembled into an overall and exhaustive volume showing its

---

2 The reference to Manchester's liberalism is in Marx 186h. On Henry Carey see in particular the chapter XXII, *National Differences of Wages* from *Capital* 1 (Marx 1867a: 562–563), and *Economic Manuscripts of 1857–1858* (Marx 1857–1861a: 5–16, 499–516). Cf. Perelman 1987: 10–26.

historical value for the interpretation of the Civil War. Marx's writings on the Civil War only started attracting significant attention during the 1930s. W.E.B. Du Bois, C.L.R. James and Raya Dunayevskaya explored them in order to establish the centrality of slavery and racism – and the *Negro's Revolutionary History* against slavery and racism – in the history of the Civil War as well as in American history and politics in general (James 1939 and James 1943; Dunayevskaya 2000: 81–91). The U.S. Communist party's publishing house issued a selection of Marx's writings on the Civil War in 1937. But there were not many other editions during the 20th century. Only recently, on the occasion of the anniversaries of the Civil War and the birth of Marx, the publication of new anthologies has turned the lights of history onto the dialogue between Lincoln and Marx (Morais 1937; Padover 1972; Wiene 1980; Kulikoff 2018; Blackburn 2011).

In the light of this renewed interest, this essay stitches together the fragments of Marx's work on the United States that are scattered in newspaper articles, letters, notes, in some digressions in his early writings, in his economic manuscripts and in *Capital* (1867). The main aim is to show that what we can call a *global history of the civil war* emerges from his pen: a history that is global not simply in a geographical sense, that is, because it expands the European space beyond the Atlantic and towards the Pacific, but also because of the general meaning it takes on in the world market, the latter of which is discussed in *The German Ideology* (1845).

This emerges first of all from the Marxian notion of slavery. Although it is not present in any relevant way in either his *Communist Manifesto* nor his political histories of *The Class Struggle in France* (1850) and other workers' struggles in Europe, the notion of slavery was already central in *The Poverty of Philosophy* (1847):

> Direct slavery is just as much the pivot of bourgeois industry as machinery, credits, etc. Without slavery you have no cotton; without cotton you have no modern industry. It is slavery that gave the colonies their value; it is the colonies that created world trade, and it is world trade that is the precondition of large-scale industry. Thus, slavery is an economic category of the greatest importance.
>
> MARX 1847a: 167

From this point of view, according to Marx, Southern United States was not an archaic entity opposed to European civilization. On the contrary, as a cotton producer, the South was not only an integral part of the national economy, it was also a historical pillar of the world market. Slavery acquired its modern character of oppression and exploitation exclusively through the industrial capital that dominated the world market. Therefore, even if slavery '[is] incompatible with and disappears as a result of the development of bourgeois society', it *'implies* wage labour'. Even more important was the conclusion that Marx drew from the economic historicity of slavery: since 'a negro (a man of the black race) is a negro' and 'he only becomes a *slave* in certain relations', slavery is a 'purely industrial' institution (Marx 1849b: 211). In the third book of *Capital*, Marx wrote:

> The supervision work necessarily arises in all modes of production based on the antithesis between the labourer, as the direct producer, and the owner of the means of production. The greater this antithesis, the greater the role played by supervision. Hence it reaches its peak in the slave system.
>
> MARX 1894: 382

Furthermore, it is important to underline that the historical link Marx traced between the conditions of slave and free labour echoed the workers' discourse on *wage slavery* that had circulated on both sides of the Atlantic from the 1830s and 1840s until the Civil War:

> As long as the English cotton manufactures depended on slave-grown cotton, it could be truthfully asserted that they rested on a twofold slavery, the indirect slavery of the white man in England and the direct slavery of the black men on the other side of the Atlantic.
>
> MARX 1861b: 20

On this theoretical and historical basis, slavery and the fight against slavery immediately assumed a global meaning in the history of capitalism. From the beginning of the Civil War, Marx grasped the industrial repercussions of the slave revolt and military conflict, especially with regards the Northern naval blockade of the South, the so-called Anaconda Plan. He also emphasized the political role that the working classes in Europe, particularly in Great Britain, played in publicly affirming an abolitionist position that blocked the possible interventionist policy of the European states, again particularly that of Great Britain. Finally, because of the global meaning that slavery had assumed in the world market of industrial capital, Marx identified that democracy was at stake in the war against slavery, not merely as a contingent conquest in the United States, but as a universal horizon at which the working classes in Europe also aimed:

The first grand war of contemporaneous history is the American war. The peoples of Europe know that the Southern slaveocracy commenced that war with the declaration that the continuance of slaveocracy was no longer compatible with the continuance of the Union. Consequently, the people of Europe know that a fight for the continuance of the Union is a fight against the continuance of the slaveocracy – that in this contest the highest form of popular self-government till now realized is giving battle to the meanest and most shameless form of man's enslaving recorded in the annals of history.

MARX 1861c: 30

In this sense the Civil War marked the final stage in the historical process of democratization that Marx had followed and analysed in his writings. From the democratization of the United States discussed in *On the Jewish Question* (1844) and the European revolutionary uprisings of 1848 to British Chartism and the U.S. Civil War, he considered democracy as a political movement not immediately reducible to a form of government. If *Capital* shifted his criticism from the political history of class struggles to the study of political economy as a capitalistic science of governance in the face of the unruly presence of the working class, if the Paris Commune (1871) excluded the prospect of the reform of the state from Marxian politics, then during the Civil War democracy was still the polemical notion of his initial philosophical reflection (*Critique of Hegel's Philosophy of Right*, 1844): the ruthless criticism of democracy as 'bourgeois democracy' did not remove the possibility of its partisan appropriation. In other words, democracy still defined a field of struggle that established the conditions for the possible emancipation from slavery and wage labour.

For Marx, then, the history of the Civil War was global history because it opened the issue of emancipation to the presence of a black proletariat fighting against slavery, a presence that interacted with the European working-class movement within the world market of industrial capital (Anderson 2010; Jeannot 2007; Nimtz 2011 and Nimtz 2003; Miles 1987; Cohen 1978). Marx did not consider slavery as an endangered past in a present that would be freed from the pre-capitalist chains of command. On the contrary, for him, slavery was an anachronism that marked the present: slavery negatively affected the possibilities of emancipation because, by holding together property and race in a 'peculiar institution', it rewarded the separation of labour from property with racial superiority. In this specific sense, slavery would have survived its abolition as a 'color line' that divided labour into black and white skin (Du Bois 1900). This was exactly why, even after the Civil War, Marx chose to use the notion of emancipation again after it had been shelved in 1848. As we shall see, in light of the 'slave movement', Marx removed emancipation from the historical indeterminacy of his youthful humanism and turned it into a political notion that reflected the heterogenous, transnational – not national – composition of the working class. That is, emancipation encompassed and indicated the political connection between the different and disarticulated voices of labour – slave and free, black and white – that rejected the position assigned to them by industrial capital in the world market (Pradella 2016; Blackburn 2011; Draper 1971).

2 The Long Constitutional History of the Civil War

Marx's work on the Civil War is composed mainly of the writings that he published in 1861 and 1862 in *The New York Daily Tribune* and in *Die Presse*, and of the correspondence that he kept up above all, but not only, with Engels until the end of the 1870s. The collaboration with the most widespread U.S. newspaper of the time, which had about two hundred thousand subscribers and one million readers, began in 1851 following a meeting with Charles Dana – the newspaper's editor – in Cologne during the revolutionary uprisings of 1848. Designed to inform the public about European politics, the writings were interrupted in the first year of the war for various reasons, such as payment was not regular and the articles were often cut, modified, or published without accreditation. Moreover, thanks to Carey, the newspaper became the republican voice of the American industrial capital in a war that was also fought to defend U.S. manufacture from British trade competition (Perelman 2008). The articles that Marx published from October 1861 to February 1862 dealt with the war in an international key, giving an account of the British (and not only) attitude towards the belligerents. Nevertheless, they anticipated themes that were taken up again in the following months: criticism of the interpretation that *The Times*, *The Economist* and other British liberal press presented of the Civil War as a conflict on the customs tariff triggered by the 'Northern lust for sovereignty' (Marx 1861d: 32); condemnation of the interests in cotton that pushed the British government to choose neutrality and the British industrial capital to increase the production of cotton in India; the workers' support of the Unionist cause despite the employment crisis caused by the collapse of textile production (Marx 1862b: 137–142).

In the writings published in *Die Presse*, this international and transnational framework was built up further in terms of a *long constitutional history*, from the founding of the republic to the secession. Marx examined the series of compromises on slavery that began with the Continental Congress and continued with the expansion to the West, the federal laws (the Fugitive Slave Act of 1850 and the Kansas Nebraska Act of 1854) and the ruling of the Supreme Court (Dred Scott of 1857) that made the Union a 'slave' of the South, constitution-alizing slavery as a 'guiding star ... in the foreign, as in the domestic, policy of the United States'. Within this constitutional history, Marx reconstructed the formation of the Republican party in the years of the guerrilla warfare in Kansas and discussed the Republican platform in the presidential elections of 1856 and 1860, underlining 'its principal contents', that is, 'not a foot of fresh territory is further conceded to slavery'. Most importantly, behind the consti-tutional history that led to Lincoln's presidency, Marx saw a social process that transformed the political conflict between the North and the South into a civil war, moving the issue of slavery from constitutional compromise to a conflict that affected society:

> The present struggle between the South and North is, therefore, nothing but a struggle between two social systems, the system of slavery and the system of free labour. The struggle has broken out because the two sys-tems can no longer live peacefully side by side on the North American continent. It can only be ended by the victory of one system or the other.
> MARX 1861d: 37–38, MARX 1861e: 50

As historiography has shown, his historical reconstruction was not without errors. Marx overestimated or underestimated the military forces in the field and the popular support for the Unionist and Confederate causes (Runkle 1964). However, what is important to emphasize are the different temporal-ities – institutional and social – that Marx highlighted in his *constitutional history of the civil war*. That is the key in which we should read the pages he dedicated to the economic and demographic transformations that affected the South and the North, fragmenting the two sides along class and race lines that prevented their representation in terms of people or nation. In his view, the political expansion of the plantation system and the associated drafting of the slave constitutions of the South states were linked to the peculiar social process of concentration and separation of property from labour that made the capi-talist and the landowner coincide in the person of the slaveowner. Since 'the business in which slaves are used is conducted by *capitalists*', these latter apply the 'maxim of slave management', namely that 'the most effective economy is that which takes out of the human chattel in the shortest space of time the utmost amount of exertion it is capable of putting forth' (Marx 1861–1863b: 516). Consequently, the conquest of ever new land to make cotton, tobacco and sugar plantations productive and to stake a claim in the federal government through Senate control did not result in a distribution of slavery as property, but in its accumulation in the hands of 'the oligarchy of the 300,000 salve lords in the South *vis-à-vis* the five million whites'. The resulting separation of free labour from slave labour, which implied 'the rapid transformation of states like Maryland and Virginia ... into states which raises slaves to export into the deep South', left no alternative. As Marx noted, quoting a speech by Senator Robert Toombs, Georgia's delegate to Montgomery's secessionist Convention (February 1861) and Secretary of State of the Confederacy: 'in fifteen years without a great increase in slave territory, either the slaves must be permitted to flee from the whites, or the whites must flee from the slaves' (Marx 1861d: 30–40; Marx to Engels 7/1/1861 in MECW 41: 301).

The slave oligarchy therefore asserted its right to 'concentration, status, and resources' and to 'put down any opposition', thus imposing secession as 'usurpation'. With the exception of South Carolina, which had in John C. Calhoun the founding father of secession, 'everywhere ... there was the strongest opposition to secession'. In some letters to Engels, Marx reported a series of titles and quotations from various newspapers in the South – *The Augusta Chronicle and Sentinel* and *The Macon Journal* from Georgia, *The Mobile Advertiser* and *The North Alabamian* from Alabama, and the *New Orleans True Delta* from Mississippi – that exposed how secession had taken place 'without the authority of the people'. Through a *'coup de main'* and 'invalid act' in the legislative assemblies or through elections of special conventions that were held in 'a reign of terrorism', exercised through 'the mob' of 'poor whites' that were moved like 'Zouaves' in defense of racial superiority and the slaveowner's property (Marx to Engels 7/1/1861; Marx to Engels 7/5/1861 in MECW 41: 300–303, 305–309).

Marx therefore did not consider any Southern state to be an 'actual slave state' because the slaveowner's enterprise was conducted in a capitalist manner and because the racial line along which production was organized reinforced the separation of property from labour. With greater reason, therefore, the border states were not slave states either, not even those belonging to the Confederacy, because there the slave system and free labour struggled openly to gain the upper hand. Thus 'the South' was not 'a territory closely sealed off from the North geographically', and neither could it be represented in a people or a nation. It did not constitute a 'moral unity', but rather a 'battle-cry' that existed exclusively by 'subjugating completely ... the section of the white population that had still preserved some independence under the protection of the democratic Constitution of the Union'. Marx noted that 'between 1856 and 1860 the political spokesmen, jurists, moralists and theologians of the slaveholders' party had already sought to prove, not so much that Negro slavery is justified, but rather that colour is a matter of indifference, and the working class is everywhere born to slavery'. In the event of a Confederate victory:

> The slave system would infect the whole Union. In the Northern states, where Negro slavery is in practice impossible, the white working class would gradually be forced down to the level of helotry. This would fully accord with the loudly proclaimed principle that only certain races are capable of freedom, and as the actual labour is the lot of the Negro in the South, so in the North it is the lot of the German and the Irishman, or their direct descendants.
>
> MARX 1861e: 43, 49–50

3   The Revolutionary Turn

In his writings, Marx exalted the political rejection of the historical perspective of a 'slave republic' entangled in the *long constitutional history*. The tensions between the different institutional and social temporalities of the Civil War erupted under the pressure of the distant and disarticulated voices of individuals working as slaves and freemen. The transnational process of exploitation and accumulation through slavery was overturned by the interrelated agency of the 'slave movement', of the 'public opinion' of the working classes in Great Britain and the 'political power' of free and waged labour in New England and in the Northwest of the United States. Their claims to emancipation made '*all compromise* impossible' (Marx to Philips 5/6/1861 in MECW 41: 277) because they prevented the war from being kept within its institutional temporality: it would not have been possible to save the democratic Constitution of the Union without abolishing slavery. This was the passage from 'the *constitutional* waging of war' to 'the *revolutionary* waging of war', a historically contingent moment that found its maximum expression in the Emancipation Proclamation (January 1, 1863), but within which long-term labour action – slave and free – affected the outcome of the war (Marx 1862i: 228).

For Marx, the 'slave movement' during the Civil War was mainly a mass flight from the plantations. What Du Bois called a 'general strike' (Du Bois 2007 [1935]) forced 'a large section of the slaveholders, with their black chattels', to 'constantly migrate to the South, in order to bring their property to a place of safety'. Consequently, 'the war itself brought about a solution by radically changing the form of society in the border states'. What Weydemeyer – engaged during the war as a lieutenant and colonel in various battles in Missouri, Arkansans, Kentucky and Tennessee – defined as an 'exodus', comparable to the Irish one following the potato famine, left behind 'encroachments of ... free labour' (Marx 1862k: 257–258). Moreover, it created much tension within the Union army. Constantly informed by Engels on the events of the war, Marx wrote about this from November 1861 to the summer of 1862, reporting on the insubordination of generals and lieutenants. They enlisted the fugitive slaves as free men, violating the laws on black smuggling (Confiscation Act of 1861 and 1862) which led to their progressive revision until the drafting of the Proclamation. They also intervened publicly in favour of the abolition of slavery. From Marx's pen it emerged, therefore, how the military insubordination moved Lincoln and his Secretary of State William H. Seward away from an initial moderate and constitutional management of the war, as exemplified by the dismissal of the abolitionist General John C. Frémont from the post of commander of the district of Missouri over his emancipation edict in St. Louis. They were also forced to limit and finally dismiss General George McClellan who, on the strategic front of the Potomac River, aimed for agreements 'with constant regard to the restoration of the Union on its *old* basis'. The mass flight of slaves therefore freed the President from the political problem of 'keeping the loyal slaveholders of the border states in good humor' – a problem that 'has smitten the Union government with incurable weakness since the beginning of the war, driven it to half measures, forced it to dissemble away the principle of the war, and to spare the foe's most vulnerable spot, the root of the evil, *slavery itself*. As a result, war should no longer be waged 'in a strictly businesslike fashion', instead the 'revolutionary tendencies' that affected the peculiar institution needed to be recognized. For Marx, therefore, it was the 'slave movement' and not the 'legally cautious, constitutionally conciliatory' Lincoln that affirmed 'the battle-slogan of Abolition of Slavery' (Marx 1861e; Marx 1861f; Marx 1861g; Marx 1862e; Marx 1862f; Marx 1862g; Marx 1862h; Marx 1862i; Marx 1862m: 50–51, 115–116, 179, 186–195, 204–208, 227–228, 233–235, 266–269).

To the ears of the President and his administration this outcry was intensified by the 'chorus' that arose overseas against possible British recognition of the Confederacy and the consequent possible military intervention of the Palmerston government. Between the end of 1861 and the summer of 1862, Marx alternated discussion of the U.S. theatre with a reconstruction of the British anti-war movement. From the Trent case onwards – where a Union vessel arrested two Confederate ambassadors from a British ship – Marx underlined how 'the issue between the English people and the English Cabinet' imposed an 'anti-intervention feeling' which Palmerston and the press soon took note of. More importantly, Marx pointed out that popular opinion of 'all sections of the English people', with the exception of 'the friends of cotton', began to look like a working-class public opinion against slavery. The mass presence of workers placed a different political slant on the anti-war movement. While at the heart of people's opinion was simply support of the North against the 'anti-Republican war', in the workers' assemblies this democratic vision became 'the policy of the working class'. Once again after the Reform Bill of 1832, the abolition of the protectionist laws on wheat and the law establishing the ten-hour day, the working class imposed its will on the government, even without being represented in Parliament: Workers organized these protest actions and influenced events at a time when even adult male workers did not enjoy the suffrage, still based upon heavy property qualifications. Already in February 1862, Marx paid tribute 'to the sound attitude of the British working classes, the more so when contrasted with the hypocritical, bullying, cowardly, and stupid conduct of the official and well-to-do John Bull'. The danger of 'an English war for the slaveocrats' was averted when, on the stage of public opinion, the abstractness of the people left room for the materiality of the working class, denoting with the abolition of slavery an essential moment in the emancipation from wage labour. For Marx, a mass of migrants (mostly Irishmen and Britons) had in fact escaped and were still escaping from the European regime of wage slavery and finding 'a new home in the United States' (Marx 1861h; Marx 1862a; Marx 1862b; Marx 1862c; Marx 1862d; Marx 1862k: 128, 135, 138–142, 146, 153–154, 157–159, 259).

The voices of the black proletariat fleeing from plantations and of the working classes striking against slavery in Great Britain, that Marx politically connected within the industrial course of the world market, reached its highest note when the free labour composite, that is the self-working farmers of the Northwest and the working classes of New England, burst onto the scene, thus interrupting the institutional temporality of the *long constitutional history*. In a letter to Engels dated July 1861, Marx identified 'the extraordinary development of the Northwestern states ... with [their] rich admixture of newly-arrived Germans and Englishmen' as the long-term process that shattered the constitutional compromise by providing electoral bulk to the Republican party. Moreover, in August 1862, in two contributions to *Die Presse* preceding the October one on the Preliminary Proclamation, Marx focused on the abolitionist movement, reporting the speech that Wendell Philips – 'the leader of the Abolitionists in New England' together with William Lloyd Garrison and Gerrit Smith – gave in Abington, Massachusetts, on the anniversary of the emancipation of slaves in the British West Indies. Above all, Marx emphasized that abolitionism was rooted in the 'popular classes' of New England and the Northwest that constituted 'the main body of the army', together with the 'considerable amount of people of military experience who had immigrated to the United States in consequence of the European revolutionary unrest of

1848–1849'. These masses 'did not, of course, lend [themselves] so readily to intimidation as the gentlemen of Wall Street' who had invested in the plantation system. These masses built up 'a power that was not inclined either by tradition, temperament or mode of life to let [them] be dragged from compromise to compromise in the manner of the old Northeastern states'. They were 'determined to force on the government a revolutionary kind of warfare and to inscribe the battle-slogan of Abolition of Slavery! on the star-spangled banner'. For them, the defeat of the South and the end of the plantation slave system opened the way to realizing a historical workers' claim: the distribution of land to the West, which Lincoln conceded with the Homestead Act in May 1862 (Marx 1861d; Marx 1862f; Marx 1862i: 42, 188, 228).

The *revolutionary turn* imposed by the 'slave movement', the 'policy of the British working classes' and the 'political power' of free and waged labour in New England and the Northwest therefore shifted the war in the direction of abolitionism, impacting the cautious constitutional conduct of the President who was thus forced 'to act the lion'. In the autumn of 1862, even more important than the Union's victories on the war front and the 'symptoms of Disintegration in the Southern Confederacy' was the announcement of the Emancipation Proclamation (January 1, 1863). Although the Proclamation did not affect the owner's right to slavery in border states and states occupied by the Union army, it affected some three million slaves outside the territory controlled by the Union. For Marx, it was therefore a turning point: 'the most important document in American history since the establishment of the Union ... the manifesto abolishing slavery' (Marx 1862j: 250).

Marx knew that the manifesto would encounter several setbacks, both in the military and in the political sphere. He believed that it would be necessary to fight slavery for a long time to come. The reaction that the announcement of the Proclamation provoked in the congressional elections of November 1862, when the Republican administration suffered a defeat in favor of the Democratic party, did not constitute a mere electoral event. It was rather a sign of how slavery would survive its very abolition, along color lines that pushed the white and immigrant workers to see in the black proletariat 'a symbol of slavery and the humiliation of the working class' (Marx 1862l: 264). Yet, unlike Engels and despite the controversial events of the war, Marx was already convinced that the Proclamation would determine the outcome of the war. Two years after the conclusion of his collaboration with the Viennese newspaper, his labourious political work of weaving the fabric of the transnational connection between the different and disarticulated voices of black and white labour went public. The *Address to Abraham Lincoln* (Marx 1864b) of the International Working Men's Association (December 23, 1864), that Marx surely drafted, publicly welcomed his re-election. The letter published in *The Bee-Hive Newspaper* (November 7, 1865) declared his global view of the Civil War and the political meaning the Civil War had in the world market of industrial capital:

> The working classes of Europe understood at once ... that the slave-holders' rebellion was to sound the tocsin for a general holy crusade of property against labour, and that for the men of labour, with their hopes for the future, even their past conquests were at stake in that tremendous conflict on the other side of the Atlantic.
>
> ... While the working men ... boasted it the highest prerogative of the white-skinned labourer to sell himself and choose his own master; they were unable to attain the true freedom of labour or to support their European brethren in their struggle for emancipation, but this barrier to progress has been swept off by the red sea of Civil War.

Marx did not reduce the Civil War to the liberal triumph of free labour, which should have concluded the democratic movement begun in 1776. To him the slave-free democracy of the Thirteenth Constitutional Amendment appeared rather as a partisan conquest that revealed what the color line, the racial privilege of white labour, hid behind the doctrine of free labour: 'the great problem of the relation of labour to capital' (Marx 1864b: 19–21). Marx reacted with satisfaction to the words with which Lincoln had responded to the message from the International Workingmen's Association: 'you can understand [he wrote to Engels] how gratifying that has been for our people'. But, for him, the answer reaffirmed the President's constitutional vision. While Lincoln was convinced that the nation would emerge from the Civil War by renewing the promises of self-rule and happiness that had marked his personal and political biography in the pre-war Northwest, for Marx those promises were closed off by the war (Marx to Engels 2/10/1865 in MECW 42: 86). Not only because Marx was soon irritated by the turn of events with the murder of Lincoln and the reactionary politics of his successor Johnson (Marx 1865b: 99–100), but also because, although stripped of slavery, the West would no longer be the space in which U.S. and immigrant workers found their emancipation from wage slavery. In *Capital*, the *global history of civil war* was described using this historical and theoretical meaning. The abolition of slavery as an institution and the subsequent conquest of Black male suffrage saturated the historical movement of democracy, determining not only new social relations, but also new political conditions that offered the possibility for emancipation. This emerged in what we can call the *state moment* of the Civil War by analysing some passages on the United States scattered through Marx's work.

4 The State Moment

In his correspondence with Engels and in some passages in *Capital*, Marx identified the *state moment* of the Civil War as the fulfilment of the historical, institutional, and social process of the financial construction of the American state and the industrial transition to capitalism that was not accomplished with the war of independence (Battistini 2013). If the United States was still to be considered as a 'European colony' before the Civil War because its 'economic development' was 'a product of Europe, more especially of English modern industry', (Marx 1867a: 454) then the Civil War severed that colonial dependence. The institutional tension between state rights and the sovereignty of the Union bequeathed by the founding fathers not only did not permit the 'slave revolution' to be avoided, but in the uncertain pre-war constitutional framework it did not allow capital to find its established social form in industrial capital either. In the so-called early republic, society still defined an economically indeterminate space, where the glorious narrative of the British and U.S. political economy that elevated Robinson Crusoe to the leading role in the history of capitalism was continually upended in misadventures of capital. As Marx underlined when discussing the British imperial experience overseas in the chapter *The Modern Theory of Colonization* in the first book of *Capital*, the historical process of capital accumulation failed to reach its established European form overseas (Marx 1867a: 751–764).

In some letters where Marx discussed the economic measures, in particular the huge print-run of paper money which the Union adopted to finance the war, the *state moment* of the Civil War thus emerged as a solution to the colonial problem of accumulation. Unlike Engels, who saw 'the financial crash' approaching, Marx did not believe in the bankruptcy of the Union: 'the United States know from the time of the War of Independence ... how far one may go with depreciated paper money'. For Marx, the issue of the first national single banknote – the greenback – and its diffusion in substitution of the bonds of the slave states' banks were the economic sign of the 'confidence in them [yankees] and hence in their government [Union]'. Moreover, the depreciation of paper money and the consequent increase in interest on public debt were balanced by an increase in exports and a trade balance favoured by protectionist policies. Most importantly, the 'new system of taxation' that integrated the customs tax (Morril Act of 1861) with direct and indirect taxation (Revenue Act of 1862) guaranteed a 'reflux' of paper money that counterweighed devaluation. For Marx, 'the inherent disadvantage of the thing' was rather the 'premium for jobbing and speculation' of the capitalist who had invested in public debt (Marx to Engels 5/27/1862; Engels to Marx 10/16/1862 in MECW 41: 369–370, 419–421).

The *state moment* of the Civil War condensed the historical event of the European states overseas, establishing a centralized system of public debt that was fed by modern fiscality, based on indirect taxation, and ensured by the protectionist system that capitalized the national means of production. After the Glorious Revolution of 1688, which had inaugurated the commercial wars between the European powers, the British state systematically combined colonial policy with public debt, taxation, and protectionism 'to hasten, hothouse fashion, the process of transformation of the feudal mode of production into the capitalist mode, and to shorten the transition'. In the same way, the Civil War completed the financial construction of the American state, declaring the war of independence economically concluded: the Union concentrated and organized the 'force of society' conferring on the state 'the power ... to shorten [the] genesis of the industrial capital' (Marx 1867a: 738–739, 744–745).

What we have defined with Marx as *constitutional history*, *revolutionary turn* and *state moment* of the Civil War do not therefore determine a chronological sequence, but rather indicate a contemporaneity of temporalities – institutional and social – that synchronized the national history of the United States with the world market. In this sense, the Civil War imposed a double global twist on the making of the American state: while the Civil War institutionalized democracy as the established form of government by removing its historical movement from the claims of emancipation by black and white workers, it also transformed the American state into a player in the world market. Its politics and policies were socially linked to the government of industrial capital. In this way, what Marx defined as an 'artificial product of modern society', or rather, 'the process of separation between labourers and conditions of labour' which transformed 'the mass of the population into wage labourers, into free labouring poor', found its fulfilment also on the Western shores of the Atlantic. The irony of history was that it was those who in 1776 had renounced Britishness that realized the English 'modern theory of colonization', or rather, the accumulation of capital where it had remained incomplete (Marx 1867a: 747–748, 759–760).

It is not so important here to underline that, for Engels, the *global history of civil war* projected the United States into 'a differed position in world history within the shortest possible time' (Engels to Weydemeyer 11/24/1864 in MECW 42: 39). Rather, it is more relevant to highlight that the *state moment* of the Civil War allowed Marx to reveal what remained hidden behind the promise of self-rule and happiness that Lincoln saw in the post-war nation, that is, behind the social harmony that Carey intended to scientifically root in the 'natural law' of American capitalism. Before the Civil War, Marx himself had recorded the specificity of U.S. society. In the *Economic Manuscripts of 1857–1858*, he wrote that the abstraction of labour as a 'means to create wealth in general' was taken to its highest level for the first time overseas. In the United States, 'individuals easily pass from one kind of labour to another' because 'the particular kind of labour [is] accidental to them and therefore indifferent'. However, this indifference towards work (neither manufacturing, nor mercantile, nor agricultural work, but all types of work) that characterized the independence of producers was nothing more than a historical product of a society where free labour fought against slavery. Instead, independence of labour diminished after the war and the separation of labour from ownership removed the promised land of emancipation from wage slavery from the world market:

> ... the American Civil War brought in its train a colossal national debt, and, with it, pressure of taxes, the rise of the vilest financial aristocracy, the squandering of a huge part of the public land on speculative companies for the exploitation of railways, mines, in brief, the most rapid centralization of capital. The great republic has, therefore, ceased to be the promised land for emigrant labourers. Capitalistic production advances there with giant strides, even though the lowering of wages and the dependence of the wage worker are yet far from being brought down to the normal European level.
>
> MARX 1867a: 760

Marx, therefore, theoretically and historically understood not only the new social relations following the Civil War, but also the unprecedented political conditions that offered the possibility for emancipation. From a theoretical point of view, since the *state moment* of the Civil War solved the colonial problem of accumulation, Marx revoked any possibility of appeal to the U.S. political economy. In the 1850s, he had allowed his rival in the columns of the *New York Daily Tribune* to be 'the only original economist among the North Americans'. Carey's attempt 'to demonstrate the harmony of the relations of production at the point where the classical economists naively analyzed their antagonism' had 'at least the merit of articulating in abstract form the magnitude of American relations and of doing so in contradiction of those of the Old World'. For Marx, in fact, U.S. society allowed for an 'unprecedented scale and unprecedented conditions of freedom of movement' until the Civil War. The worker could 'appropriate a part of his surplus' and 'accumulate enough to become a farmer ... through the reproduction of earlier modes of production and [forms] of property on the bases of capital (e.g. of the independent peasantry)'. But, after the Civil War, even in the United States, 'the contradictions of bourgeois society' no longer appeared 'as transient moments'. Consequently, Carey's 'harmonious laws' lost that aforementioned merit. His economic school became dogmatic not only because it denied the antagonism between capital and labour, but also because it demanded that the 'American dogma' of harmony of interests be valid for the world: 'He is American as much in his assertion of the harmony within bourgeois society as in his assertion of the disharmony of the same relations in their world market form' (Marx 1857–1861a: 6–10, 500).

From a historical point of view, these new social relations that marked labour on both sides of the Atlantic opened up new possibilities for emancipation that Marx exalted in his *Capital* by using the notion of *civil war* no longer in exclusive reference to the United States, but also in reference to his vision of the class struggle (Dunayevskaya 1958: 81; Welsh 2002: 274–287; Zimmerman 2015: 304–336). While in a letter to Weydemeyer in 1852 Marx had admitted that the U.S. society was 'still far too immature for the class struggle to be made perceptible and comprehensible' (Marx to Weydemeyer, 3/5/1852 in MECW 39: 62), in *Capital* the notion of *civil war* was used to describe the *global history of the class struggle* for the working day. The American Civil War marked a decisive moment in 'a protracted civil war, more or less dissembled, between the capitalist class and the working class':

> In the United States of North America, every independent movement of the workers was paralyzed so long as slavery disfigured a part of the Republic. Labour cannot emancipate itself in the white skin where in the black it is branded. But out of the death of slavery a new life at once arose. The first fruit of the Civil War was the eight hours' agitation, that ran with the seven-leagued boots of the locomotive from the Atlantic to the Pacific, from New England to California.
>
> MARX 1867a: 303, 305

5   The Issue of Emancipation as a Global Question

Before and after the Paris Commune, Marx repeatedly returned to reflect on the labour movement in the United States in interviews given to the U.S. press in New York and Chicago and in writings written on behalf of the International Working Men's Association. This latter moved to New York after 1871 not only to remove it from the anarchist and socialist influence of Europe, but also because of the importance the United States had been gaining in the world market.[3] From the beginning of the decade it had dozens of branches in different industrial areas of the country, from Boston to San Francisco, passing through New York, New Jersey, St. Louis and Chicago. Besides, as Marx wrote in the *Preface* to the first edition of *Capital* dated July 25, 1867, quoting the words of Benjamin Franklin Wade, a radical republican firmly against the policies of President Johnson: 'after the abolition of slavery, a radical change of the relations of capital and of property in land is next upon the order of the day' (Marx 1867a: 1, 11). Within this new agenda, the working-class voices in Europe, that during the Civil War had raised the cry against slavery, could not ignore the labour movement in the United States and could not even confine the class struggle to within the racial boundary of white labour. The issue of emancipation needed to be opened to the presence of a black proletariat: emancipation should face the political problem of slavery, no longer as property but as a principle of racial superiority, determined along the color line that divided the white working class from the black proletariat. As was written in the International's message sent to the National Labor Union, the main organization in the United States at that time which led the fight for eight hours, Marx did not forget that the victory against slavery had given an unprecedented 'moral impetus' to the 'class movement'. 'The glorious task' that the Civil War bequeathed on both sides of the Atlantic was therefore 'to prove to the world' that 'the working classes are bestriding the scene of history no longer as servile retainers, but as independent actors' (Marx 1869c: 54). However, from the start this challenge seemed all the more difficult the more global a scene the Civil War imposed on the issue of emancipation. Marx wrote to Engels about this already at the end of 1858:

> The proper task of bourgeois society is the creation of the world market, at least in outline, and of the production based on that market. Since the world is round, the colonization of California and Australia and the opening up of China and Japan would seem to have completed this process. For us, the difficult question is this: on the Continent revolution is imminent and will, moreover, instantly assume a socialist character. Will it not necessarily be crushed in this little corner of the earth, since the movement of bourgeois society is still in the ascendant over a far greater area?
>
> MARX to ENGELS 10/8/1858 in MECW 40: 347

---

3   Please refer to the two interviews that Marx gave to the *World* in New York on July 18, 1871, and to the *Tribune* in Chicago on January 5, 1879, Foner 1973: 240–262.

In conclusion, the importance of reading Marx lies in his theoretical vision of the American Civil War as a 'world-historical fact' that materially changed not only U.S. history, but also the history of capitalism because it changed the historical, institutional, and social temporalities in which individuals at work in a racially connoted way experienced democracy, the state, its politics and policy of accumulation, the world market and its industrial capital. Although sceptical of the national ways to emancipation, up to *Manifesto* Marx had thought of emancipation in the political terms of an international alliance of the European proletariat. Between the 1850s and 1860s, in light of the events in the United States, the issue of emancipation could only be tackled at the world market level. Marx acknowledged that the world market revoked the exclusive character of national histories because it framed individuals as 'empirically universal individuals', that is, the world market framed individuals materially connected by 'a power alien to them'. In this specific sense, the Civil War for Marx was not just a national war that historically brought to fruition the democratic constitution, marking the triumph of free labour. Nor was it just an international war that allowed capital to take control of U.S. society and lead domestic industry to success in the commercial competition between national economies. Behind these wars, another civil war was raging: a real movement of individuals at work in different and distant points of the world market who, pitting themselves against the power that connected them, determined new social and political conditions that offered the possibility for emancipation. For this reason, reconstructing the history of the Civil War through Marx did not just bring to light a historical contingency in which actors other than the European white working class, to which the *Manifesto* had entrusted the task of communism, made their appearance. Marx's *global history of the civil war* also, and above all, brought to light his theoretical attempt to think of emancipation as a global issue. In other words, the problem – both historical and theoretical – that his work on the United States left unresolved in the pages of *Capital* was how to solve the issue of emancipation when it was placed in a world market where the presence of a racially connoted and divided proletariat, the saturation of the democratic movement and the accumulation policy of the states prevented the identification of a single point from which to deploy a new political history of the class struggle. His *global history of civil war* was not in this sense 'a collection of dead facts', but it was a history of the present (Marx and Engels 1845–1846: 43–53).

CHAPTER 16

England as the Metropolis of Capital
Marx, the International and the Working Class

Mario Piccinini

It is very difficult to say what England was for Marx. There is not much point in revising and updating the canonical account of Marxism's three sources in French materialism, German classical philosophy, and English political economy. But if we ask what England was for Marx politically or what England was for political Marx – which are slightly different things – the question is still complex but loosens up a little. *Marx and England* primarily means *Marx and the International.*

I have chosen to analyse a seemingly minor text, the *Circulaire du Conseil Général de l'Association International au Conseil Fédéral de la Suisse Romande* (Marx 1870b: 84–91), in which Marx lays out his overall position on England. The date is significant: January 1870, the year before the Commune. On 2 September 1864, Marx had attended the meeting that opened the way to the foundation of the International Working Men's Association (IWMA), convinced that it would include 'people who really count', meaning not men of ideas, but 'real powers', referring, on the British side, to the exponents of the new reality of workers' unionism expressed in the London Trades Council. Marx had limited knowledge of this new reality, which was very different to that which he had found on his arrival in England, which had been marked by Chartism and its crisis. His involvement in the construction of the IWMA in the weeks following the meeting was the result of a happy intuition whose validity would soon be confirmed, transforming 'the mute figure on the platform' into the main guarantor of the political construction of the International (Marx to Engels 11/4/1864 in MECW 42: 11 18). When Marx was in the process of writing the text of the *Circulaire* five years later, these conditions had changed. From 1867 to 1869 there had been a period of stagnation in the relationship between the International and the English situation (Collins and Abramsky 1965: 82–101). In the latter, unlike on the continent, the worker's organization had stopped expanding and there was a drop in political militancy within the union sectors that had been responsible for its initial growth. In this period Marx's point of view was aligned, and not always critically, with the London Trades Council, to the detriment of other components of London unionism

(Coltham 1964–1965). He had acquired a more conscious and disenchanted understanding both of the British workers' movement as a whole and of the organizational components of the political class that in various ways partici-pated in the IWMA, as well as of the limits of their relationship with the wider working-class reality outside of London, particularly with the large industrial concentrations in the North. He did not go back to his 1864 intuition but trans-lated it into the articulation of strategy and tactics that confronted the particu-lar circumstances of the political phase. The *Circulaire*'s treatment of England should be understood in this context. The fact that it locates a specific moment of struggle within the International, and finds its performative function there, does not mean it should be dismissed as a piece of mere rhetoric legitimising the General Council.

It is crucial to understand the context in which he was writing, which we will now briefly outline. In the final months of 1869, two Swiss newspapers, the *Égalité* and the *Progrès,* which had formal links with the International Association, contested the work of the General Council in London, accusing it of not properly complying with the decisions of the International, which were binding by statute. At first it seemed to refer to the General Council's failure to uphold their obligation to produce a bulletin providing periodic informa-tion, in particular on the development of the labour market and on workers' cooperatives and on workers' conditions in various countries (*L'Égalité* 1972 vol 1/42). Marx's disappointment was understandable. The bulletin – which was also forcefully proposed in the resolutions of the London Conference and else-where – was his idea. It brought to the fore the question of class-consciousness, which was the main question of his writings on statistics and workers inquiry. Although, due to financial problems and the failure of the sections to supply data, it had encountered difficulties that were formally acknowledged, it had not been abandoned (*Documents* 1963–1968, 3: 298). For the Swiss, the bulletin was not a tool, but a forum. On 6 November 1869, *L'Égalité* published a brief resolution by the General Council in London on amnesty for Irish militants imprisoned for the spring 1867 insurrectionary attempt, followed by almost two columns of editorial entitled *Réflexions* (*L'Égalité* 1972 vol 1/47). In short, they were saying: we are publishing your deliberations, but we do not understand the reasons behind them. Their challenge was not so much against the General Council's praise for the Irish as against the council's conduct. The interest of the workers, according to *L'Égalité*, was not 'to improve existing governments, but to radically suppress them by substituting the existing political, authori-tarian, religious and legal state with the new social organization which guaran-tees to each person the whole product of his labour along with all which that entails'. The Swiss did not deny that the General Council in London might have its own specific good reasons for getting involved in a local movement such as that of the Irish militants, but they argued that the Council certainly did not do so as a general body of an association that was *'répandue dans l'univers'*, acting instead in the manner of a regional body of the English sections. The appeal that l'*Égalité* made to all *confrères* was to press the London Council to finally set up an autonomous English regional council.

On 1 January 1870, Marx used emergency procedure to submit to the sub-committee of the General Council a long communication responding to this criticism. The General Council did not address the two Swiss newspapers, which were increasingly assuming the character of the 'official oracles' of positions attributable to Bakunin. It instead sent a resolution to the Geneva Council, accusing the latter of having tolerated the usurpation of its prerogatives, allowing objections and peremptory demands to be publicly stated by those who had no right to do so. Such an attitude should have been the exclusive purview of the Swiss Federal Council. Marx took a position which, in rather cutting terms, meticulously referred to the Statutes and Rules which the International Association had given itself and to the decisions which had been made in the various congresses. This was a very coherent stance since it was on this ground that the role and position of the London Council was being questioned. Yet he devoted most of the text to the subject of the relations between the General Council and the British situation. On this issue he began from a question of statutory legality. He pointed out that this was not the first time the question of a regional council for England had been raised. In fact, it had already been discussed on various occasions in the General Council but had always been rejected almost unanimously. While maintaining a flexible attitude in relation to affiliation to the association, from its constitution the International had urged its members to make the utmost effort 'to combine the disconnected workingmen's societies of their respective countries into national bodies, represented by central national organs' (Marx 1868b: 334). Thus, England was an anomaly in the field of organization that had to be politically understood.

'Although revolutionary initiative will probably come from France, England alone can serve as the lever for a serious economic Revolution' (Marx 1870b: 86). Marx introduces his considerations with a judgment that, at the beginning of 1870, seems to be endowed with prognostic value on the unpredictable events of the following months, but in fact should be understood instead as referring to the debates and the subjective composition of the movement in France whose growing tremors the Marxian seismograph carefully recorded (Cervelli 2009). It would happen first in France, but the French trigger, if it ever happened, would be insufficient to break the hard shell of the societal relationship. Only

England offered the *possible* conditions to do this properly, that is, to combine radicality and expansiveness. The image of the lever is crucial: it reorganizes the political significance of an argument, literally overturning the order of the contested points. First of all, the organizational anomaly of the English situation was not a local reality which needed to be justified as such, but on the contrary, it was something that had to be vindicated, precisely by beginning from England's uniqueness. *Only* in England was it possible to recognize the absence of a significant class of peasant-owners, as a consequence of the heavy concentration of land ownership and the predominance of the *capitalist form* in production, i.e., of 'combined labour on a large scale under capitalist masters'. The mass of wage labourers formed the majority of the population. In addition, only in England had class struggle and the organization of the working class through the trade unions reached a 'certain degree of maturity and universality'. Moreover, English predominance in the world market implied that every revolution on the *economic* terrain would have unmediated [*immédiatement*] repercussions everywhere. This was not so much a variation on the idea of England as the 'Workshop of the World', as a decisive issue for the strategy and *organization* of the International. England was the classic location of land concentration and capitalism, where the *material* conditions for their destruction were most mature. For Marx it was of utmost importance that the General Council should take direct charge of British affairs. This would put it in the fortunate position of being free of intermediaries in getting its hands on 'this great lever of the proletarian revolution', a lever which it would be a folly, indeed a crime to let fall into English hands alone. The image of the lever, which Marx uses repeatedly, projects England out of England. It was no accident that the list of elements that characterized British uniqueness ended with the world market. The General Council *had to* take care of British affairs itself (Marx 1870b: 86–87).

However, it would be wrong to give Marx's position a *subjectivist* reading. The General Council itself was in many ways still a *British thing* (Robinson 1976: 59–72) and Marx was aware of that. Its composition, however, allowed for the maintenance of a terrain of political confrontation which, even in its discontinuity, was very far from the catastrophic outcomes it would have had had it dealt with the doctrinarism of continental *socialism* without mediation by the English. Marx rapidly rose to a central role – which, although not formal, was acknowledged by almost everyone. But it would be mistaken to imagine that this happened due to any deference by the leaders of the London workers' association to an intellectual, however high-profile. It was on this particular organizationally defined ground, that those who saw themselves as *communists* were able to *bring out each time* – and not without some effort – political majorities that operated in the direction of the autonomy of the workers as a class. This was contrary to the accusations levelled against them which suggested that they provided the Association with an impossible and unrealistic doctrinal homogeneity.

'The English', writes Marx, 'have all the *material* necessary for social revolution. What they lack is the *spirit of generalization* and *revolutionary ardour*'. In this respect the General Council is unique in playing a compensatory role that 'can accelerate the truly revolutionary movement in this country, and consequently *everywhere*'. The indicator is always that of becoming autonomous, of the transformation of the potential of the new trade-unionism and workers' radicalism into an independent movement. In the face of the threat posed by Gladstonian progressivism, this meant consolidating and widening a clear working-class separateness from the middle class. Marx argued that the constitution of the Land and Labour League, which had taken place a few months earlier as the direct initiative of the IWMA, showed how it was possible for the General Council to 'initiate measures which later, in the process of their execution, will appear to the public as spontaneous movements of the English working class' (Marx 1870b: 87). The League saw itself as an autonomous workers' intervention on the question of large land ownership, which had been previously raised by the Land Tenure Reform Association, founded by John Stuart Mill with the aim of liberalising land from the constraints associated with primogeniture. Unlike the Reform Association, the League demanded the nationalization of land, in line with what had been established by the Basel Congress (September 1869), in which Bakunin's position that had isolated the question of hereditary rights, 'aiming to make it the starting point of the social movement', had been defeated with the support of the British delegates. The nationalization of land was concretely articulated in relation to the unemployed and in open opposition to the positions of the *emigrationists*, who were always present in workers' associations (Harrison 1953). It was precisely the idea of emigration as the only possible solution that had been evoked by the workers' delegates after the failure of the great Preston strike of 1853 (Lowe 1860: 232), the last in which the Chartist left had played a somewhat effective role. The explicit aim of the League was to link struggle to rent and capital. Not surprisingly, the League's *Inaugural Address* closely echoed that written by Marx for the IWMA.

Beyond the outcomes of this affair, Marx's reference to the League sheds light on what he had in mind. The English anomaly of the General Council made it possible for English 'maturity' and European revolutionary experience to communicate, linking a material condition that had not yet found an adequate subjective form and a subjective disposition largely burdened down by the past, which was struggling to assume consciousness of a properly capitalist reality that was becoming a world market. It was not simply a matter of the English and the continentals: the legacy of the long season of the European workers' 1848, in which Chartism was seen by Marx as having played an integral part, was also understood *as a problem* (Chase 2015). Defending the anomaly was not only about making space for direct initiative on English soil, but also about binding the *English component* of the General Council to that role, preventing a federal duplication of the International's presence (the autonomous British regional council) from undermining its position of authority vis-à-vis the reality of workers' unionism. Moreover, the centre of gravity of British participation had shifted in the late 1860s towards the emerging reality of the City and East End workers' clubs and organizations, and this further complicated the problem (Robinson 1976: 7). In Marx's eyes this would result in an impoverishment of the General Council, decreasing the active participation of the British members and the trade-unionist component, which was constantly at risk of falling back into the dynamics of the political system to which the London scene was constantly exposed. The National Reform League included a significant number of people also involved in the International, attempting to revive the Chartist watchword of *manhood suffrage*. Its unsatisfactory outcomes are still pressing and, in some respects, constituted one of the central elements of the subtext of Marx's considerations. This should not have been the subject of journalistic attacks and polemics like that of the Swiss on the 'improper accumulation of functions' that the General Council in London had given itself. What was not understood was 'that England cannot to be treated simply as a country along with other countries. It must be treated as *the metropolis of capital*' (Marx 1870b: 87).

This should be read in connection with the General Council's intervention in favour of amnesty for Fenian militants. Two points are raised by Marx. The first is what we might call the extraterritoriality of the relation between rent and profit. If the *European* bastion of capitalism and large landed property is England, the bastion of *English* landed property is Ireland, and the standing army guarantees it. English rule is maintained only by virtue of a disguised military occupation, which Marx does not hesitate to call colonial, without which a social revolution, 'though in outmoded form', would be inevitable and irresistible, given the unsustainable situation of the Irish people. Irish emancipation passes through the rejection of the Act of Union, the refusal of which would have involved not only the loss of an immense source of wealth for the English landlords, but also of their 'greatest moral force, i.e., that of *representing the domination of England over Ireland*'. By endorsing the power of their landlords over Ireland 'the English proletariat makes them invulnerable in England itself' (Marx 1870a: 120). This first point moves into the second, which is centred on the political composition of the English working class. In these passages, Marx's text brings together dispersed considerations on the position of Ireland, which only *subsequently* initiated a heated political and historiographical debate on the coexistence of different modes of production and on the nexus between industrialization and de-industrialization. For Marx the point was rather the political element of the English working class's international composition. It is not just a question of the use made of the forced migration of the Irish poor to keep down (*debaisser*) the working class *in* England, but of the real division produced within the latter.

> *In all the big industrial centres in England* there is a profound antagonism between Irish proletarian and English proletarian. The average [Marx in French uses the word *vulgaire*, meaning average, but also naïve] English worker hates the Irish worker as a competitor who lowers wages and the standard of life. He feels national and religious antipathy for him. He regards him somewhat like the *poor whites* in the Southern States of North America regarded black slaves.
>
> MARX 1870b: 88

This attitude is clearly reciprocated and is projected along all the migratory lines of Irish poverty, especially in the United States, with the same divisive effects. The symbolic value of domination over Ireland supports and surrounds the division between English and Irish workers, in a social construct that unfolds on both sides of the Atlantic, artificially nurtured and cultivated by the bourgeoisie and with respect to which the American reference to the opposition between free and slave labour has particular significance.

The forceful idea of a *grand coup* in Ireland was not so much an attempt at *big politics* on the part of the International as the concrete political necessity of bringing together different strata of workers in England who were divided by *nationality* just like in the United States. This was not an appeal to international justice, but a catchword directly aimed at a re-composition that was *only* possible on the terrain of the political autonomy of the class. In the background was the American situation in which 'the Irish, chased from their native soil by the *bulls* and the sheep, reassemble in North-America where they constitute a huge, ever-growing section of population', but there were also 'the big industrial centres in England' (Marx 1870b: 88), whose situation, at an organizational level, had little connection with the London-centric world with which the General Council interacted and in which it was difficult to move without taking the Irish into account. For the International it was a question of initiating measures that should have been carried out within the working class in England. It is significant how much Marx stressed the General Council's work on this matter, also in terms of financial contributions, which included printing the resolutions on Ireland to ensure they reached all trade unions, given that the major London workers' newspaper, the *Bee Hive,* was censoring them.

> I have become more and more convinced – and the thing now is to drum this conviction into the English working class – that they will never be able to do anything decisive here in England before they separate their attitude towards Ireland quite definitely from that of the ruling classes, and not only make common cause with the Irish, but even take the initiative in dissolving the union established in 1801, and substituting a free federal relationship for it. And this must be done not out of sympathy for Ireland, but as a demand based on the interests of the English proletariat.
>
> MARX to KUGELMANN 11/29/1869 in MECW 43: 390

Marx's lack of interest in envisaging the constitutional profiles of the Irish solution is significant. The option of a federal outcome *after* Irish independence had little to do with a future scenario of international relations, aiming rather at imagining non-subaltern modes of communication between the *backward forms* of the agrarian revolution and the multinational industrial proletariat. This is the opposite of a 'decisive geopolitical investment in the Irish *peasantry*' (Rodden 2008). Ireland was a problem internal to the working class in England, to its political composition, to its possibility of movement. 'But since the English working class undoubtedly throws decisive weight into the scale of social emancipation generally, the lever has to be applied here'. (Marx to Kugelmann 11/27/1869 in MECW 43: 391). The English lever, the Irish lever: it is not a question of putting together the pieces of a puzzle, but of setting forces in motion. It is about articulating two moments, the *objective* one of the attack on the land blockade by the landlords in Ireland who 'to a large extent [are] the *same persons* as the English landlords' (Marx to Kugelman 11/29/1896 in MECW 43: 390) and the *communicative* one that makes the English workers, or at least the 'intelligent section of the *working class* here' (Marx to Engels 11/7/1867 in MECW 42: 464), take up the task of repealing the Act of Union as a condition for class re-composition in England. On the level of organization, the directive was to constitute autonomous *Irish* sections in England within the International and in direct relation with the General Council. In London, but also in the industrial cities of the North, the Irish sections would be an attempt at a response, albeit a partial one. The same would happen to some extent in the United States. The order of consequentiality between the two moments is suspended and tends to be translated into contemporaneity, or even inverted. The vicious circle could only be broken on the terrain of the relationship between class composition and class organization, between *English* workers and workers *in England*. On this ground, too, England is projected out of England, 'it should be treated as the *metropolis of* capital' (Marx 1870b: 87).

The International's resolution on amnesty demonstrates the full transnational relevance of the Fenian insurgency, attempting to make it a resource, without any illusions about its actual actors and their reliability. Yet more generally it was the anti-Irish backlash following the bloody events in Manchester on 18 September 1867, not only amongst the middle class but also amongst the working class, that indicated that the *cosmopolitanism* that had characterized the years of the Chartist movement's rise was now gone. The segmentation of the working class connected to the reorganization of the economic cycle (Berta 1979: 88–120) tended to take on the feature of a 'racialization' on the social level (Virdee 2014: 32–40) of those strata that did not neatly fit into the schemes of inclusivity deployed by the bourgeois project for governing the pressing processes of democratization. Thus, Marx points to an uncomfortable and even dangerous terrain, which, as the General Council's own discussions record (*Documents* 1963–1968, 2: 174–182; *Documents* 1963–1968, 3: 178–190), encounters censure, hostility and indifference, but which is vital to the revolutionary process in England 'and so everywhere'. It is the terrain on which you either move forwards or go backwards, as the following decades would dramatically demonstrate. So much for the *local question*.

Marx was right on the question of the autonomous British regional council. When at the London Conference in September 1871 John Hales proposed creating a specific British Federal Council, Marx did not object (*Documents* 1963–1968, 4: 446). The Paris Commune had just come to an end and the general situation had changed again, bringing with it new priorities. The arrival of the Parisian refugees absorbed most of the council's energy and, as a result of their presence in London, its composition changed, altering its previous dynamics. In May 1872, Hales and other English members submitted a proposal to the General Council to place the Irish sections under the jurisdiction of the British Federal Council, with the intention of denying the specific *project* of those sections. The proposal was rejected by a majority, but it brought out previously unexploded tensions. The episode is known to us only through Engels's notes on his own heavy-handed intervention, because it was believed that making the full minutes of the session public would have seriously damaged the International and its image. Engels caustically argued:

If the motion was adopted by the Council, the Council would inform the Irish working men, in so many words, that, after the dominion of the English aristocracy over Ireland, after the dominion of the English middle class over Ireland, they must now look forth to the advent of the dominion of the English working class over Ireland.

Documents 1963–1968, 5: 297–300

The 'political nullity' of the English workers, as Engels would furiously brand the British situation in the 1880s (Engels to Bebel 8/30/1883 in MECW 47: 55), also finds *one* of its roots there. Returning to the *Circulaire*, we understand why Marx gets straight to the point, which is the relation between *politics* and *economics*. The doctrines of the Swiss followers of Bakunin 'on the *connexion* or, rather, on the *non-connexion between the social movement and the political movement have never*, as far we known, been recognized by any of our International congresses. *They run counter to our Rules*'. And he refers to the passage in the preamble to the IWMA Rules, which states that 'the economical emancipation of the working classes is therefore the great end to which every political movement ought to be subordinated *as a means*'. Marx stresses this last expression (*as a means, as an instrument*), which the first translations produced by the French sections had omitted, along with other decisive points such as 'the abolition of all class rule' (Marx 1870b: 89, 90). What is most striking, however, is the triangulation that the term *social movement* has with the other two terms, *economic emancipation* and *political movement*. What the Swiss would contest a few months later would also have its centrality formally recognized. 'The relation between political action and the social movement of the working class' would be announced as the second point of the Mainz Congress, but the congress never took place.

As is well known, *after* the Commune the relationship between social transformation and the acquisition of political power would condense around the figure of the State, redetermining and exacerbating the clash with the Bakuninists. The ninth resolution of the second conference in London, which replaced the Mainz Congress, entitled the *Political Action of the Working Class,* was focused – here we can see the hand of Engels – on the need for the working class to constitute itself as 'a political party, distinct from, and opposed to, all old parties formed by the propertied classes', as an indispensable condition of the *Social Revolution* and – as its ultimate goal – the abolition of the classes (*Documents* 1963–1968, 4: 444–445). Certainly, there is some difference between the Marxian *Inaugural Address* of 1864 – which spoke of the duty of the working classes to take political power and the consequent *political* reorganization of the workers' party – and the formulation of the London resolution. Strictly speaking, however, what was reaffirmed in the resolution was the very *raison d'être* of the International. This certainly made sense, but the point initially on the agenda, of working-class political action, still remained out of focus.

Nevertheless, the English experience of the International was presented as an important reference point. Not a key, but a frame of reference in contrasting colours, which had had a mix of successes and defeats and in which not all the defeats had been failures. In the IWMA the relationship between the *economic* plan and politics had been implicit from the outset. By the end of the 1850s a new strike movement had hit British industry, reinforcing organizational structures whose coverage guaranteed 'a certain universality' and a territorial dimension as important as the London area (Knudsen 1988). George Potter, the *man of strikes* and the movementist face of the new unionism, was notably absent from those who would join the International or develop a stable relationship with it, which included workers' leaders and *societies* who were more focused on the maintenance and development of the organizational dimension than he was (Coltham 1964–1965). It was from the latter that a new drive towards politics came, after a long decade of icy separateness.

The meeting that opened the way to the IWMA was convened on the *political* theme of solidarity with the Polish insurrection of the previous year, but precisely for this reason it immediately set out its opposition to John Bright and Richard Cobden's Radicals (Collins and Abramsky 1965: 29), laying the ground for an independent initiative. The intertwining of the international dimension and the British situation would be confirmed shortly afterwards, with a message congratulating Lincoln on re-election in the same year (*Documents* 1963–1968, 1: 51–53). If the *text*, drafted by Marx, summarized his protracted reflection on the global significance of the American war, the *act* not only signalled the protagonism of the British workers on the abolitionist scene, in which the International took up the baton against Palmerston *and* Gladstone, but also sealed a phase of bitter conflict that had divided the old worker political class (Harrison 1965: 40–69). But it is the question of suffrage that provides the test case. It is completely understandable that the *Inaugural Address* and the *Provisional Rules* make no mention of it. It was no longer politically or theoretically possible to make the *Charter* the basis for 'something more' (Harney 1968). It is in this way that the Chartist left exhausted itself in its last attempt to seek out the legacy of 1848.

The lucidity of Marxian analyses produced in the mid-1850s had the flavour of a farewell:

> The last illusions disappeared in 1842 ... Since that day there has no longer been any doubt about the meaning of universal suffrage. Nor about its name. It is the *Charter of* the people and implies the assumption of

political power as a means of satisfying their social needs. Universal suffrage, which was regarded as the motto of universal brotherhood in the France of 1848, has become a battle cry in England. There universal suffrage was the direct content of the revolution; here, revolution is the direct content of universal suffrage.

MARX 1855d: 243

All idealization was out of the picture, and with it the possibility of bringing *manhood suffrage* in line with *representative government*. These pages indicate the political limit on which any claim to replace the *Charter* with an administrative reform was destined to run aground. There was no lack of revolutionary optimism, not unlike when, celebrating the fourth anniversary of *The People's Paper*, Marx concluded by saying that capital would be judged by the court of history, of which the proletariat would be the executor. However, the speech began in a more thoughtful way:

The so-called revolutions of 1848 were but poor incidents – small fractures and fissures in the dry crust of European society. However, they denounced the abyss. Beneath the apparently solid surface, they betrayed oceans of liquid matter, only needing expansion to render into fragments continents of hard rock.

MARX 1856b: 655–656

With this geological metaphor he reshaped on a different scale what would be the agenda for the party of the revolution for some time. The mole had to start digging again, leaving behind the 1848 inspired image of an *immediately* social revolution of which politics was simply a carbon copy.

When, however, the assembly of 21 April 1865 founded the National Reform League, six elected members in the General Council and seven out of ten in the Executive Committee belonged to the IWMA. Marx was genuinely enthusiastic about this, and even Engels, who up to then had been rather cold and detached in relation to the affairs of the International, began to show signs of interest. The connection between the League and the IWMA changed the picture and reproposed the issue of *one man, one vote* from a radically different perspective. Yet the Reform League affair marked an overall defeat for the International.

In the sequence of events that resulted in the enactment of Disraeli's Second Reform Act, the Reform League played an important mobilizing role (Harrison 1965: 78–136), which was not limited to the parliamentary ambit (for an opposing point of view, see, Cowling 1967). However, it did not keep to the central point of its programme, i.e., *manhood suffrage* versus *household suffrage*, and failed to represent a politically stable reference point in the composite of the various people who supported the franchise. Indeed, the contortions of the organization had a negative impact on the General Council of the International. Marx followed the League's events with growing disappointment, becoming more interested in the conflicts of the leadership cadre and the International's diminishing grip on it than in the extent of workers' mobilizations and the subjective richness underlying them (Foot 2006: 130–170). There was a growing gap and confrontation between the movement's leading group and those who took part in street mobilization and there was little recognition of this. It certainly could not be perceived by leaders such as George Howell who understood electoral reform as a vehicle for the social mobility of the *respectable* working class, but neither could it be by those for whom it could be a resource, i.e., neither by Marx nor his followers. One passage is particularly significant on this point. At this time, and with much hesitation, but forced by the fall of Gladstone, the League promoted the second major demonstration in Hyde Park for 6 May, which would see two hundred thousand people defy the Home Secretary's ban, with the latter being forced to abandon his planned show of military strength in response, and to resign. Harrison speaks of it as the day on which the Chartist humiliation of 10 April 1848 was 'avenged' (Harrison 1965: 78–136). It was a historic day in which people's behaviour and composition transcended the importance of the occasion and where there was no shortage of those *plebeians* who would be excluded from the Reform Act and who had in part been organized by the sections in the East End.

At the General Council meeting of 16 April 1867, at Marx's request Lafargue presented a note criticising George Odger, Secretary of the League and President of the IWMA, who had proposed a resolution congratulating Bismarck on giving the subjects of the North German Confederation the right to vote (*Documents* 1963–1968, 2: 111). At the 30 April meeting of the General Council, Joseph Collett, a French journalist who was a member, read a public letter to Odger without encountering any opposition, which dissuaded Odger from breaking the ban (*Documents* 1963–1968, 2: 116–118). The contrast is stark: it is reasonable to assume that, had he been present, Marx would have objected (Robinson 1976: 158–159), but even afterwards he made no record of 6 May. This is not simply anecdotal, but a revealing snapshot of the situation. To call it political short-sightedness would be easy, but perhaps unfair. Marx was caught up in the publication of *Das Kapital*, i.e., what for him would be *the* book – and *that* book was also a weapon – and his justified belief that a workers' *advance* on the suffrage question was no longer on the agenda led him to take a distance from it. The Reform Act, which received royal assent on 15 August, closed an epochal passage in which workers' mobilization played a real role, but whose *governance* was completely in the hands of the bourgeoisie and whose outcome projected a division between a *virtuous* working class and the *residuum* of those excluded from it. They are no longer the *two cities* of which Disraeli wrote, but a mobile and regulated frontier, although no less effective for that. Paradoxically, the judgement of 1855 was confirmed: what lay at the heart of the *Charter* was not something that could be fully integrated in the representative apparatus.

On the other hand, on the ground of *organization* any recrimination would have been fanciful, and Marx, despite his propensity for invective, was a realistic politician. Both the role of the General Council and the connection with the men of the trade unions were forcefully reiterated. The suffragist option, which Marx would *always* support, beyond any fetishism of *pure* democracy, also remained: the universality of suffrage was seen as one of the conditions that made the Commune possible. But something changed in Marx's relationship with *politics*, and the efforts made after the defeat of *manhood suffrage*, although conditioned by circumstances and forces, painted a different picture.

The perspective of the *conquest of political power* identifies the working class as a class and not as a social *group*, however large or even numerically in the majority it was. But the central questions now were its composition, the making and unmaking of its boundaries along the lines marked by class struggle, and *within this* the question of politics as the constant intervention of the working class on itself, on its own *form*. It might be seen as a politics *of reflexivity*. This disrupts any separation between the economic and the political, but also determines something in the unresolved nature of the expression *to conquer power*, recalling the relationship between the economic and the political on which the *General Address* insisted regarding the legislation on the reduction of the working day. Workers' *political* struggle is a necessary condition and at the same time a limit on any discourse on power in which reference to the state remains inescapable, but it is by no means constitutive of it (Ricciardi, in this volume). The perspective of political struggle is not recomposed in the state, just as workers' critique does not recompose itself in labour. At the end of November 1871, two months before the London Conference, Marx wrote a long letter to Friedrich Bolte, where he clarified and developed his point about politics and sketched out *his* history of the International. According to Marx, it was founded in order to replace the socialist or semi-socialist sects with a real workers' movement, which would have been unfeasible if they had not fallen into ruin.

> For all that, what history exhibits everywhere was repeated in the history of the International. What is antiquated tries to reconstitute and assert itself within the newly acquired form ... And the history of the International was a *continual struggle of the General Council* against the sects and attempts by amateurs to assert themselves within the International itself against the real movement of the working class.
>
> MARX to BOLTE 11/23/1871 in MECW 44: 252

As historians, we know that things are more complicated, at least in relation to the history of the General Council. But Marx's 1864 intuition was confirmed to be correct. The conquest of political power naturally requires class organization, which finds the origin of its development in economic struggles.

> But on the other hand, every movement in which the working class comes out as a class against the ruling classes and tries to coerce them by PRESSURE FROM WITHOUT is a POLITICAL MOVEMENT.

If the struggle against a single capitalist to reduce working time in a single factory can be considered an economic struggle, this is not the case for its generalization: the movement to impose an eight-hour day as law was a political movement.

And in this way, out of the separate economic movements of the workers there grows up everywhere a political movement, that is to say a movement of the class, with the object of achieving its interests in a general form, in a form possessing general, socially binding force.

Once again organization is the focus: 'Though these movements presuppose a certain degree of PREVIOUS organization, they are in turn equally a means of developing this organization' (Marx to Bolte 11/23/1871 in MECW 44: 258). If we think back to the polemic with the anarchists, this is an indication that *also* helps to understand what Marx means when he speaks of 'a serious economic Revolution' (Marx 1870b: 86), that is, not only the political form of emancipation, but its political practice.

A final remark: When Marx applied for British citizenship in 1874, the Home Office refused to grant it to him. But when he had applied to regain his Prussian citizenship in 1861, he had also been refused.

Works of Karl Marx and Friedrich Engels

Karl Marx

1837

Marx to his Father, 10–11 November. In MECW (1975), Volume 1: 10–21.

1842

a) Proceedings of the Sixth Rhine Province Assembly. Third Article Debates on the Law on Thefts of Wood. In MECW (1975), Volume 1: 224–263.
b) The Philosophical Manifesto of the Historical School of Law. In MECW (1975), Volume 1: 203–210.

1843

Marx to Feuerbach, 3 October. In MECW (1975), Volume 3: 349–351.
Contribution to the Critique of Hegel's Philosophy of Law. In MECW (1975), Volume 3: 3–187.

1844

Marx to Feuerbach, 11 August. In MECW (1975), Volume 3: 354–357.
a) Economic and Philosophic Manuscripts of 1844. In MECW (1975), Volume 3: 229–348.
b) On the Jewish Question. In MECW (1975), Volume 3: 146–174.
c) Contribution to the Critique of Hegel's Philosophy of Law. Introduction. In MECW (1975), Volume 3: 175–187.
d) Comments on James Mill, Elémens d'économie politique. In MECW (1975), Volume 3: 211–228.
e) Critical Marginal Notes on the Article 'The King of Prussia and Social Reform. By a Prussian'. In MECW (1975), Volume 3: 189–206.
f) Letters from the *Deutsch-Französische Jahrbücher.* In MECW (1975), Volume 3: 133–145.

1845

Draft of an Article on Friedrich List's Book: *Das Nationale System der Politischen Oekonomie.* In MECW (1975) Volume 4: 265–293.

1846

Peuchet: On Suicide. In MECW (1975), Volume 4: 597–612.

1847

a)   The Poverty of Philosophy. Answer to the *Philosophy of Poverty* by M. Proudhon. In MECW (1976), Volume 6: 105–212.

b)   Moralising Criticism and Critical Morality. A Contribution to German Cultural History Contra Karl Heinzen. In MECW (1976), Volume 6: 312–340.

1848

a)   To the editor of the newspaper *L'Alba*, 29 June. In MECW (1977), Volume 7: 11–12.

b)   German Foreign Policy and the Last Events in Prague. *Neue Rheinische Zeitung*, 12 July. In MECW (1977), Volume 7: 212–215.

c)   English-French Mediation in Italy. *Neue Rheinische Zeitung*, 21 October. In MECW (1977), Volume 7: 480–481.

d)   Speech on the Question of Free Trade. In MECW (1976), Volume 6: 450–465.

e)   The Bourgeoisie and the Counter-Revolution. *Neue Rheinische Zeitung*, 10 December. In MECW (1977), Volume 8: 154–178.

f)   The Bill Proposing the Abolition of Feudal Obligations. *Neue Rheinische Zeitung*, 29 July. In MECW (1977), Volume 7: 290–295.

1849

a)   The Revolutionary Movement. *Neue Rheinische Zeitung*, 1 January. In MECW (1977), Volume 8: 213–215.

b)   Wage Labour and Capital. *Neue Rheinische Zeitung*, 5 April. In MECW (1977), Volume 9: 197–228.

1850

a)   The Class Struggles in France 1848–1850. *Neue Rheinische Zeitung*, January–November. In MECW (1978), Volume 10: 45–146.

b)   Review of F. Guizot, *Pourquoi la révolution d'Angleterre a-telle réussi? Discours sur l'histoire de la révolution d'Angleterre. Neue Rheinische Zeitung*, 2 November. In MECW (1978), Volume 10: 251–256.

1852

Marx to Weydemeyer, 5 March. In MECW (1983), Volume 39: 60–66.

Marx to Engels, 6 May. In MECW (1983), Volume 39: 100–102.

a)   The Eighteenth Brumaire of Louis Bonaparte. In MECW (1979), Volume 11: 99–197.

b)   The Elections in England. Tories and Whigs. In MECW (1979), Volume 11: 327–332.

1853

Marx to Engels, 14 June. In MECW (1983), Volume 39: 344–348.

a)   Defense – Finances – Decrease of the Aristocracy – Politics. *The New York Daily Tribune*, 8 February. In MECW (1979), Volume 11: 502–507.

b)   Forced Emigration – Kossuth and Mazzini – The Refugee Question – Election Bribery in England – Mr. Cobden. *The New York Daily Tribune*, 4 March. In MECW (1979), Volume 11: 528–534.

c)   The Indian Question – Irish Tenant Right. *The New York Daily Tribune*, 28 June. In MECW (1979), Volume 12: 157–162.

d)   The War Question – British Population and Trade Returns – Doings of Parliament. *The New York Daily Tribune*, 12 August. In MECW (1979), Volume 12: 245–256.

e)   The Italian Insurrection – British Politics. *The New York Daily Tribune,* 11 February. In MECW (1979), Volume 11: 508–512.

f)   The Attack on Francis Joseph – The Milan Riot – British Politics – Disraeli's speech – Napoleons Will. *The New York Daily Tribune*, 22 February. In MECW (1979), Volume 11: 513–521.

g)   Kossuth and Mazzini – Intrigues of the Prussian government – Austro-Prussian Commercial Treaty – The Times and the Refugees. *The New York Daily Tribune*, 4 April. In MECW (1979), Volume 11: 535–541.

h)   Exzerpte aus Augustin Thierry: Essai sur l'histoire de la formation et des progrès du Tiers État. In Marx-Engels-Gesamtausgabe MEGA² (2007), IV. Exzerpte, Notizen, Marginalien. Berlin: Akademie Verlag. Volume 12: *Exzerpte und Notizen September 1853 bis Januar 1855*, 513–580.

i)   The Future Results of British Rule in India. *The New York Daily Tribune*, 22 July. In MECW (1979), Volume 12: 217–222.

j)   The British Rule in India. *The New York Daily Tribune*, 10 June. In MECW (1979), Volume 12: 125–133.

k)   The Russo–Turkish Difficulty.–Ducking and Dodging of the British Cabinet. –Nesselrode's Last Note. –The East India Question. *The New York Daily Tribune,* 12 July. In MECW (1979), Volume 12: 192–200.

l)   Affairs in Holland.–Denmark.–Conversion of the British Debt.–India, Turkey and Russia. *The New York Daily Tribune*, 24 May. In MECW (1979), Volume 12: 101–106.

m)   The Turkish War Question.–The *New-York Tribune* in The House of Commons.–The Government of India. *The New York Daily Tribune*, 5 July. In MECW (1979), Volume 12: 174–184.

n)   The East India Company–Its History and Results. *The New York Daily Tribune*, 24 June. In MECW (1979), Volume 12: 148–156.

o)   The Russian Humbug.–Gladstone Failure–Sir Charles Wood's East India Reforms. *The New York Daily* Tribune, 7 June. In MECW (1979), Volume 12: 115–124.

p)   The War Question.–Doings of Parliament.–India. *The New York Daily Tribune*, 19 July. In MECW (1979), Volume 12: 209–216.

1854

Marx to Engels, 27 July. In MECW (1983), Volume 39: 472–476.

Marx to Engels, 2 December. In MECW (1983), Volume 39: 501–504.

a)   The Austrian Bankruptcy. *The New York Daily Tribune*, 22 March. In MECW (1980), Volume 13: 43–49.

b)   Revolutionary Spain, Articles for *the New York Daily Tribune*. In MECW (1980), Volume 13: 389–446.

c)   Mazzini and Napoleon. *The New York Daily Tribune*, 11 May. In MECW (1986), Volume 15: 485–489.

1855

a)   Ireland's Revenge. *Neue Oder-Zeitung*, 13 March. In MECW (1980), Volume 14: 78–80.

b)   Lord John Russell. *Neue Oder-Zeitung*, 25 July–1 August. In MECW (1980), Volume 14: 373–393.

c)   Sardinia. 27 November. In Marx K and Engels F (1959), *Sul Risorgimento italiano*. Roma: Editori Riuniti, 128–130.

d)   The Association for Administrative Reform. People's Charter. In MECW (1980), Volume 14: 240–244.

1856

a)   Sardinia. *The People's Paper*, 31 May. In MECW (1986), Volume 15: 3–7.

b)   Speech at the Anniversary of *The People's Paper* Delivered in London, 14 April. In MECW (1980), Volume 14: 655–656.

1857

Marx to Engels, 15 August. In MECW (1983), Volume 40: 151–153.

a)   British Incomes in India. *The New York Daily Tribune*, 21 September. In MECW (1986), Volume 15: 349–352.

b)   The Revolt in the Indian Army. *The New York Daily Tribune*, 30 June. In MECW (1986), Volume 15: 297–300.

c) Indian News. *The New York Daily Tribune*, 31 July. In MECW (1986), Volume 15: 315–317.

d) The Indian Insurrection. *The New York Daily Tribune*, 14 August. In MECW (1986), Volume 15: 327–330.

e) The Revolt in India. *The New York Daily Tribune*, 17 July. In MECW (1986), Volume 15: 305–308.

f) The Revolt in India. *The New York Daily Tribune,* 1 September. In MECW (1986), Volume 15: 342–348.

g) The Indian Revolt. *The New York Daily Tribune*, 4 September. In MECW (1986), Volume 15: 353–356.

h) English Atrocities in China. The New York Daily Tribune. 10 April 1857. In MECW (1986), Volume 15: 232–235.

1857–1861

a) Economic Manuscripts of 1857–61. In MECW (1986), Volume 28.

b) Economic Manuscripts of 1857–61. In MECW (1987), Volume 29.

1858

Marx to Engels, 16 January. In MECW (1983), Volume 40: 248–250.

Marx to Engels, 14 February. In MECW (1983), Volume 40: 265–267.

Marx to Engels, 29 April. In MECW (1983), Volume 40: 319–311.

Marx to Engels, 15 August. In MECW (1983), Volume 40: 151–152.

Marx to Engels, 8 October. In MECW (1983), Volume 40: 346–347.

a) Imprisonment of Lady Bulwer-Lytton. In MECW (1986), Volume 15: 596–601.

b) The Excitement in Ireland. *The New York Daily Tribune*, 29 December. In MECW (1980), Volume 16: 134–138.

c) The Approaching Indian Loan. *The New York Daily Tribune*, 22 January. In MECW (1986), Volume 15: 443–446.

d) History of the Opium Trade. *The New York Daily Tribune*, 3 September. In MECW (1980), Volume 16: 17–20.

e) Bolivar y Ponte. *The New American Cyclopaedia*. Vol. III. In MECW (1987), Volume 18: 219–233.

f) Lord Canning's Proclamation and Land Tenure in India. *The New York Daily Tribune,* 25 May. In MECW (1986), Volume 15: 546–548.

g) Taxation in India. *The New York Daily Tribune*, 24 June. In MECW (1986), Volume 15: 575–579.

h) Investigation of Tortures in India. *The New York Daily Tribune, 28 August.* In MECW (1986), Volume 15: 336–341.

i)   The Annexation of Oude. *The New York Daily Tribune*, 14 May. In MECW (1986), Volume 15: 533–538.

1859

Marx to Lassalle, 4 February. In MECW (1983), Volume 40: 380–383.

Marx to Engels, 9 April. In MECW (1983), Volume 40: 412–413.

Marx to Lassalle, 22 November. In MECW (1983), Volume 40: 536–539.

a)   A Contribution to the Critique of Political Economy. In MECW (1988), Volume 29: 257–420.

b)   Fair Professions. *The New York Daily Tribune,* 18 May. In MECW (1980), Volume 16: 307–309.

c)   Spree and Mincio. *Das Volk*, 25 June. In MECW (1980), Volume 16: 380–383.

d)   What has Italy Gained? *The New York Daily Tribune*, 27 July. In MECW (1980), Volume 16: 407–409.

e)   The Treaty of Villafranca. *The New York Daily Tribune*, 4 August. In MECW (1980), Volume 16: 416–420.

f)   The Current Position of Italy. 16 September. In Marx K and Engels F (1959) *Sul Risorgimento italiano.* Roma: Editori Riuniti, 345–348.

g)   Great Trouble in Indian Finances. *New York Daily Tribune*, 8 April. In MECW (1980), Volume 16: 279–282.

h)   Trade With China. *New York Daily Tribune*, 3 December. In MECW (1980), Volume 16: 536–539.

1860

Marx to Engels, 11 January. In MECW (1985), Volume 41: 3–5.

a)   Sicily and the Sicilians. *The New York Daily Tribune*, 17 May. In MECW (1981), Volume 17: 370–372.

b)   British Commerce. *New York Daily Tribune*, 16 July. In MECW (1981), Volume 17: 406–409.

1861

Marx to Philips, 6 May. In MECW (1985), Volume 41: 276–279.

Marx to Engels, 1 July. In MECW (1985), Volume 41: 300–303.

Marx to Engels, 5 July. In MECW (1985), Volume 41: 305–309.

a)   The Intervention in Mexico. *The New York Daily Tribune*, 23 November. In MECW (1984), Volume 19: 71–78.

b)   The British Cotton Trade. *The New York Daily Tribune*, 14 October. In MECW (1984), Volume 19: 17–20.

c)   The London Times on the Orleans Princes in America. *The New York Daily Tribune*, 7 November. In MECW (1984), Volume 19: 27–31.

d) The North American Civil War. *Die Presse*, 25 October. In MECW (1984), Volume 19: 32–42.

e) The Civil War in the United States. *Die Presse*, 6 November. In MECW (1984), Volume 19: 43–52.

f) The Dismissal of Frémont. *Die Presse*, 26 November. In MECW (1984), Volume 19: 86–88.

g) The Crisis over the Slavery Issue. *Die Presse*, 11 December. In MECW (1984), Volume 19: 115–116.

h) The Opinion of the Newspapers and the Opinion of the People. *Die Presse*, 31 December. In MECW (1984), Volume 19: 127–130.

1861–1863

a) Economic Manuscripts of 1861–1863. In MECW (1989), Volume 34.

b) Economic Manuscripts of 1861–1863. In MECW (1989), Volume 31.

c) Economic Manuscripts of 1861–1863. In MECW (1989), Volume 32.

d) Economic Manuscripts of 1861–1863. In MECW (1989), Volume 33.

1862

Marx to Engels, 6 March. In MECW (1985), Volume 41: 347–351.

Marx to Engels, 27 May. In MECW (1985), Volume 41: 369–370.

Marx to Engels, 20 November. In MECW (1985), Volume 41: 431.

a) A Pro-America Meeting. *Die Presse*, 5 January. In MECW (1984), Volume 19: 134–136.

b) English Public Opinion. *The New York Daily Tribune*, 1 February. In MECW (1984), Volume 19: 137–142.

c) A London Workers' Meeting. *Die Presse*, 2 February. In MECW (1984), Volume 19: 153–156.

d) Anti-Intervention Feeling. *Die Presse*, 4 February. In MECW (1984), Volume 19: 157–159.

e) American Affairs. *Die Presse*, 3 March. In MECW (1984), Volume 19: 178–181.

f) The American Civil War I. *Die Presse*, 26 March. In MECW (1984), Volume 19: 186–190.

g) The American Civil War II. *Die Presse*, 26 March. In MECW (1984), Volume 19: 191–195.

h) The Situation in the American Theatre of War. *Die Presse*, 30 May. In MECW (1984), Volume 19: 204–208.

i) A Criticism of American Affairs. *Die Presse*, 9 August. In MECW (1984), Volume 19: 226–229.

j) Comments on the North American Events. *Die Presse*, 12 October. In MECW (1984), Volume 19: 248–251.

k)   The Situation in North America. *Die Presse*, 10 November. In MECW (1984), Volume 19: 256–259.

l)   The Election Results in the Northern States. *Die Presse*, 23 November. In MECW (1984), Volume 19: 263–265.

m)   The Dismissal of McClellan. *Die Presse*, 29 November. In MECW (1984), Volume 19: 266–269.

1863

Marx to Engels, 13 February. In MECW (1985), Volume 41: 453–454.

1864

Marx to Engels, 4 November. In MECW (1987), Volume 42: 11–18.

Marx to Engels, 2 December. In MECW (1987), Volume 42: 49–51.

a)   Provisional Rules of the Workingmen's International Association. In MECW (1985), Volume 20: 14–19.

b)   Address of the International Workingmen's Association. To Abraham Lincoln, President of the United States of America, 23 December. In MECW (1985), Volume 20: 19–21.

1865

Marx to Engels, 10 February. In MECW (1987), Volume 42: 84–86.

Marx to Engels, 20 November. In MECW (1987), Volume 42: 198–199.

a)   To Abraham Lincoln President of the United States of America. In MECW (1985), Volume 20: 19–21.

b)   Address from the Working Men's International Association to President Johnson, 20 May. In MECW (1985), Volume 20: 99–100.

1866

Marx to Engels, 17 December. In MECW (1987), Volume 42: 338–339.

Marx to Engels, 13 February. In MECW (1987), Volume 42: 227–228.

Marx to Engels, 20 February. In MECW (1987), Volume 42: 231–232.

1867

Marx to Engels, 7 November. In MECW (1987), Volume 42: 464–465.

Marx to Engels, 28 November. In MECW (1987), Volume 42: 478–479.

Marx to Engels, 30 November. In MECW (1987), Volume 42: 484–487.

Marx to Kugelmann, 11 October. In MECW (1987), Volume 42: 440–443.

a)   Capital. A Critique of Political Economy. Book 1, in MECW (1996), Volume 35.

b)   Outline of a Report on the Irish Question Delivered to the German
     Workers' Educational Society in London on December 16, 1867. In MECW
     (1985), Volume 21: 194–206.
c)   Record of a Speech on the Irish Question Delivered by Karl Marx to the
     German Workers' Educational Society in London on December 16, 1867.
     In MECW (1985), Volume 21: 317–319.
d)   Instructions for the Delegates of the Provisional General Council. The
     Different Questions. In MECW (1985), Volume 20: 185–194.

1868

Marx to Kugelmann, 12 May. In MECW (1988), Volume 43: 173–175.
Marx to Engels, 7 November. In MECW (1988), Volume 43: 154.
a)   Record of Marx's Speech on the Consequences of Using Machinery
     under Capitalism, 28 July. In MECW (1985), Volume 21: 382–384.
b)   The International Working Men's Association. Its Establishment,
     Organization, Political and Social Activity, and Growth. In MECW (1985),
     Volume 21: 322–380.

1869

Marx to Kugelmann, 29 November. In MECW (1988), Volume 43: 389–391.
Marx to Engels, 10 December. In MECW (1988), Volume 43: 396–399.
a)   Report of the General Council to the Fourth Annual Congress of the
     International Working Men's Association. In MECW (1985), Volume
     21: 68–82.
b)   Ireland from the American Revolution to the Union of 1801 – Extracts
     and Notes. In MECW (1985), Volume 21: 212–282.
c)   Address to the National Labor Union of the United States, 12 May. In
     MECW (1985), Volume 21: 53–55.

1870

a)   Confidential Communication, 28 March. In MECW (1985), Volume
     21: 112–124.
b)   The General Council to the Federal Council of Romance Switzerland. In
     MECW (1985), Volume 21: 84–91.

1871

Marx to Bolte, 23 November. In MECW (1989), Volume 44: 251–259.
The Civil War in France. Address of the General Council of the International
Working Men's Association. In MECW (1986), Volume 22: 307–398.

1872

Letter to *Il gazzettino rosa*. 18 May, quoted in Marx K and Engels F (1959) *Sul Risorgimento italiano*. Rome: Editori Riuniti, 39.

1875

a)   Critique of the Gotha Programme. In MECW (1989), Volume 24: 75–99.
b)   Notes on Bakunin's Book Statehood and Anarchy. In MECW (1989), Volume 24: 485–526.

1877

Marx to Otechestvenniye Zapiski, November. In MECW (1989), Volume 24: 196–201.

1878

Exzerpte und Notizen zur Geologie, Mineralogie und Agrikulturchemie – März Bis September 1878 (MEGA 2011). Berlin: Akademie Verlag.

1880–1882

The Ethnological Notebooks of Karl Marx (1974). Assen: Van Gorcum.

1881

Marx to Danielson, 19 February. In MECW (1993), Volume 46: 60–64.
Marx to Zasulič, 8 March. In MECW (1993), Volume 46: 71–72.
Marx to Zasulič, 3 August, First draft. In MECW (1989), Volume 24: 346–360.
Marx to Zasulič, 3 August, Second draft. In MECW (1989), Volume 24: 362–364.
Marx to Zasulič, 3 August. In MECW (1989), Volume 24: 370–371.

1881–1882

Marginal Notes on Adolph Wagner's *Lehrbuch der politischen Oekonomie*. In MECW (1989), Volume 24: 531–559.

1882

Preface to the Second Russian Edition of the 'Manifesto of the Communist Party'. In MECW (1989), Volume 24: 425–426.

1885

Capital. A Critique of Political Economy. Book 2, in MECW (1997), Volume 36.

1894

Capital. A Critique of Political Economy. Book 3, in MECW (1998), Volume 37.

1981
Die technologisch-historischen Exzerpte Historisch-kritische Ausgabe. Frankfurt am Main-Berlin-Wien: Ullstein.

1982
Capital. A Critique of Political Economy, Volume 1. Harmondsworth: Penguin.

1983
Mathematical Manuscripts of Karl Marx. Clapham, London: New Park Publications.

Friedrich Engels

1844
Outlines of a Critique of Political Economy. In MECW (1975), Volume 3: 418–443.

1845
The Condition of the Working-Class in England. From Personal Observation and Authentic Sources. In MECW (1975), Volume 4: 295–583.

1847
The Constitutional Question in Germany. In MECW (1976), Volume 6: 75–91.

1848
Germany's Foreign Policy. *Neue Rheinische Zeitung*, 3 July. In MECW (1977), Volume 7: 165–167.

1858
The Revolt in India. *New York Daily Tribune*, 17 September. In MECW (1980), Volume 15: 607–611.

1862
Engels to Marx, 16 October. In MECW (1985), Volume 41: 418–419.

1864
Engels to Weydemeyer, 24 November. In MECW (1987), Volume 42: 37–39.

1875
Engels to Bebel, 18–28 March. In MECW (1989), Volume 24: 67–74.
On Social Relations in Russia. In MECW (1989), Volume 24: 39–50.

1883

Engels to Bebel, 30 August. In MECW (1995), Volume 47: 52–55.

1884

The Origin of the Family, Private Property and the State. In MECW (1990), Volume 26: 129–256.

Karl Marx and Friedrich Engels

1845

The Holy Family, or Critique of Critical Criticism. In MECW (1975), Volume 4: 5–294.

1845–1846

The German Ideology. In MECW (1976), Volume 5: 19–539.

1847

On Poland. 29 November. In MECW (1976) Volume 6: 388–390.

1848

The Communist Manifesto. In MECW (1976), Volume 6: 477–519.

1850

Reviews from the Neue Rheinische Zeitung. Politisch-ökonomische Revue No. 2. G. Fr. Daumer, Die Religion des neuen Weltalters. Versuch einer combinatorisch-aphoristischen Grundlegung. In MECW (1978), Volume 10: 241–246.

References

Abensour M (1997) *La Démocratie contre l'État. Marx et le moment machiavélien.* Paris: PUF.

Abensour M (2013) *Utopiques I. Le procès des Maîtres rêveurs.* Paris: Sens&Tonka.

Abensour M (2016) *Utopiques IV. L'histoire de l'utopie et le destin de sa critique.* Paris: Sens&Tonka.

Adler PS (1990) Marx, Machines, and Skill. *Technology and Culture* vol 31(4): 780–812.

Anderson KB (2002) Marx's Late Writings on Non-Western and Precapitalist Societies and Gender. *Rethinking Marxism* vol 14(4): 89–93.

Anderson KB (2010) *Marx at the Margins: On Nationalism, Ethnicity, and Non-Western Societies.* Chicago: Chicago University Press.

Aricó J (2013) *Marx and Latin America.* London: Routledge.

Arthur CJ (2009) Il concetto di denaro. In Bellofiore R and Fineschi R (eds) *Marx in questione. Il dibattito 'aperto' dell'International Symposium on Marxian Theory.* Napoli: La Città del Sole, 9–83.

Assoun P-L (1978). *Marx et la répétition historique.* Paris: PUF.

Bachofen JJ (1870) *Die Sage Von Tanaquil: eine Untersuchung uber den Orientalismus in Romund Italien.* Heidelberg: JCB Mohr.

Balibar É (1970[1965]) On the Basic Concepts of Historical Materialism. In Althusser L and Balibar É, *Reading Capital.* London: NLB, 201–308.

Balibar É (1974) *Cinq études de matérialisme historique.* Paris: François Maspero.

Balibar É (1997) *La crainte des masses. Politique et philosophie avant et après Marx.* Paris: Galilée.

Balibar É (2011) Le contrat social des marchandises: Marx et le sujet de l'échange. In Balibar É *Citoyen sujet et autres essais d'anthropologie philosophique.* Paris: PUF, 315–342.

Balibar É (2014) 'Klassenkampf' als Begriff des Politischen. In Jaeggi R and Loik D (eds) *Nach Marx. Philosophie, Kritik, Praxis.* Frankfurt am Main: Suhrkamp: 445–462.

Ballarin R (1985–86) *L'"Hegelismo liberale" di Eduard Gans e la sua influenza nella formazione del pensiero di K. Marx.* Dissertation in Philosophy, Università degli Studi di Padova.

Barrett M (1980) *Women's Oppression Today: Problems in Marxist Feminist Analysis.* New York: Verso.

Basso L (2012[2008]) *Marx and Singularity: From the Early Writings to the Grundrisse.* Leiden-Boston: Brill.

Basso L (2015[2012]) *Marx and the Common: From Capital to the Late Writings.* Leiden-Boston: Brill.

Battistini M (2004), '... lo si costringerà ad essere libero'. Appunti marxiani sulla Rivoluzione francese. *Scienza & Politica. Per una storia delle dottrine* vol 16(30): 3–27.

Battistini M (2013) A National Blessing: debito e credito pubblico nella fondazione atlantica degli Stati Uniti d'America. *Scienza & Politica* vol 25(48): 13–31.

Battistini M (2021) Karl Marx and the Global History of the Civil War: The Slave Movement, Working-Class Struggle, and the American State within the World Market. *International Labor and Working-Class History* vol 100(2): 158–185.

Bauer B (1844) Neueste Schriften über die Judenfrage. *Allgemeine Literatur-Zeitung* vol 4: 10–19.

Beckert S and Rockman S (2016) *Slavery's Capitalism. A New History of American Economic Development.* Philadelphia: Pennsylvania University Press.

Bensaïd D (2004) *A Marx for Our Times: Adventures and Misadventures of a Critique.* London: Verso.

Bentham J (2001[1796]) *Essays on the Subject of the Poor Laws.* In Quinn M (eds) *Writings on the Poor Laws.* Oxford: Clarendon Press, Volume I, 3–140.

Bentham J (1830) *Rationale of Rewards.* London: sn.

Berman M (1988) *All That Is Solid Melts into Air. The Experience of Modernity.* New York: Penguin Books.

Berresford EP (1972) *A History of the Irish Working Class.* London: Victor Gollancz Ltd.

Berta G (1979) *Marx, gli operai inglesi e i cartisti.* Milano: Feltrinelli.

Bertani C (2004) *Eduard Gans e la cultura del suo tempo.* Napoli: Guida.

Blackburn R (ed) (2011) *Marx and Lincoln. The Unfinished Revolution.* London: Verso Books.

Bongiovanni B (1981) *L'universale pregiudizio. Le interpretazioni della critica marxiana della politica.* Milano: La salamandra.

Bongiovanni B (1989a) Democrazia, dittatura, lotta di classe. Appunti su Marx e la rivoluzione francese. *Studi Storici* vol 4: 775–802.

Bongiovanni B (1989b) *Le repliche della storia. Karl Marx fra la Rivoluzione francese e la critica della politica.* Torino: Bollati Boringhieri.

Boostels J (2010) *Marx and Latin America Revisited,* Fall 2010 Janey Lecture, New School for Social Research: New York.

Bosio G (1955) Introduzione. In Marx K and Engels F *Scritti italiani.* Roma-Milano: Ed. Avanti!, (reprint by Samonà & Savelli in 1972): 5–17.

Bourdieu P (1976) Les modes de domination. *Actes de la recherche en sciences sociales* vol 2(2–3): 122–132.

Boylan TA and Foley TP (1992) *Political Economy and Colonial Ireland. The Propagation and Ideological Function of Economic Discourse in the Nineteenth Century.* London: Routledge.

Bradley A (2011) *Originary Technicity: The Theory of Technology from Marx to Derrida.* Basingstoke-New York: Palgrave MacMillan.

Braudel F (1981) *Civilization and Capitalism, 15–18th century*. London: Collins.

Braudel F (1992) *The Mediterranean and the Mediterranean World in the Age of Philip II*. New York: HarperCollins.

Braun J (1980) Der Besitzrechtsstreit zwischen F. C. von Savigny und Eduard Gans. *Quaderni fiorentini per la storia del pensiero giuridico moderno* vol 9: 457–506.

Breckman W (1999) *Marx, the Young Hegelians, and the Origins of Radical Social Theory: Dethroning the Self*. Cambridge: Cambridge University Press.

Broeze FJA (1982) Private Enterprise and the Peopling of Australasia 1831–50. *The Economic History Review* vol 35(2): 235–253.

Brown H (2012) *Marx on Gender and the Family. A Critical Study*. Leiden-Boston: Brill.

Brunner O (1968) Das 'ganze Haus' und die alteuropäische 'Ökonomik'. In *Neue Wege der Verfassungs– und Sozialgeschichte*. Göttingen, Vandenhoeck & Ruprecht: 103–127.

Canale D (2000) *La costituzione delle differenze: giusnaturalismo e codificazione del diritto civile nella Prussia del Settecento*. Torino: Giappichelli.

Carver T (2013) Marx and Gender. *Deutsche Zeitschrift für Philosophie/Sonderband* vol 34: 193–207.

Carver T (2005) Marx's Illegitimate Son or Gresham's Law in the World of Scholarship. In Carver T. *Marx's Myths and Legends*: https://www.marxists.org/subject/marxmyths/terrell-carver/article.htm.

Carwardine R and Sexton J (eds) (2011) *The Global Lincoln*. New York: Oxford University Press.

Cazzaniga GM (2004) *Marx, le macchine e la filosofia della storia:* https://www.unesco.chairephilo.uqam.ca/textes/caza-1.pdf.

Cervelli I (2009) Verso la Comune. A margine di una lettera di Marx a Kugelmann. *Studi Storici* vol 50(4): 837–963.

Chakrabarty D (2000) *Provincializing Europe: Postcolonial Thought and Historical Difference*. Princeton: Princeton University Press.

Chase M (2015) Chartism, Democracy and Marx and Engels. *Theory and Struggle* vol 116: 32–37.

Clochec P (2019) Le jeune Marx et la question de l'origine du droit. *Droit & Philosophie* vol 10: 41–53.

Cohen GA (1978) *Karl Marx's Theory of History: A Defense*. Oxford: Clarendon Press.

Collina V (1990) *Le democrazie nella Francia del 1840*. Firenze: D'Anna.

Collins H and Abramsky C (1965) *Karl Marx and the British Labour Movement. Years of the First International*. London: Macmillan.

Coltham S (1964–1965) George Potter, the Junta, and the Bee-Hive. *International Review of Social History* vol 9(3): 391–432, vol 10(1): 23–65.

Consolati I (2018) Verso una teoria del presente storico globale. Marx e il problema della contemporaneità. *Storia del pensiero politico* vol 2: 283–294.

Consolati I (2019) Marx e gli accidenti della storia universale. L'India, lo Stato e il mercato mondiale. *Scienza & Politica. Per una storia delle dottrine* vol 31(61): 153–170.

Corbellini G (2013) *Scienza*. Torino: Bollati Boringhieri.

Cornell JF (1984) Analogy and Technology in Darwin's Vision of Nature. *Journal of the History of Biology* vol 17: 303–344.

Cornu A (1948) *Karl Marx et la révolution du 1848*, Paris: PUF.

Cornu A (1962) *Karl Marx et Friedrich Engels: leur vie et leur oeuvre*, tome III: *Marx à Paris*. Paris: PUF.

Cornu A (1971) *Marx e Engels. Dal liberalismo al comunismo*. Milano: Feltrinelli.

Cowling M (1867) *Disraeli, Gladstone and Revolution. The Passing of the Second Reform Bill*. Cambridge: Cambridge University Press.

Croce B (2016[1900]) *Historical materialism and the economics of Karl Marx*. London: Forgotten Books.

Dal Pane L (1939) Intorno alle origini del materialismo storico. *Giornale degli economisti* vol 1: 874–885.

Dardot P and Laval C (2012) *Marx, prénom Karl*. Paris, Gallimard.

Dardot P and Laval C (2014) *Commun. Essai sur la révolution au XXIe siècle*. Paris: La Découverte.

Darwin C (1859) *On the Origin of Species by Means of Natural Selection or the Preservation of Favored Races in the Struggle for Life*. London: Murray.

Delphy C (1984) *Close to Home: A Materialist Analysis of Women's Oppression*. Amherst, MA: University of Massachusetts Press.

Demirovic A (2014). Kritik der Politik. In Jaeggi R and Loik D (eds) *Nach Marx. Philosophie, Kritik, Praxis*, Frankfurt am Main: Suhrkamp, 463–485.

Desmond A and Moore J (1991) *Darwin*. London: Michael Joseph.

De Mauro T (1958) Storia e analisi semantica di 'classe'. In De Mauro T (1971) *Senso e significato. Studi di semantica teorica e storica*. Bari: Laterza, 163–227.

De Palma A (1971) *Le macchine e l'industria da Smith a Marx*. Torino: Einaudi.

Documents of the First International 1864–1872 (1963–1968). *The General Council of the First International. Minutes*. Moscow: Progress Publishers/London: Lawrence and Wishart.

Dörig JA (ed) (1960) *Marx contra Rußland. Der russische Expansionsdrang und die Politik der Westmächte. Berichte von Karl Marx als europäischer Korrespondent der New York Daily Tribune 1853–1856*. Tübingen: Seewald.

Doyle D (2015) *The Cause of All Nations. An International History of the American Civil War*. New York: Basic Books.

Drach M (ed.) (2004), *L'argent. Croyance, mesure, spéculation*. Paris: La Découverte.

Draper H (1971) The Principle of Self-Emancipation in Marx and Engels. *Socialist Register*. Available at socialistregister.com

Draper H (1972) The concept of the lumpenproletariat in Marx and Engels. *Economies et Sociétés.* vol 6(12): 285–312.

Ducange J-N and Burlaud A (eds) (2018) *Marx, une passion française.* Paris: La Découverte.

Ducange J-N (2015) Marx, le marxisme et le 'Père de la lutte des classes' Augustin Thierry. *Actuel Marx* vol 58: 13–27.

Dunayevskaya R (2000[1958]) *Marxism and Freedom.* Amherst, NY: Humanity Books.

Du Bois WEB (1900) *To the Nations of the World*, remarks given on July 25 at the first Pan African Convention, London.

Du Bois WEB (2007[1935]) *Black Reconstruction in America.* New York: Oxford University Press.

Eden FM (1797) *The State of The Poor: Or an History of the Labouring Classes in England, from the Conquest to the Present Period*, Volume 1–3. London: Devis.

Espinoza Pino M and Mezzadra S (2018) Cartografie globali. Il concetto di mercato mondiale in Marx tra giornalismo e teoria. In Petrucciani S (ed) *Il pensiero di Karl Marx.* Roma: Carocci, 177–208.

Fallot J (1966) *Marx et le machinisme.* Paris: Cujas.

Farrer DG (1972) Thierry, Saint-Simon and the Theory of Class Struggle. *Il Politico* vol 37: 582–596.

Federici S (2017) Notes on Gender in Marx's Capital. *Continental Thought & Theory: A Journal of Intellectual Freedom* vol 1(4): 19–37.

Ferrari R (2017) A Victorian Woman in the 'weird Marxian world'. In Potter B *On Marx and the Politics of Economic Discourse. Two Unpublished Manuscripts and Other Writings*, ed. by Ferrari R. In Quaderni di Scienza & Politica, vol 6: 7–89: http://amsacta.unibo.it/5597/1/quaderno_n_6.pdf.

Finelli R (2015) *A Failed Parricide: Hegel and the Young Marx.* Leiden-Boston: Brill.

Fioravanti M (1979) *Giuristi e costituzione politica nell'Ottocento tedesco.* Milano: Giuffrè.

Folbre N (1987) A Patriarchal Mode of Production. In Albelda R, Gunn C and Waller W (eds) *Alternatives to Economic Orthodoxy: Reader in Political Economy.* Armonk, NY: M.E. Sharpe Inc: 323–338.

Foner PS (ed) (1973) *Karl Marx Remembered.* San Francisco: Imprint.

Foot P (2006) *The Vote. How It was Won and how It was Undermined.* London: Penguin Books.

Foster JB (2000), *Marx's Ecology. Materialism and Nature*, New York: Monthly Review Press.

Foster JB and Clark B (2018) Women, Nature, and Capital in the Industrial Revolution. *Monthly Review* vol 69(8): 1–24.

Frosini F (2009) *Da Gramsci a Marx. Ideologia, verità, politica.* Roma: Derive Approdi.

Furet F (1986) *Marx et la Révolution française.* Paris: Flammarion.

Gans E (1827) *System des römischen Civilrechts*. Berlin: F. Dümmler.

Gans E (2005[1832–1833]) *Naturrecht und Universalrechtsgeschichte*. Tübingen: Mohr Siebeck.

Gans E (1839) Über die Grundlage des Besitzes. Eine Duplik. In: Gans E (1971) *Philosophische Schriften*. Glashutten im Taunus: Auvermann.

García Linera A (1991) *De demonios escondidos y momentos de revolución. Marx y la revolución social en las extremidades del cuerpo capitalista*. La Paz: Ofensiva Roja.

Garo I (2012) *Marx et l'invention historique*. Paris: Syllepse.

Geierhos W (1977) *Vera Zasulič und die russische revolutionäre Bewegung*. München-Wien: Oldenbourg.

Genovese E (1971) *In Red and Black: Marxian Explorations in Southern and Afro-American History*. New York: Pantheon Books.

Gitermann V (1945) *Geschichte Rußlands*. Zürich: Büchergilde Gutenberg. Volume 1–2.

Gossman L (1976) Augustin Thierry and Liberal Historiography. *History and Theory. Studies in the Philosophy of History* vol 15(4): 3–6.

Gould SJ (1977) *Ever since Darwin*. New York: W.W. Northon & Co.

Gramsci A (1971) *Selections from the Prison Notebooks*. London: Lawrence & Wishart.

Gramsci A (1995) *Further Selections from the Prison Notebooks*. London: Lawrence & Wishart.

Gramsci A (2007) *Prison Notebooks*. New York: Columbia University Press. Volume 1–3.

Gray R (1990) The Aristocracy of Labour in Nineteenth-Century Britain c.1850–1914. In Clarkson LA (ed) *British Trade Union and Labour History. A Compendium*. London: MacMillan, 137–208.

Gray P (2002) The Peculiarities of Irish Land Tenure, 1800–1914: From Agent of Impoverishment to Agent of Pacification. In Winch D and O'Brien PK (eds) *The Political Economy of British Historical Experience 1688–1914*. New York: The British Academy/Oxford University Press: 139–162.

Grenier J-Y (1996) *L'économie d'Ancien Régime. Un monde de l'échange et de l'incertitude*. Paris: Albin Michel.

Grün K (1845) *Neue Anekdota*. Darmstadt: Leske.

Guastini R (1974) *Marx: dalla filosofia del diritto alla scienza della società. Il lessico giuridico marxiano 1842–1851*. Bologna: Il Mulino.

Guerraggio A and Vidoni F (1982) *Nel laboratorio di Marx: scienze naturali e matematica*. Milano: F. Angeli.

Guizot F (1856) Introductory Discourse of the History of the Revolution of England. In Guizot F *History of the English Revolution of 1640*. London: H.G. Bohn, 1–78.

Guizot F (1875) *The History of Civilization from the Fall of the Roman Empire to the French Revolution*. London: George Bell & Sons, Volume I.

Gunawardana RALH (1976) The Analysis of Pre-colonial Social Formations in Asia in the Writings of Marx. *The Indian Historical Review* vol 2(2): 365–388.

Habib I (2006) Introduction: Marx's Perception of India. In Husain I, Habib I and Patnaik P (eds) *Karl Marx on India*. Delhi: Tulika Books, xix–lxviii.

Hall S (2003) Marx's Notes on Method. A 'Reading' of the '1857 Introduction'. *Cultural Studies* vol 17(2): 113–149.

Hardt M and Negri A (2009) *Commonwealth*. Cambridge: Harvard University Press.

Harney GJ (1968[1850]), The Charter, and Something More. In *The Democratic Review, 1849–1850*. London: The Merlin Press, 349–352.

Harootunian H (2015) *Marx After Marx. History and Time in the Expansion of Capitalism*. New York: Columbia University Press.

Harrison R (1953) The Land and Labour League. *Bulletin of International Institute of Social History* vol 8: 169–195.

Harrison R (1965) *Before the Socialists. Studies in Labour and Politics 1861 to 1881*. London: Routledge.

Hartmann H (1979) The Unhappy Marriage of Marxism and Feminism: Towards a More Progressive Union. *Capital & Class* vol 3: 1–33.

Hartog F (2015) *Regimes of Historicity. Presentism and Experiences of Time*. New York: Columbia University Press, 2015.

Harvey D (1981) The Spatial Fix. Hegel, Von Thunen, and Marx. *Antipode* 3: 1–12.

Harvey D (2003) *The New Imperialism*. Oxford: Oxford University Press.

Haug WF (2013) *Das ,Kapital' lesen – aber wie?*. Hamburg: Argument Verlag.

Hecker R (2014) Nikolaj F. Daniel'son und die russische 'Kapital'-Übersetzung. In Vollgraf C-E, Sperl R and Hecker R (eds) *Beiträge zur Marx-Engels Forschung. Neue Folge 2012, Marx und Russland*. Hamburg: Argument, 135–147.

Hegel GWF (1977) *Phenomenology of the Spirit*. Oxford: Oxford University Press.

Hegel GWF (1981) *Lectures on the Philosophy of World History*. London-New York-New Rochelle-Melbourne: Cambridge University Press.

Hegel GWF (1991) *Elements of the Philosophy of Right*. Cambridge: Cambridge University Press.

Hill C (1948) The English Civil War Interpreted by Marx and Engels. *Science & Society* vol 12(1): 130–156.

Hindess B and Hirst P (1977) *Mode of Production and Social Formation. An Auto-Critique of 'Pre-Capitalist Modes of Production'*. Atlantic Highlands: Humanities Press.

Hobsbawm EJ (1965) Introduction. In Marx K *Pre-Capitalist Economic Formations*. New York: Lawrence & Wishart.

Hobsbawm EJ (1984) Marx and History. *Diogenes* vol 32(25): 103–114.

Hoff J (2017) *Marx Worldwide. On the Development of the International Discourse on Marx since 1965*. Leiden: Brill.

Holmstrom N (1984) A Marxist Theory of Women's Nature. *Ethics* vol 94(3): 456–473.

Holmstrom N (2002) *The Socialist Feminist Project*. New York: Monthly Review Report.

hooks b (1981) *Ain't I a Woman. Black Women and Feminism*. Boston: South End Press.

Iacono AM (1988) Bachofen e l'Origine della famiglia di Engels. *Annali della Scuola Normale Superiore di Pisa. Classe di Lettere e Filosofia. Classe di Lettere e Filosofia* vol 18(2): 749–766.

Il'enkov EV (1982[1960]) *The Dialectics of the Abstract and the Concrete in Marx's Capital.* Moscow: Progress Publishers.

Irigaray L (1985) *The Sex which is not One.* Ithaca: Cornell University Press.

Jaeck H-P (1988) Marx und Guizot. *Zeitschrift für Geschichtswissenschaft* vol 36: 403–497.

James CLR (1939) The Revolution and the Negro. *New International* vol 5 (December): 339–343.

James CLR (1943) Negroes in the Civil War: Their Role in the Second American Revolution. *New International* vol 11(December): 338–342.

James S and Dalla Costa MR (1972) *Women and the Subversion of the Community, by Mariarosa Dalla Costa; and A woman's Place, by Selma James.* Bristol: Falling Wall Press.

Janoska J (ed) (1994) *Das "Methodenkapitel" von Karl Marx. Ein historischer und systematischer Kommentar.* Basel: Schwabe & Co.

Jeannot T (2007) Marx, Capitalism, and Race. *Radical Philosophy Today* vol 5: 69–92.

Kaiser B (1967) *Ex libris Karl Marx und Friedrich Engels. Schicksal und Verzeichnis einer Bibliothek.* Berlin: Dietz.

Kelley DR (1976) Vera Philosophia: The Philosophical Significance of Renaissance Jurisprudence. *Journal of the History of Philosophy* vol 14: 67–79.

Kelley DR (1978) The Metaphysics of Law: An Essay on the very Young Marx. *The American Historical Review* vol 83(2): 350–367.

Kittrel ER (1965) The Development of the Theory of Colonization in English Classical Political Economy. *Southern Economic Journal* (3): 189–206.

Kittrel ER (1973) Wakefield's Scheme of Systematic Colonization and Classical Economics. *American Journal of Economics and Sociology* vol 32(1): 87–111.

Knudsen K (1988) The Strike History of the First International. In van Holthoon FL and van der Linden M (eds) *Internationalism in the Labour Movement: 1830–1940.* Leiden-Boston: Brill, Volume 1, 304–322.

Koselleck R (1988) *La Prussia tra riforma e rivoluzione 1791–1848.* Bologna: Il Mulino.

Koselleck R (2004) *Futures Past: On the Semantics of Historical Time.* New York-Chichester, West Sussex: Columbia University Press.

Kouvélakis E (2000) *Commentaire à Karl Marx, L'introduction à la Critique de la Philosophie du droit de Hegel.* Paris: Elipses, 25–64.

Krader L (1974) Introduction. In Marx K. *Ethnological Notebooks.* Assen: Van Gorcum.

Krader L (1975) *The Asiatic Mode of Production: Sources, Development and Critique in the Writings of Karl Marx.* Assen: Van Gorcum.

Krader L (1978) Evoluzione, rivoluzione e Stato: Marx e il pensiero etnologico. In *Storia del marxismo.* Torino: Einaudi, Volume 1, 211–244.

Krätke M (2018) Marx and World History. *International Review of Social History* vol 63(1): 91–125.

Kulikoff A (ed) (2018) *Abraham Lincoln and Karl Marx in Dialogue.* New York: Oxford University Press.

Lacascade JL (2002) *Les métamorphoses du jeune Marx.* Paris: PUF.

Larrain E (1991) Classical Political Economist and Marx on Colonialism and "Backward" Nations. *World Developments* vol 3(2): 225–243.

Lefebvre H (2016) *Marxist Thought and the City.* Minneapolis, MN: University of Minnesota Press.

L'Égalité, journal de l'Association internationale des travailleurs de la Suisse romande. Milano: Feltrinelli, 1972.

Lenin VI (1908[1899]) *Razvitie kapitalizma v Rossii.* St. Petersburg: Pallada.

Levine N (1987) The German Historical School of Law and the Origins of Historical Materialism. *Journal of the History of Ideas* vol 48(3): 431–451.

Lichtheim G (1964) *Marxism. An Historical and Critical Study.* Oxford: Routledge.

Lim J-H (1992) Marx's Theory of Imperialism and the Irish National Question. *Science&Society* vol 56(2): 163–178.

Lloyd D (2010) Nomadic Figures: The 'Rhetorical Excess' of Irishness in Political Economy. In O'Connor M (ed) *Back to the Future of Irish Studies. Festschrift for Tadgh Foley.* Bern: Peter Lang, 41–64.

Lowe J (1860) Account of the strike and lock-out in cotton trade at Preston in 1853. In *National Association for the Promotion of Social Science, Trades' Societies and Strikes. Report of the Committee on Trade Societies.* London: Parker, 207–263.

Lunghini G (1977) *La crisi dell'economia politica e la teoria del valore.* Milano: Feltrinelli.

Luporini C (1978) Critica della politica e critica dell'economia politica in Marx. *Critica marxista* vol 1: 17–50.

Luxemburg R (1971[1912]) Women's Suffrage and Class Struggle. In Howard D (ed.) *Selected Political Writings of Rosa Luxemburg.* New York: Monthly Review Press, 216–222.

Luxemburg R (1913) *Die Akkumulation des Kapitals.* Berlin: Vorwärts.

MacDonagh O (1962) The Anti-Imperialism of Free Trade. *The Economic History Review* vol 14(3): 489–501.

Maffi B (2008) Prefazione. In Marx K *India, Cina, Russia.* Milano: il Saggiatore, 19–35.

MacKenzie D (1984) Marx and the Machine. *Technology and Culture* vol 25(3): 473–502.

Mascat MHJ (2019) Marx et le vol de bois. Du droit coutumier au droit de classe. *Droit & Philosophie* vol 10: 55–76.

Mazauric C (2009) *L'histoire de la Révolution française et la pensée marxiste.* Paris: PUF.

Mazzini G (2009) *A Cosmopolitanism of Nations.* Princeton: Princeton University Press.

McCormick T (2009) *William Petty and the Ambitions of Political Arithmetic.* Oxford: Oxford University Press.

Meek RL (1953) *Marx and Engels on Malthus*. London: Lawrence and Wishart.

Mezzadra S (2008) *La condizione postcoloniale. Storia e politica nel presente globale.* Verona: ombre corte.

Mezzadra S (2014) *Nei cantieri marxiani. Il soggetto e la sua produzione.* Roma: Manifestolibri.

Mezzadra S and Neilson B (2013) *Border as Method, or, The Multiplication of Labor.* Duhram and London: Duke University Press.

Mezzadra S and Samaddar R (2020) Colonialism. In Musto M (ed.) *Marx Revival. Key Concepts and New Interpretations.* Cambridge: Cambridge University Press, 247–265.

Miles R (1987) *Capitalism and Unfree Labour: Anomaly or Necessity.* London: Tavistock.

Mohri K (1970) Marx and 'Underdevelopment'. *Monthly Review* vol 30(11): 32–42.

Montanari G (1804) Della Moneta. Trattato Mercantile. In Custodi P (ed) *Scrittori classici italiani di economia politica. Parte antica. Tomo III.* Milan: De Stefani.

Morais HM (ed.) (1937) *The Civil War in the United States: Karl Marx and Frederick Engels.* New York: International Publishers.

Mosolov VG (1973) I quaderni di Kreuznach: gli studi storici del giovane Marx nella genesi della concezione materialistica della storia. *Critica marxista* vol 2: 159–179.

Mundt T (1844) *Die Geschichte der Gesellschaft in ihren neuen Entwicklungen und Problemen.* Berlin: Simion.

Musto M (2020) *The Last Years of Karl Marx. An Intellectual Biography.* Stanford: Stanford University Press.

Natalizi M (2006) *Il caso Cernysevskij.* Milano: Bruno Mondadori.

Negri A (1991) *Marx beyond Marx. Lessons on the* Grundrisse. London: Pluto Press.

Neocleous M (2011) War on Waste: Law, Original Accumulation and the Violence of Capital. *Science&Society* vol 75(4): 506–528.

Newsinger J (1982) 'A great blow must be struck in Ireland': Karl Marx and the Fenians. *Race & Class* vol XIV(2): 151–167.

Nimtz AH (2003) *Marx, Tocqueville, and Race in America. The 'Absolute Democracy' or 'Defiled Republic'.* Lanham, MD: Lexington Books.

Nimtz A (2004) The Eurocentric Marx and Engels and Other Related Myths. In Bartolovich C and Lazarus N (eds) *Marxism, Modernity, and Postcolonial Studies,* Cambridge: Cambridge University Press, 65–80.

Nimtz AH (2011) Marx and Engels on the US Civil War: The Materialist Conception of History in Action. *Historical Materialism* vol 19(4): 169–192.

Padover SK (ed) (1972) *Karl Marx on America and the Civil War.* New York: McGraw-Hill Book Company.

Panzieri R (1961) Sull'uso capitalistico delle macchine nel neocapitalismo. *Quaderni rossi* vol 1: 53–72.

Pappe HO (1951) Wakefield and Marx. *The Economic History Review* vol 4(1): 88–97.

Pateman C (2018) *The Sexual Contract.* Redwood City: Stanford University Press.

Patterson TC (2009) *Karl Mar. Anthropologist.* New York: Berg.

Perelman M (1987) *Marx's Crises Theory. Scarcity, Labor and Finance.* New York: Praeger.

Perelman M (2000) *The Invention of Capitalism. Classical Political Economy and the Secret History of Primitive Accumulation.* Duhram and London: Duke University Press.

Perelman M (2008) *Political Economy and the Press: Karl and Henry Carey at the New York Tribune:* https://michaelperelman.wordpress.com/2008/05/19/political-economy-and-the-press-karl-marx-and-henry-carey-at-the-new-york-tribune/.

Perini L (1976) *Introduzione.* In Marx K *Rivoluzione e reazione in Francia 1848–1850.* Torino: Einaudi: VII–LVIII.

Poggio PP (2017) *La rivoluzione russa e i contadini. Marx e il populismo rivoluzionario.* Milano: Jaca Book.

Pradella L (2015) *Globalization and the Critique of Political Economy.* Abingdon: Routledge.

Pradella L (2016) Crisis, Revolution and Hegemonic Transition: The American Civil War and Emancipation in Marx's Capital. *Science & Society* vol 80(4): 454–467.

Rabinbach A (1990) *The Human Motor. Energy, Fatigue and Rise of Modernity.* Basic Books: New York.

Raggi L (1980) Savigny e Marx. *Quaderni fiorentini per la storia del pensiero giuridico* vol 9: 567–574.

Raimondi F (2018) Marx: il lavoro e le macchine. In Basso L, Basso M, Raimondi F and Visentin S (eds) *Marx: la produzione del soggetto.* Roma: Derive Approdi, 199–223.

Rancière J (1973) *Critica e critica dell'economia politica. Dai 'Manoscritti del 1844' al 'Capitale'.* Milano: Feltrinelli.

Rancière J (1992) *Les mots de l'histoire. Essai de poétique du savoir.* Paris: Seuil.

Rancière J (1996) Le concept d'anachronisme et la vérité de l'historienne. *L'Inactuel* vol 6: 53–68.

Raymond H (1988) Marx et Engels devant la marginalité: la découverte du lumpenprolétariat. *Romantisme* vol 59: 5–17.

Read J (2003) *The Micro-Politics of Capital. Marx and the Prehistory of the Present.* Albany, NY: State University of New York Press.

Reissner HG (1965) *Eduard Gans: Ein Leben in Vormärz.* Tübingen: Mohr Siebeck.

Ricciardi M (2001) *Rivoluzione.* Bologna: Il Mulino.

Ricciardi M (2012) La società di tutto il popolo. Linee storiche sui concetti politici del socialismo tedesco dopo il 1848. In Ruocco G and Scuccimarra L (eds) *Il governo del popolo 2. Dalla Restaurazione alla guerra franco-prussiana.* Roma: Viella, 289–309.

Ricciardi M (2019) *Il potere temporaneo. Karl Marx e la politica come critica della società.* Milano: Meltemi editore.

Riesser G (1843) Gegen Bruno Bauer. 2. Die neue Welt und der freie Staat. *Konstitutionelle Jahrbücher* vol 3: 14–57.

Riot-Sarcey M (1998) *Le réel de l'utopie. Essai sur le politique au XIXe siècle.* Paris: Alvin Michel.

Robinson K (1976) *Karl Marx, the International Working Men's Association, and London Radicalism 1864–1872.* Unpublished PhD Dissertation, University of Manchester.

Rodden J (2008) The Lever Must Be Applied in Ireland': Marx, Engels, and the Irish Question. *The Review of Politics* vol 70: 609–640.

Rodgers DT (2003) *The Age of Fracture.* Cambridge: Harvard University Press.

Rosanvallon P (1985) *Le moment Guizot.* Paris: Gallimard.

Rosdolsky R (1977) *The Making of Marx' Capital.* London: Pluto Press.

Rosdolsky R (1986) *Engels and the 'Nonhistoric' Peoples: The National Question in the Revolution of 1848.* Glasgow: Critique Books.

Rubel M (1957) Les cahiers de lecture de Karl Marx: I. 1840–1853. *International Review of Social History* vol 2(3): 392–420.

Rubel M (1971) *Karl Marx. Essai de biographie intellectuelle,* Paris: Rivière et Cie.

Rückert J (2002) Thibaut-Savigny-Gans: Der Streit zwischen 'historischer' und 'philosophischer' Rechtsschule. In: Bänkner R, Göhler G and Waszek N (eds) *Eduard Gans (1797–1839). Politischer Professor zwischen Restauration und Vormärz.* Leipzig: Leipziger Universitätsverlag, 247–311.

Rude F (2007) *Les révoltes des canuts 1831–1834,* Paris: La Decouverte.

[Ruge A] (1975[1844]) Der König von Preußen und die Sozialreform. *Vorwärts! Pariser deutsche Zeitschrift,* 27 July, Reprint: Leipzig, Zentralantiquariat der deutschen demokratischen Republik.

Runkle G (1964) Karl Marx and the American Civil War. *Comparative Studies in Society and History* vol 6(4): 117–141.

Said EW (1978) *Orientalism.* London: Routledge.

SAP-Société des Amis du Peuple (1832), *Procès des quinze,* Paris: Auguste Mie.

Savigny FC von (1865 [1803]) *Das Recht des Besitzes: Eine civilistische Abhandlung.* Vienna: Gerold.

Schmidt A (1971) *The Concept of Nature in Marx.* London: NLB.

Scocozza A (1983) Il Bolìvar di Karl Marx. In: Cacciatore G and Lomonaco F (eds) *Marx e i marxismi cent'anni dopo.* Napoli: Guida.

Semmel B (1961) The Philosophic Radicals and Colonialism. *Journal of Economic History* vol 21(4): 513–525.

Semmig H (1845) Communismus, Socialismus und Humanismus. *Rheinische Jahrbücher zur gesellschaftlichen Reform* vol 1: 167–174.

Sereni P (2007) *Marx. La personne et la chose.* Paris: L'Harmattan.

Sereni P (2010) *La communauté en question, Tome 1: Chose publique et bien commun chez Marx.* Paris: L'Harmattan.

Shanin T (ed) (1983) *Late Marx and the Russian Road. Marx and the Peripheries of Capitalism.* London: Routledge & Kegan.

Shaw WH (1979) 'The Handmill Gives You the Feudal Lord': Marx's Technological Determinism, *History and Theory* vol 18(2): 155–176.

Slater E and McDonough T (2008) Marx on Nineteenth-century Colonial Ireland. Analyzing Colonialism as a Dynamic Social Process. *Irish Historical Studies* vol 142: 153–172.

Smith A (1838[1776]) *An Inquiry into the Nature and Causes of the Wealth of Nations.* Edinburgh: sn.

Smith R and Marx L (eds) (1994) *Does Technology Drive History? The Dilemma of Technological Determinism.* Cambridge-London: The MIT Press.

Sofri G (1969) *Il modo di produzione asiatico. Storia di una controversia marxista.* Torino: Einaudi.

Spivak GC (1981) French Feminism in an International Frame. *Yale French Studies* vol 62: 154–184.

Spivak GC (1993) *Outside in the Teaching Machine.* London: Routledge.

Spivak GC (1999) *A Critique of Postcolonial Reason. Toward a History of the Vanishing Present.* Cambridge: Harvard University Press.

Spivak GC (2018) Global Marx? In Burzack T Garnett R Mcintyre R (eds) *Knowledge, Class, and Economic. Marxism without Guarantees.* New York and London: Routledge, 265–287.

Stedman Jones G (1984) Some Notes on Karl Marx and the English Labour Movement. *History Workshop* vol 18: 124–137.

Sue E (1844) *Les mystères de Paris.* Bruxelles: Societé typographique belge. Volume 1–4.

Terray E (1969) *Le marxisme devant les sociétés primitives: deux études.* Paris: François Maspero.

Theis L (2008) *François Guizot.* Paris: Fayard.

Thierry A (1859) *The Formation and Progress of the Tiers État or Third Estate in France.* London: Henry G. Bohn.

Tomasello F (2012) Dal popolo al proletariato. Marx e la costruzione del soggetto rivoluzionario. In Scuccimarra L and Ruocco G (eds) *Il governo del popolo.* Volume 2: *Dalla Restaurazione alla guerra franco-Prussiana,* Roma: Viella, 261–287.

Tomasello F (2018a) *La questione francese. Marx e la critica della politica,* Milano: Mimesis.

Tomasello F (2018b) *L'inizio del lavoro. Teoria politica e questione sociale nella Francia di prima metà Ottocento,* Roma: Carocci.

Tomba M (2002) *Crisi e critica in Bruno Bauer. Il principio di esclusione come fondamento politico.* Napoli: Bibliopolis.

Tosel A, Luporini C and Balibar É (1979) *Marx et sa critique de la politique,* Paris: Maspero.

Tronti M (1977) *Stato e rivoluzione in Inghilterra.* Roma: Editori Riuniti.

Tvardovskaja VA (1969) *Sotsjalisticeskaja mysl Rossii na rubeze 1870–1880-ch godov.* Moskow: Nauka.

Vadée M. (1998) *Marx penseur du possible.* Paris-Montreal: L'Harmattan.

Venturi F (1972) *Il populismo russo.* Torino: Einaudi.

Vilar P (1973) Marxist History, a History in the Making. Towards a Dialogue with Althusser. *The New Left Review* vol 1(80): 65–106.

Virdee S (2014) *Racism, Class and the Racialized Outsider*. London: Palgrave.

Vogel L (1983) *Marxism and the Oppression of Women: toward a Unitary Theory*. New Brunswick: Rutgers University Press.

Wakefield EG (1833) *England and America. A Comparison of the Social and Political State of Both Nations*. London: R. Bentley. Volume 1–2.

Walicki A (1969) *The Controversy over Capitalism: Studies in the Social Philosophy of the Russian Populists*. Oxford: Clarendon Press.

Welsh JF (2002) Reconstructing Capital: The American Roots and Humanist Vision of Marx's Thought. *Midwest Quarterly* vol 13(3): 274–287.

White H (1975) *Metahistory. The Historical Imagination in Nineteenth Century Europe*. Baltimore: The Johns Hopkins University Press.

Wiene R (1980) Karl Marx's Vision of America: A Biographical and Bibliographical Sketch. *The Review of Politics* vol 12(4): 465–503.

Winch D (1963) Classical Economics and the Case for Colonization. *Economica*, New Series 120: 387–399.

Winch D (1966) The Classical Debate on Colonization: Comment. *Southern Economic Journal* (3): 341–345.

Wood EM (2008) Historical Materialism in 'Forms which Precede Capitalist Production'. In Musto M (ed) *Karl Marx's Grundrisse. Foundations of the Critique of Political Economy 150 Years Later*. New York: Routledge, 79–92.

Xifaras M (2002) Marx, justice et jurisprudence une lecture des 'Vols de bois'. *Revue Française d'Histoire des Idées Politiques* vol 15: 63–112.

Zimmerman A (2015) Marxism, the Popular Front, and the American Civil War. In Downs GP and Masur K (eds) *The World the Civil War Made*. Chapel Hill: The University of North Carolina Press, 304–336.

Index